PIERRE

HERMÉ
MACARON

PIERRE

HERMÉ

MACARON

The Ultimate Recipes from the Master Pâtissier

Photographs by **Laurent Fau** and **Bernhard Winkelmann**
Recipe text and artistic direction by **Coco Jobard**

Translated from the French by Zachary R. Townsend

Abrams
New York

To Valérie, my love

Refer to the book's removable pamphlet, "Pierre Hermé Macaron Kitchen Guide," for step-by-step instructions on how to make macaron shells, chocolate ganache, buttercream, Italian meringue, and crème anglaise, as well as how to assemble the macarons and what equipment to use.

Please note that throughout, the weight (gram) measurements should be regarded as more precise than the volume measurements. Note that ideal cooking temperature may vary from oven to oven; the temperature should not be so high that the shells change color or begin to brown as they cook.

Contents

The Real Story of the Macaron

By Pierre Hermé and Charles Znaty

We sometimes question the origin of the macaron, and it is a question that has been asked of us many times. In deciding to publish this second book devoted entirely to the macaron,[1] the idea immediately came to us to write an introductory story titled "The Real Story of the Macaron." We hope our readers will appreciate the nod because, with macarons, there are so many stories, and everyone has his own "real" one. But such certainty is reassuring, and in an age where almost all information is just a click away, readers will trust this story as true.

The use of the definite article in the title of this story intentionally places other possibilities of the history of the macaron in the background. We are aware of the controversy that this claim will create. From Saint-Émilion to Saint-Jean-de-Luz and throughout Nancy, protests will occur! We know that in the town of Astérix, the people fear nothing and no one. The only arguments they lose are the ones among themselves.

It will be understood that our "real story" is kindly created from different sources yet has become unique. Far from intending to hurt anyone's reputation, this "real story" is simply "our story." This is the story of the macaron as we, Pierre and Charles, the founders of Pierre Hermé Paris, have lived it and experienced it together since we first met in 1990. The facts, dates, and numbers quoted in this story are true and are included here to leave nothing to chance.

The first story about the macaron came to us from Pit Oberweis who, along with his wife, Monique, founded the pastry shop Oberweis in Luxembourg in 1964. Pit is now famous, and his talented children

Tom and Jeff carry on the family tradition. In 1958, Pit Oberweis was employed as a baker for the prestigious pastry house Sprüngli, founded in 1836 by David Sprüngli and headquartered on Paradeplatz Square in Zurich. Working alongside him was another apprentice, Camille Studer, also a native of Luxembourg. During their time at Sprüngli, the young Camille had the idea of joining together two almond cookie shells with a buttercream center. Fortunately, her creation pleased Richard Sprüngli, who was the fifth generation to serve as head of the family business. It was he who decided to name this creation *Luxemburgerli*, as a tribute to the birthplace of his apprentice. (Adding the ending of *–li* to a pastry name is a common tradition of the Rhine Valley.) The *Luxemburgerli* is still a specialty of the Sprüngli house today, and it is under this name that the people of Zurich refer to the macaron. Sprüngli released *Luxemburgerli* in different flavors throughout the year but in a substantially smaller size than ours. The recent popularity of macarons and the growing interest by its customers has encouraged Sprüngli to give this delicate confection a greater presence in its windows and to transform and modernize the historic Paradeplatz store in Zurich.

Meanwhile, Georges Hermé, Pierre Hermé's father, was making several types of *petits fours* including *Spiegli*, which are small hazelnut-paste cones filled with praline, and *Zungli*. These specialties were intended as after-dinner treats or for afternoon tea. Georges Hermé was also making *Makrönli*, a type of small cookie made from almonds, granulated sugar, and eggs. At this time, German-Swiss pastry was the model for all pastry chefs and chocolatiers around the world, as reflected through the COBA school (Basel School of Chocolate), directed by Jules Perlia, whose contribution was significant in modern chocolate.[2] Signaling the importance of this school of thought, the renowned French pastry chef Gaston Lenôtre traveled once or twice a year beyond the Vosges and never failed to visit his colleagues in Zurich.

When Pierre Hermé began his apprenticeship in 1976 in the grand Parisian pastry shop run by Monsieur and Madame Lenôtre, the making of macarons there was an important task that was strictly regimented. From a technical approach, making macarons consisted of incorporating homemade almond paste into egg whites. For the fledgling apprentice Pierre Hermé, this technique was completely innovative. The final product was too sweet for his tastes, but he was surprised to see how popular they were with the local clientele along rue d'Auteuil. And most important, the young apprentice admired the skill that was displayed each day by the team in charge of making them. Successfully making macarons as demanded by Gaston Lenôtre required an iron discipline and was a veritable *tour de force* each day. In his kitchen, only a few bakers were allowed to make macarons. The process required skills that no beginning pastry chef or apprentice possessed. The Lenôtre kitchens produced vanilla macarons, which consisted of joining two shells together with no filling, and you can still find them on the menu at the restaurant Le Louis XV by Alain Ducasse at the Hôtel de Paris in Monte Carlo.

At the shop of Monsieur Lenôtre, the shells were baked on sheets of paper similar to newspaper. Once baked, it was necessary to pour water under the baking paper so that the shells, still warm from the oven, could be stuck together two by two. This was a very physical and tricky task because you had to hold a hot baking sheet extended out with your arm above the sink while at the same time pouring a small trickle of water underneath the baking paper to lightly moisten the macarons but without getting them wet. The shells were baked on a hearth, so it was necessary to place each baking sheet one after the other in such a way as to control their temperature, and this was done by balancing on a small stool specifically designed for this purpose.

Among the staff at the Lenôtre pastry shop, only Alain Rousseau and Richard Lecoq were allowed to make the macaron batter (the "mass," as it's called in pastry language). Therefore, it required much persuasion and patience by Pierre Hermé to eventually be trusted to work at their side; learning to prepare the batter with them was a privilege of which he needed to prove himself worthy. Also integral were pastry chefs Raguin Michel and Jean-Pierre Desprès, who taught Pierre Hermé how to make macarons. Additionally, the story would not be complete without evoking the memory of baker Michel Malzis, a centerpiece of the process, who, in a Homeric fashion, completed a considerable amount of work each day.

After taking over the pastry kitchen at Fauchon, Pierre Hermé discovered a different method for making macarons. At its location at Place de la Madeleine, the technique was to mix ground almonds with confectioners' sugar and beaten egg whites. Starting in 1986, Pierre Hermé began to develop new macaron flavors: rose, lemon, pistachio, and caramel. He then decided to take a slightly different approach to making them, using an Italian meringue base. At that time, many pastry shops had their own approaches for making macarons, such as the pastry shop Pons, located just across from the Jardin du Luxembourg (and now a Dalloyau location) or the pastry shop Carette that served passersby around the Trocadero. Among other major pastry shops was that of Monsieur Peltier, who learned from Gaston Lenôtre. All of Paris flocked to his shop on rue de Sèvres.

When we met in 1990, Marianne Comolli, head writer for the food section of *Marie Claire* magazine, described the macarons at Fauchon as "the best in Paris," and this resulted in our very first photo, taken by photographer Jean-Louis Bloch-Lainé and styled by designer 'Yan D. Pennor's, which was a still life in black and white consisting of three macarons balanced on the corner of a Fauchon pastry box. Next came the publication of the cookbook *Secrets Gourmands*, the first edition published by Larousse, in which the almond was featured as one of the primary ingredients at the pastry shop. As a sign of our progress, together we came up with the idea of La Maison du Macaron and we registered this name with the National Institute of Industrial Property (INPI) in 1993.

In 1995, Pierre Hermé began to experiment with the combination of different flavors in macarons. This approach, which was characteristic of his pastry style, resulted in such combinations as lime and basil; rose, lychee and raspberry; and chocolate and caramel. Starting on January 1, 1997, after more than a year of discussions on the conditions and outlines of our future collaboration with Ladurée, and with the consent of Serge Guillon, who ran the family group of Madame Prémat that owned Fauchon, we began to write a new page in the history of the macaron.

After leaving Fauchon and moving to Ladurée, Pierre Hermé began by establishing, in writing, the basic approaches to pastry for the pastry shop. The shop located on rue Royale had been sold two years earlier by the family of Jean-Marie Desfontaines to the bakery group Boulangeries Paul. Jean-Marie Desfontaines therefore left the rue Royale location and settled in at the Pradier pastry house on rue de Bourgogne. Like many of his colleagues, Monsieur Desfontaines verbally communicated instructions to his teams, who, as a result, became more or less the trusted keepers of that information. Pierre Hermé, on the other hand, began by creating his famous "recipe cards" to which every pastry chef who worked with him would become accustomed. Strict management of technique, which was inherited from Gaston Lenôtre, was always emphasized in both the written instructions and in practice.

The following year, the Ladurée launch included the creation of a new store located on the Champs-Élysées, which was to include a large production facility, so we took the opportunity to consolidate the production of macarons at the shop on rue Royale and to focus the message of Ladurée on what we considered to be one of the most promising of its products. As a result, the window displays were filled with macarons—bittersweet chocolate, vanilla, coffee, pistachio, raspberry, chestnut, coconut, and so on. And in the span of one year's time, the shop on rue Royale was significantly transformed. Pierre Hermé bought a convection oven and a machine for piping the shells, while those defecting from Fauchon, led by pastry chefs Richard Ledu, Colette Petremant,[3] and many others, came to our side to strengthen our production teams.

The enthusiastic response to our macarons after our presentation to the press in Paris, Tokyo, and New York during 1997 encouraged us to introduce the macarons everywhere possible that would welcome this type of confection. The research to find possible historical records from the pastry shop, led by Valerie Taieb, our assistant at the time, was unsuccessful. Without any real means to investigate further, and pressured by the thousands of tasks that the launch required, we settled on communicating the story of Louis Ernest Ladurée as we envisioned it. For us, the objective was clear: The macaron was to become a flagship product of the Pierre Hermé collection because "these little grams of happiness" (as Pierre likes to call them) offer an ideal outlet for his creativity. First because of the technical challenge of making the macaron (during the last twenty years, Pierre Hermé has continued to reinterpret its recipe, and the production techniques are the focus of great care and constant change in our shop), and second because of the endless creative possibilities with flavors, which is Pierre Hermé's field of experience. We have released and sold more than a hundred different flavors, and dozens more are jotted down in the notebooks where he records the ideas that pop into his head. On August 28, 2001, during the opening of the 72 rue Bonaparte location in Paris, 'Yan D. Pennor's, who designed the shop, displayed empty boxes in the shop windows on which he balanced several macarons echoing, in color, the photography of Jean-Louis Bloch-Lainé, who had the idea ten years earlier.

In 2005, in order to invite our pastry colleagues who were members of Relais Desserts to be involved with macarons, we created "Macaron Day." The idea was to popularize the product by giving them away for an entire day. Giving away what usually sells easily can quickly become bad business, so we were mindful of limits and requested of the lucky customers who benefited from the free macarons that they offer a donation to a good cause in exchange. Nine years later, the success of Macaron Day has far exceeded our expectations. The event takes place in Japan, London, and Hong Kong, where we organize it, but other bakeries have led the event in major cities in Europe and most recently in the United States. The monies raised are used to fund initiatives by such organizations as Vaincre La Muscoviscidose (End Cystic Fibrosis), the Make-a-Wish Foundation (an organization that grants wishes for children with life-threatening medical conditions), and Nanbyo-net (an organization that provides vacation destinations for sick children).

The macaron is now available many places around the world, including in major retailers that have built their reputations on burgers, fries, and soda. We have even recently seen advertising campaigns that use the macaron rather than the loaf of bread as a symbol of France. In short, this is why we felt it was time to dedicate a new book to the macaron.

Several of Pierre Hermé's macarons have become classics. Almost anywhere in the world one can find pink macarons that are inspired by Ispahan (rose, raspberry, and lychee), or yellow ones that are lightly dusted with specks of cocoa as a tribute to Mogador (milk chocolate and passion fruit), or even with bi-colored shells like Mosaïc (pistachio and cherry). However, it is rare to see the Infiniment Truffe Blanche Macaron (white truffle and Piedmont hazelnuts), which appeared in 2002 as part of our collection "Blanc Cousu Main" (Hand-Stitched White); this flavor is for real connoisseurs. Other "Infiniment" macarons have been added to this collection, such as the Infiniment vanille (see page 20), composed of a bouquet of vanilla beans from Mexico, Tahiti, and Madagascar to best capture the essence of each of these botanical varieties, making up a distinct house vanilla flavor. In 2006, Pierre Hermé introduced the idea that the single origin chocolates he used, given their intrinsic qualities, deserved a special recipe. We therefore released several chocolate macarons at the same time so that our customers could appreciate the nuances of each one. Thus was born Infiniment Chocolat Porcelana—Pure Origin Venezuela Porcelana Dark Chocolate from the Pedregal Domaine and Infiniment Chocolate Chuao—Pure Origin Venezuelan Dark Chocolate, Village of Chuao (see page 14). Fleeting in nature, these macarons, whose chocolate is made from a single cacao bean variety that is harvested on a specific plantation, are subject to the unpredictable nature of the seasons. More recently, Pierre Hermé Paris shops simultaneously offered two Infiniment Café macarons that featured two single origin coffees with very distinct flavors: Bourbon pointu de la Réunion coffee and Iapar rouge du Brésil coffee (see pages 26 and 68). Among the latest recipes envisioned by Pierre Hermé are the "Jardins" and the "Velouté" collections, which are featured prominently in the following pages. The recipes for many of these special offerings are included here to provide less fleeting access to these acclaimed creations.

In 2008, motivated by the same passions that have continued to drive us since we started working together, we undertook opening our first store: Macarons & Chocolats Pierre Hermé Paris. Fate gave us a chance to discover a quiet shop, located at No. 4 rue Cambon where, not long ago, at the other end of the street, Coco Chanel would cross when she came and went from her apartments at the Ritz to her design studio at number 31. As surprising as it may seem, the obstacles to this project were not easy to overcome. Whatever you decide to undertake, there is always someone who will try to predict your future: "What? A Pierre Hermé shop with no pastries? Insane!" was the prevailing thought. However, this didn't matter. Our determination was decided by our needs: our shops on rue Bonaparte and rue de Vaugirard had become too small to house all of our creations that had been added over the years. We needed a setting whose scale was worthy of the magnitude of our macarons and chocolates. With the worst behind us, and encouraged by our initial success, we decided to move forward. Our macarons began to travel. First to London, then Strasbourg, then into Japan as we started expanding. The rue Cambon location was particularly promising since the late Philippe Séguin, then president of the *Cour des Comptes* (Court of Financial Auditors) sometimes made an impromptu visit, as well as Françoise Montenay, president of Chanel, who agreed to become our sponsor after our entry into the *Comité Colbert*.

The macaron culture is now widespread—in hotels, bistros, and gourmet restaurants. It has become a kind of universal language. Many countries persist in writing the word "macaroons," because the language of Shakespeare dominates. But this is a huge error! The word "macaroon" is a *faux ami*. For many Americans, the term always refers to a dry cookie made with coconut. A prominent example of this confusion of terminology can be seen in the final twist of the second season of the show *Gossip Girl*. Blair the heroine finds her lover again whom she thought had left, and he explains his absence by saying "I was in Paris to get you your favorite macaroons from Pierre Hermé."[4] At our first location in London in 2010, we took pleasure in printing the word [makarɔ̃] phonetically on the cover of the brochures given to each customer.

Since 2012, we have strived to strengthen our international presence. Today, our macarons and our chocolates can be found in nearly a dozen countries.

1. See *Pierre Hermé: Macarons*, Grub Street Publishing, 2011.

2. See *Le Chocolat Apprivoisé* by Pierre Hermé, Éditions PHP, 2013.

3. Respectively, president of Maison Pierre Hermé Paris in Japan and director of Manufacturing for Macarons & Chocolats Pierre Hermé Paris.

4. *Gossip Girl*, television series created by Josh Schwartz and Stephanie Savage, from the books by Cecily von Ziegesar, season 2, episode 25, 2008–2009.

FROM APPRENTICE TO INVENTOR

The Classics from My Apprenticeship
and Their Reinterpretation

Macaron Chocolat

This is the recipe for macaron shells that I learned when I was an apprentice at Lenôtre in Plaisir, France. It was made with raw almonds so the skins had to be removed first. Then the blanched almonds had to be left to dry for 48 hours before being used.

MAKES ABOUT 72 MACARONS
(OR ABOUT 144 SHELLS)

PREPARATION TIME: **20 MINUTES**
(2 DAYS IN ADVANCE) + 40 MINUTES

COOKING TIME: **2 MINUTES (2 DAYS IN ADVANCE) + 35 MINUTES**

RESTING TIME: **48 HOURS + 1 HOUR**

REFRIGERATION TIME: **2 HOURS + 24 HOURS**

FOR THE CHOCOLATE MACARON SHELLS
1⅔ cups (240 g) whole almonds, with skins
4¾ cups (480 g) confectioners' sugar
¼ cup (20 g) unsweetened cocoa
8 drops / ⅛ teaspoon (0.5 g) liquid carmine red food color
Generous 1 teaspoon (5 g) water
2⅓ large (70 g) fresh egg whites
1 tablespoon (20 g) apricot puree

TO FINISH THE MACARON SHELLS
3½ large (110 g) fresh egg whites

FOR THE CHOCOLATE GANACHE
11¼ ounces (320 g) Valrhona Extra-bitter 61% cacao dark chocolate
1 cup minus 1 tablespoon (220 g) fresh whole milk
½ cup minus 1 tablespoon (100 g) fine French unsalted butter, preferably *beurre de la Viette*, room temperature

TWO DAYS IN ADVANCE, PLACE THE ALMONDS IN BOILING WATER FOR 2 MINUTES. Drain, then immediately remove the skins. Spread the skinned almonds out on several layers of paper towels. Let dry for 48 hours at room temperature.

PREPARE THE CHOCOLATE MACARON SHELLS. The day before, process the almonds in a food processor with a little bit of the confectioners' sugar. Add the rest of the confectioners' sugar then process again until the almonds are finely ground. Sift and press the confectioners' sugar–almond mixture through a medium sieve. Re-process any remaining large almond pieces with the sifted confectioners' sugar–almond mixture until all of the almonds are very finely ground and will fit through the sieve. Dilute the cocoa and the food color in the water then add this along with the 2⅓ (70 g) egg whites and the apricot puree and process again until the mixture forms a rough mass.

Lightly beat the 3½ (110 g) egg whites just until frothy then add them to the food processor. Process to combine, then transfer the batter to a pastry bag fitted with a plain #11, ½-inch (11-mm to 12-mm) pastry tip.

Line baking sheets with parchment paper. Pipe disks about 1½ inches (3.5 cm) in diameter and ¾ inch (2 cm) apart on the lined baking sheets. Set aside for at least 1 hour at room temperature to allow a skin to form.

Preheat a convection oven to 300°F (150°C). Place the baking sheets in the oven. Bake for 15 minutes, quickly opening and closing the oven door twice during baking to release moisture. Remove the shells from the oven and slide them still on the parchment paper onto a work surface.

PREPARE THE CHOCOLATE GANACHE. Chop the chocolate using a serrated knife then melt it to between 113°F (45°C) and 122°F (50°C) set over a bain-marie or in a microwave.

In a saucepan, bring the milk to a boil. Pour the hot milk in thirds into the melted chocolate, stirring after each addition starting in the center then in increasingly wider concentric circles toward the sides of the bowl. Using an immersion blender, blend the ganache until smooth.

Add the butter in small pieces. Blend again until smooth. Pour the ganache into a baking dish. Cover it by gently pressing plastic wrap onto its surface. Refrigerate for 2 hours, just until the ganache has developed a creamy consistency. Transfer the ganache to a pastry bag fitted with a plain #11, ½-inch (11-mm to 12-mm) pastry tip.

Turn half of the shells over with the flat sides up onto a new piece of parchment paper. Fill them with the ganache. Close them with the rest of the shells, pressing down lightly.

Refrigerate the macarons for 24 hours. Remove them from the refrigerator 2 hours before eating them.

Macaron Infiniment Chocolat Chuao

MAKES ABOUT 72 MACARONS
(OR ABOUT 144 SHELLS)
PREPARATION TIME: **5 MINUTES (5 DAYS
IN ADVANCE, SEE "MACARON SHELLS
STEP-BY-STEP" IN THE KITCHEN GUIDE)**
COOKING TIME: **15 TO 18 MINUTES**
RESTING TIME: **30 MINUTES**
REFRIGERATION TIME: **3 HOURS +
2 HOURS + 24 HOURS**

**FOR THE CHUAO
CHOCOLATE PIECES**
½ teaspoon (2 g) fleur de sel sea
salt, preferably *fleur de sel de
Guérande*
5¼ ounces (150 g) Valrhona Chuao
68% cacao dark chocolate

**FOR THE CHOCOLATE
MACARON SHELLS**
4¼ ounces (120 g) Valrhona 100%
cocoa paste
3 cups (300 g) confectioners' sugar
2 cups plus 2 tablespoons (300 g)
ground almonds
8 drops / ⅛ teaspoon (0.5 g) liquid
carmine red food color
**7 large (220 g) "liquefied" egg
whites, divided (see "Macaron
Shells Step-by-Step" in the Kitchen
Guide)
¼ cup plus 1 tablespoon (75 g) still
mineral water
1½ cups (300 g) superfine
granulated sugar
Edible glittering (or "pearl") ruby
red dust, for sprinkling

**FOR THE CHUAO
CHOCOLATE GANACHE**
13 ounces (370 g) Valrhona Chuao
68% cacao dark chocolate
**1½ cups minus 2 teaspoons
(340 g)** light whipping cream
(32%–35% fat)
**½ cup minus ¾ teaspoon
(110 g)** fine French unsalted butter,
preferably *beurre de la Viette*,
room temperature

Chuao chocolate is one of the most highly prized chocolates in the world due to its rarity, exceptional aromatic flavor profile of blond tobacco and spices, supple texture, and lingering finish. Its origins are the little village of Chuao, situated north of Venezuela, accessible only from the sea.

PREPARE THE CHUAO CHOCOLATE PIECES. The day before, using a rolling pin, crush the sea salt on top of a piece of parchment paper.

Chop the chocolate using a serrated knife then melt it to between 113°F (45°C) and 122°F (50°C) set over a bain-marie or in a microwave. Stir the crushed sea salt into the chocolate. Transfer the melted chocolate to a large plastic storage bag (such as a plastic freezer bag) and smooth it into a thin layer using a narrow metal spatula. Place weights on top of the bag to keep it flat. Refrigerate for at least 3 hours. When the chocolate has set, use a rolling pin to break it into pieces approximately ¼ inch (6 mm) to ½ inch (12 mm) in size while still in the bag. Refrigerate until needed.

PREPARE THE CHOCOLATE MACARON SHELLS. Chop the cocoa paste using a serrated knife then melt it to between 113°F (45°C) and 122°F (50°C) set over a bain-marie or in a microwave. Sift the confectioners' sugar and almonds together in a bowl.

Combine the food color with half of the "liquefied" egg whites. Pour this into the confectioners' sugar–almond mixture without mixing.

→ Add the remaining "liquefied" egg whites to the bowl of a stand mixer fitted with the wire whisk. In a saucepan, boil the mineral water and granulated sugar to 244°F (118°C). As soon as the syrup reaches 239°F (115°C), begin beating the egg whites on high speed.

When the syrup reaches 244°F (118°C), reduce the mixer speed to medium–high and pour the syrup in a steady stream down the inside edge of the bowl into the beaten egg whites. Beat the meringue until it cools to 122°F (50°C). Fold about one–third of the meringue into the melted cocoa paste then add this mixture to the confections' sugar–almond mixture along with the rest of the meringue. Fold it with a silicone spatula until the mixture loses volume. Transfer the batter to a pastry bag fitted with a plain #11, $^1/_2$-inch (11-mm to 12-mm) pastry tip.

Line baking sheets with parchment paper. Pipe disks about $1^1/_2$ inches (3.5 cm) in diameter and $^3/_4$ inch (2 cm) apart on the lined baking sheets. Rap the baking sheets on a work surface covered with a clean kitchen towel to gently smooth out the disks. Lightly dust the disks with the red dust. Set aside for at least 30 minutes at room temperature to allow a skin to form.

Preheat a convection oven to 350°F (180°C). Place the baking sheets in the oven. Bake for 12 minutes, quickly opening and closing the oven door twice during baking to release moisture. Remove the shells from the oven and slide them still on the parchment paper onto a work surface.

PREPARE THE CHUAO CHOCOLATE GANACHE. Chop the chocolate using a serrated knife then melt it to between 113°F (45°C) and 122°F (50°C) set over a bain-marie or in a microwave.

In a saucepan, bring the cream to a boil. Pour the hot cream in thirds into the melted chocolate, stirring after each addition starting in the center then in increasingly wider concentric circles toward the sides of the bowl. Using an immersion blender, blend the ganache until smooth.

Add the butter in small pieces. Blend again until smooth. Pour the ganache into a baking dish. Cover it by gently pressing plastic wrap onto its surface. Refrigerate for 2 hours, just until the ganache has developed a creamy consistency. Transfer the ganache to a pastry bag fitted with a plain #11, $^1/_2$-inch (11-mm to 12-mm) pastry tip.

Turn half of the shells over with the flat sides up onto a new piece of parchment paper. Fill them with the ganache. Gently place some of the fleur de sel chocolate pieces in the center. Pipe a dab of ganache on top of the chocolate pieces. Close them with the rest of the shells, pressing down lightly.

Refrigerate the macarons for 24 hours. Remove them from the refrigerator 2 hours before eating them.

In Chuao, the agricultural cooperative partnership produces twenty-four metric tons of cacao beans per year. Only a few buyers get the privilege to share each year's beans, whose quality is matched only by their rarity.

Macaron Vanille

These vanilla macarons are macarons with no filling at all. They were the tradition when I was at Lenôtre. The batter is flavored simply with vanilla powder. This recipe requires pouring water underneath the baking paper to release the shells.

MAKES ABOUT 72 MACARONS
(OR ABOUT 144 SHELLS)
PREPARATION TIME: 20 MINUTES
(2 DAYS IN ADVANCE) + 30 MINUTES
COOKING TIME: 2 MINUTES +
13 MINUTES
RESTING TIME: 48 HOURS + 1 HOUR
REFRIGERATION TIME: 24 HOURS

FOR THE VANILLA MACARON SHELLS
1⅔ **cups (240 g)** whole almonds, with skins
4¾ **cups (480 g)** confectioners' sugar
2⅓ **large (70 g)** fresh egg whites
1 **tablespoon (20 g)** apricot puree
1 **tablespoon plus 2 teaspoons (10 g)** vanilla powder

TO FINISH THE MACARON SHELLS
3½ **large (110 g)** fresh egg whites

TWO DAYS IN ADVANCE, PLACE THE ALMONDS IN BOILING WATER FOR 2 MINUTES. Drain, then immediately remove the skins. Spread the skinned almonds out onto several layers of paper towels. Let dry for 48 hours at room temperature.

PREPARE THE VANILLA MACARON SHELLS. The day before, process the almonds in a food processor with a little bit of the confectioners' sugar. Add the rest of the confectioners' sugar then process again until the almonds are finely ground. Sift and press the confectioners' sugar–almond mixture through a medium sieve. Re-process any remaining large almond pieces with the sifted confectioners' sugar–almond mixture until all of the almonds are very finely ground and will fit through the sieve. Add the 2⅓ (70 g) egg whites, apricot puree, and vanilla powder and process again until the mixture forms a rough mass.

Lightly beat the 3½ (110 g) egg whites just until frothy then add them to the food processor. Process to combine, then transfer the batter to a pastry bag fitted with a plain #11, ½-inch (11-mm to 12-mm) pastry tip.

Line baking sheets with parchment paper. Pipe disks about 1½ inches (3.5 cm) in diameter and ¾ inch (2 cm) apart on the lined baking sheets. Set aside for at least 1 hour at room temperature to allow a skin to form.

Preheat a convection oven to 300°F (150°C). Place the baking sheets in the oven. Bake for 13 minutes, quickly opening and closing the oven door twice during baking to release moisture. Remove the baking sheets from the oven and immediately pour a little bit of cold water underneath the parchment paper. Slide the parchment onto a cooling rack then stick the shells together two by two, pressing them firmly enough for them to stick together.

Refrigerate the macarons for 24 hours. Remove them from the refrigerator 2 hours before eating them.

Macaron Infiniment Vanille

I wanted to create my own distinct vanilla flavor by combining several vanilla beans from different origins. The Tahitian bean has depth of flavor that is intense and exuberant; the Madagascar bean has woody notes, and the Mexican bean is floral.

PREPARE THE VANILLA MACARON SHELLS. The day before, sift together the confectioners' sugar, almonds, and vanilla powder.

Pour half of the "liquefied" egg whites into the confectioners' sugar–almond–vanilla mixture without mixing.

Add the remaining "liquefied" egg whites to the bowl of a stand mixer fitted with the wire whisk. In a saucepan, boil the mineral water and granulated sugar to 244°F (118°C). As soon as the syrup reaches 239°F (115°C), begin beating the egg whites on high speed.

When the syrup reaches 244°F (118°C), reduce the mixer speed to medium-high and pour the syrup in a steady stream down the inside edge of the bowl into the beaten egg whites. Beat the meringue until it cools to 122°F (50°C). Fold it with a silicone spatula into the confectioners' sugar–almond–vanilla mixture until the mixture loses volume. Transfer the batter to a pastry bag fitted with a plain #11, ½-inch (11-mm to 12-mm) pastry tip.

Line baking sheets with parchment paper. Pipe disks about 1½ inches (3.5 cm) in diameter and ¾ inch (2 cm) apart on the lined baking sheets. Rap the baking sheets on a work surface covered with a clean kitchen towel to gently smooth out the disks. Set aside for at least 30 minutes at room temperature to allow a skin to form.

Preheat a convection oven to 350°F (180°C). Place the baking sheets in the oven. Bake for 12 minutes, quickly opening and closing the oven door twice during baking to release moisture. Remove the shells from the oven and slide them still on the parchment paper onto a work surface.

PREPARE THE VANILLA GANACHE. Scrape the seeds out of the vanilla beans using a knife and stir the seeds into the cream along with the vanilla bean pods. In a saucepan, bring the cream to a boil. Remove from the heat then cover and let stand for 30 minutes to infuse.

Chop the white chocolate using a serrated knife then melt it to between 113°F (45°C) and 122°F (50°C) set over a bain-marie or in a microwave.

Strain the cream then bring it back to a boil. Pour the hot cream in thirds into the melted white chocolate, stirring after each addition starting in the center then in increasingly wider concentric circles toward the sides of the bowl.

Pour the ganache into a baking dish. Cover it by gently pressing plastic wrap onto its surface. Refrigerate for 6 hours, just until the ganache has developed a creamy consistency. Transfer the ganache to a pastry bag fitted with a plain #11, ¹/₂-inch (11-mm to 12-mm) pastry tip.

Turn half of the shells over with the flat sides up onto a new piece of parchment paper. Fill them with the ganache. Close them with the rest of the shells, pressing down lightly.

Refrigerate the macarons for 24 hours. Remove them from the refrigerator 2 hours before eating them.

MAKES ABOUT 72 MACARONS (OR ABOUT 144 SHELLS)

PREPARATION TIME: **5 MINUTES (5 DAYS IN ADVANCE, SEE "MACARON SHELLS STEP-BY-STEP" IN THE KITCHEN GUIDE)**
COOKING TIME: **18 TO 20 MINUTES**
INFUSION TIME: **30 MINUTES**
RESTING TIME: **30 MINUTES**
REFRIGERATION TIME: **6 HOURS + 24 HOURS**

FOR THE VANILLA MACARON SHELLS
3 cups (300 g) confectioners' sugar
2 cups plus 2 tablespoons (300 g) ground almonds
1½ teaspoons (3 g) vanilla powder
7 large (220 g) "liquefied" egg whites, divided (see "Macaron Shells Step-by-Step" in the Kitchen Guide)
¼ cup plus 1 tablespoon (75 g) still mineral water
1½ cups (300 g) superfine granulated sugar

FOR THE VANILLA GANACHE
2 Tahitian vanilla beans, halved lengthwise
2 Madagascar vanilla beans, halved lengthwise
2 Mexican vanilla beans, halved lengthwise
1½ cups minus 1 tablespoon (335 g) light whipping cream (32%–35% fat)
13¼ ounces (375 g) Valrhona Ivoire 35% white chocolate

Macaron Café

MAKES ABOUT 72 MACARONS
(OR ABOUT 144 SHELLS)

PREPARATION TIME: 20 MINUTES
(2 DAYS IN ADVANCE) + 40 MINUTES

COOKING TIME: 2 MINUTES (2 DAYS IN
ADVANCE) + ABOUT 25 MINUTES

RESTING TIME: 48 HOURS + 1 HOUR

REFRIGERATION TIME: 24 HOURS

FOR THE COFFEE MACARON SHELLS
1⅔ cups (240 g) whole almonds, with skins
4¾ cups (480 g) confectioners' sugar
2⅓ large (70 g) fresh egg whites
1 tablespoon (20 g) apricot puree
1 tablespoon (16 g) coffee extract, preferably Trablit
Scant ½ teaspoon (1.5 g) liquid yellow food color

TO FINISH THE MACARON SHELLS
3½ large (110 g) fresh egg whites

FOR THE ITALIAN MERINGUE
2 large (65 g) egg whites
2 tablespoons plus 1 teaspoon (35 g) still mineral water
⅔ cup (130 g) superfine granulated sugar, divided

FOR THE CRÈME ANGLAISE
⅓ cup plus 2 teaspoons (90 g) fresh whole milk
3½ large (70 g) egg yolks
3 tablespoons plus ½ teaspoon (40 g) superfine granulated sugar

FOR THE COFFEE BUTTERCREAM
2 cups (450 g) fine French unsalted butter, preferably *beurre de la Viette*, room temperature
1½ teaspoons (3 g) instant coffee
¾ teaspoon (3 g) still mineral water
¾ teaspoon (3 g) coffee extract, preferably Trablit
1 recipe Crème Anglaise (see above)
1½ cups (175 g) Italian Meringue (see above)

The filling that I learned at Lenôtre for a coffee macaron was a coffee buttercream. The flavor comes from instant coffee and coffee extract.

TWO DAYS IN ADVANCE, PLACE THE ALMONDS IN BOILING WATER FOR 2 MINUTES. Drain, then immediately remove the skins. Spread the skinned almonds out onto several layers of paper towels. Let dry for 48 hours at room temperature.

PREPARE THE COFFEE MACARON SHELLS. The day before, process the almonds in a food processor with a little bit of the confectioners' sugar. Add the rest of the confectioners' sugar then process again until the almonds are finely ground. Sift and press the confectioners' sugar–almond mixture through a medium sieve. Re-process any remaining large almond pieces with the sifted confectioners' sugar–almond mixture until all of the almonds are very finely ground and will fit through the sieve. Add the 2⅓ (70 g) egg whites, apricot puree, coffee extract, and food color and process again until the mixture forms a rough mass.

Lightly beat the 3½ (110 g) egg whites just until frothy then add them to the food processor. Process to combine, then transfer the batter to a pastry bag fitted with a plain #11, ½-inch (11-mm to 12-mm) pastry tip.

Line baking sheets with parchment paper. Pipe disks about 1½ inches (3.5 cm) in diameter and ¾ inch (2 cm) apart on the lined baking sheets. Set aside for at least 1 hour at room temperature to allow a skin to form.

Preheat a convection oven to 300°F (150°C). Place the baking sheets in the oven. Bake for 13 minutes, quickly opening and closing the oven door twice during baking to release moisture. Remove the shells from the oven and slide them still on the parchment paper onto a work surface.

PREPARE THE ITALIAN MERINGUE. Add the egg whites to the bowl of a stand mixer fitted with the wire whisk. In a saucepan, boil the mineral water and all but 1¼ teaspoons (5 g) of the granulated sugar. When the syrup starts to boil, wipe down the inside of the saucepan with a dampened pastry brush. As soon as the syrup reaches 239°F (115°C), begin beating the egg whites on high speed with the rest of the granulated sugar until the peaks are almost firm and droop slightly in the shape of a "bird's beak" when the whisk is lifted. When the syrup reaches 250°F (121°C), reduce the mixer speed to medium and slowly pour the syrup in a steady stream down the inside edge of the bowl into the beaten egg whites, continuing to beat until the meringue has cooled.

PREPARE THE CRÈME ANGLAISE. In a saucepan, bring the milk to a boil. In a separate saucepan, whisk together the egg yolks and the granulated sugar until lightened. Slowly add the hot milk to the yolk-sugar mixture while whisking vigorously. Place the saucepan over low heat and cook to 185°F (85°C) while stirring continuously—rich in eggs, this cream has a tendency to stick to the bottom of the saucepan. Strain the cooked cream then transfer it to a stand mixer fitted with the wire whisk. Beat on medium speed until cooled.

PREPARE THE COFFEE BUTTERCREAM. In a stand mixer fitted with the paddle attachment, beat the butter on high speed for 5 minutes. Meanwhile, dilute the instant coffee in the mineral water and coffee extract. Add the cooled crème anglaise and coffee mixture to the butter. Beat again to combine.

Using a silicone spatula, fold in the 1½ cups (175 g) Italian meringue a little at a time. Transfer the mixture to a pastry bag fitted with a plain #11, ½-inch (11-mm to 12-mm) pastry tip.

Turn half of the shells over with the flat sides up onto a new piece of parchment paper. Fill them with the coffee buttercream. Close them with the rest of the shells, pressing down lightly.

Refrigerate the macarons for 24 hours. Remove them from the refrigerator 2 hours before eating them.

Macaron
Infiniment Café

Infiniment Café is the expression of my work with coffee with Hippolyte Courty, founder of l'Arbre à Café in Paris. The Iapar rouge du Brésil coffee is both potent and soft, with aromatic notes of chocolate, cinnamon, spice, and a sharp touch of eucalyptus. It's an exceptional coffee!

MAKES ABOUT 72 MACARONS
(OR ABOUT 144 SHELLS)

PREPARATION TIME: **5 MINUTES (5 DAYS
IN ADVANCE, SEE "MACARON SHELLS
STEP-BY-STEP" IN THE KITCHEN GUIDE)**

COOKING TIME: **16 TO 18 MINUTES**

INFUSION TIME: **3 MINUTES**

RESTING TIME: **30 MINUTES**

REFRIGERATION TIME: **6 HOURS +
24 HOURS**

○

**FOR THE COFFEE MACARON
SHELLS**
3 cups (300 g) confectioners' sugar
2 cups plus 2 tablespoons (300 g)
ground almonds
2 tablespoons (30 g) coffee
extract, preferably Trablit
7 large (220 g) "liquefied" egg
whites, divided (see "Macaron
Shells Step-by-Step" in the Kitchen
Guide)
¼ cup plus 1 tablespoon (75 g) still
mineral water
1½ cups (300 g) superfine
granulated sugar

PREPARE THE COFFEE MACARON SHELLS. The day before, sift together the confectioners' sugar and almonds.

Combine the coffee extract with half of the "liquefied" egg whites. Pour this into the confectioners' sugar–almond mixture without mixing.

Add the remaining "liquefied" egg whites to the bowl of a stand mixer fitted with the wire whisk. In a saucepan, boil the mineral water and granulated sugar to 244°F (118°C). As soon as the syrup reaches 239°F (115°C), begin beating the egg whites on high speed. When the syrup reaches 244°F (118°C), reduce the mixer speed to medium–high and pour the syrup in a steady stream down the inside edge of the bowl into the beaten egg whites. Beat the meringue until it cools to 122°F (50°C). Fold it with a silicone spatula into the confectioners' sugar–almond mixture until the mixture loses volume. Transfer the batter to a pastry bag fitted with a plain #11, ½-inch (11-mm to 12-mm) pastry tip.

PREPARE THE COFFEE GANACHE. Chop the white chocolate using a serrated knife then melt it to between 113°F (45°C) and 122°F (50°C) set over a bain-marie or in a microwave.

Grind the coffee beans. In a saucepan, bring the cream to a boil. Add the ground coffee and stir. Cover and let infuse for 3 minutes. Strain the hot cream through a fine-mesh sieve then pour it in thirds into the melted white chocolate, stirring after each addition starting in the center then in increasingly wider concentric circles toward the sides of the bowl.

 Line baking sheets with parchment paper. Pipe disks about 1¹⁄₂ inches (3.5 cm) in diameter and ³⁄₄ inch (2 cm) apart on the lined baking sheets. Rap the baking sheets on a work surface covered with a clean kitchen towel to gently smooth out the disks. Set aside for at least 30 minutes at room temperature to allow a skin to form.

Preheat a convection oven to 350°F (180°C). Place the baking sheets in the oven. Bake for 12 minutes, quickly opening and closing the oven door twice during baking to release moisture. Remove the shells from the oven and slide them still on the parchment paper onto a work surface.

Pour the ganache into a baking dish. Cover it by gently pressing plastic wrap onto its surface. Refrigerate for 6 hours, just until the ganache has developed a creamy consistency. Transfer the ganache to a pastry bag fitted with a plain #11, ¹⁄₂-inch (11-mm to 12-mm) pastry tip.

Turn half of the shells over with the flat sides up onto a new piece of parchment paper. Fill them with the ganache. Close them with the rest of the shells, pressing down lightly.

Refrigerate the macarons for 24 hours. Remove them from the refrigerator 2 hours before eating them.

FOR THE COFFEE GANACHE
15¾ ounces (450 g) Valrhona Ivoire 35% white chocolate
½ cup (30 g) Iapar rouge du Brésil coffee beans, preferably from l'Arbre à Café
2¼ cups (520 g) light whipping cream (32%–35% fat)

I have always taken the time to fully understand every ingredient that I use, to know its history, its origins, and how it's produced.

Macaron Framboise

The filling for this raspberry macaron is neither a ganache nor a cream, but rather a raspberry jam with its seeds. This is the jam recipe I learned as an apprentice at Lenôtre.

MAKES ABOUT 72 MACARONS
(OR ABOUT 144 SHELLS)

PREPARATION TIME: 20 MINUTES
(2 DAYS IN ADVANCE) + 30 MINUTES

COOKING TIME: ABOUT 20 MINUTES

RESTING TIME: 48 HOURS + 1 HOUR

REFRIGERATION TIME: 24 HOURS

FOR THE RASPBERRY JAM
1½ pints (**500 g**) fresh raspberries
or frozen whole or chopped
raspberries
1½ cups (**300 g**) superfine
granulated sugar
2½ teaspoons (**7.5 g**) pectin
or 1 packet of Vitpris pectin
3 tablespoons plus 1 teaspoon
(**50 g**) freshly squeezed lemon juice
(from 1 lemon)

**FOR THE RASPBERRY
MACARON SHELLS**
1⅔ cups (**240 g**) whole almonds,
with skins
4¾ cups (**480 g**) confectioners'
sugar
¼ teaspoon (**1 g**) liquid raspberry
red food color
1 tablespoon (**20 g**) apricot puree
2⅓ large (**70 g**) fresh egg whites

**TO FINISH THE MACARON
SHELLS**
3½ large (**110 g**) fresh egg whites

TWO DAYS IN ADVANCE, PLACE THE ALMONDS FOR THE MACARON SHELLS IN BOILING WATER FOR 2 MINUTES. Drain, then immediately remove the skins. Spread the skinned almonds out onto several layers of paper towels. Let dry for 48 hours at room temperature.

PREPARE THE RASPBERRY JAM. The day before, using an immersion blender, process the raspberries for 10 minutes. Add the sugar and the pectin then process for another 30 seconds. Place the pureed raspberries in a heavy-bottomed stainless-steel saucepan and bring to a boil for 4 to 5 minutes. Remove the saucepan from the heat and stir in the lemon juice.

Pour the jam into a baking dish. Let cool. Cover it by gently pressing plastic wrap onto its surface. Refrigerate until the next day.

PREPARE THE RASPBERRY MACARON SHELLS. Process the almonds in a food processor with a little bit of the confectioners' sugar. Add the rest of the confectioners' sugar then process again until the almonds are finely ground. Sift and press the confectioners' sugar–almond mixture through a medium sieve. Re-process any remaining large almond pieces with the sifted confectioners' sugar–almond mixture until all of the almonds are very finely ground and will fit through the sieve. Dilute the food color and the apricot puree in the 2⅓ (70 g) egg whites then add this to the food processor and process again until the mixture forms a rough mass.

Lightly beat the 3½ (110 g) egg whites just until frothy then add them to the food processor. Process to combine, then transfer the batter to a pastry bag fitted with a plain #11, ½-inch (11-mm to 12-mm) pastry tip.

Line baking sheets with parchment paper. Pipe disks about 1½ inches (3.5 cm) in diameter and ¾ inch (2 cm) apart on the lined baking sheets. Set aside for at least 1 hour at room temperature to allow a skin to form.

Preheat a convection oven to 300°F (150°C). Place the baking sheets in the oven. Bake for 13 minutes, quickly opening and closing the oven door twice during baking to release moisture. Remove the shells from the oven and slide them still on the parchment paper onto a work surface.

Transfer the jam to a pastry bag fitted with a plain #11, ½-inch (11-mm to 12-mm) pastry tip.

Turn half of the shells over with the flat sides up onto a new piece of parchment paper. Fill them with the jam. Close them with the rest of the shells, pressing down lightly.

Refrigerate the macarons for 24 hours. Remove them from the refrigerator 2 hours before eating them.

Macaron Infiniment Framboise

I reinterpreted the traditional raspberry macaron filling made with raspberry jam that has seeds. I wanted to create a raspberry flavor that was as natural as possible to impart the freshest flavor in the mouth rather than the candied taste of raspberry jam.

PREPARE THE RASPBERRY MACARON SHELLS. The day before, sift together the confectioners' sugar and almonds.

Combine the food color with half of the "liquefied" egg whites. Pour this into the confectioners' sugar–almond mixture without mixing.

Add the remaining "liquefied" egg whites to the bowl of a stand mixer fitted with the wire whisk. In a saucepan, boil the mineral water and granulated sugar to 244°F (118°C). As soon as the syrup reaches 239°F (115°C), begin beating the egg whites on high speed.

When the syrup reaches 244°F (118°C), reduce the mixer speed to medium–high and pour the syrup in a steady stream down the inside edge of the bowl into the beaten egg whites. Beat the meringue until it cools to 122°F (50°C). Fold it with a silicone spatula into the confectioners' sugar–almond mixture until the mixture loses volume. Transfer the batter to a pastry bag fitted with a plain #11, ½-inch (11-mm to 12-mm) pastry tip.

Line baking sheets with parchment paper. Pipe disks about 1½ inches (3.5 cm) in diameter and ¾ inch (2 cm) apart on the lined baking sheets. Rap the baking sheets on a work surface covered with a clean kitchen towel to gently smooth out the disks. Set aside for at least 30 minutes at room temperature to allow a skin to form.

Preheat a convection oven to 350°F (180°C). Place the baking sheets in the oven. Bake for 12 minutes, quickly opening and closing the oven door twice during baking to release moisture. Remove the shells from the oven and slide them still on the parchment paper onto a work surface.

PREPARE THE RASPBERRY CREAM. Chop the white chocolate using a serrated knife then melt it to between 113°F (45°C) and 122°F (50°C) set over a bain-marie or in a microwave.

Puree the raspberries using a food mill. In a saucepan, bring the puree to a boil with the lemon juice. Pour the hot puree in thirds into the melted white chocolate, stirring after each addition starting in the center then in increasingly wider concentric circles toward the sides of the bowl.

Pour the raspberry cream into a baking dish. Cover it by gently pressing plastic wrap onto its surface. Refrigerate for 6 hours, just until the cream has developed a creamy consistency. Transfer the cream to a pastry bag fitted with a plain #11, ¹⁄₂-inch (11-mm to 12-mm) pastry tip.

Turn half of the shells over with the flat sides up onto a new piece of parchment paper. Fill them with the raspberry cream. Place a half raspberry in the center then pipe a dab of the cream on top. Close them with the rest of the shells, pressing down lightly.

Refrigerate the macarons for 24 hours. Remove them from the refrigerator 2 hours before eating them. Because of the fresh raspberry, these macarons will last only about 48 hours.

MAKES ABOUT 72 MACARONS
(OR ABOUT 144 SHELLS)
PREPARATION TIME: **5 MINUTES (5 DAYS
IN ADVANCE, SEE "MACARON SHELLS
STEP-BY-STEP" IN THE KITCHEN GUIDE)
+ 1 HOUR 30 MINUTES**
COOKING TIME: **18 TO 20 MINUTES**
RESTING TIME: **30 MINUTES**
REFRIGERATION TIME: **6 HOURS +
24 HOURS**

**FOR THE RASPBERRY
MACARON SHELLS**
3 cups (300 g) confectioners' sugar
2 cups plus 2 tablespoons (300 g)
ground almonds
Generous 2 teaspoons (10 g) liquid
raspberry red food color
7 large (220 g) "liquefied" egg
whites, divided (see "Macaron
Shells Step-by-Step" in the Kitchen
Guide)
¼ cup plus 1 tablespoon (75 g) still
mineral water
1½ cups (300 g) superfine
granulated sugar

FOR THE RASPBERRY CREAM
13¼ ounces (375 g) Valrhona Ivoire
35% white chocolate
1½ pints (500 g) fresh raspberries
(to make 1½ cups/335 g raspberry
puree)
1 tablespoon (15 g) freshly
squeezed lemon juice (from
½ lemon)

FOR THE FILLING
40 fresh raspberries, halved

MY
NEW
CLASSICS

Macaron Infiniment Rose

The rose macaron was one of the first macaron flavors that I created. While on a trip to Bulgaria in 1986, I discovered numerous savory and sweet local specialties using roses. As a result, I created this Infiniment Rose Macaron. Eleven years later, the Ispahan creation was born—a flavor association of lychee, rose, and raspberry.

PREPARE THE ROSE MACARON SHELLS. The day before, sift together the confectioners' sugar and almonds.

Combine the food color with half of the "liquefied" egg whites. Pour this into the confectioners' sugar–almond mixture without mixing.

Add the remaining "liquefied" egg whites to the bowl of a stand mixer fitted with the wire whisk. In a saucepan, boil the mineral water and granulated sugar to 244°F (118°C). As soon as the syrup reaches 239°F (115°C), begin beating the egg whites on high speed.

When the syrup reaches 244°F (118°C), reduce the mixer speed to medium-high and pour the syrup in a steady stream down the inside edge of the bowl into the beaten egg whites. Beat the meringue until it cools to 122°F (50°C). Fold it with a silicone spatula into the confectioners' sugar–almond mixture until the mixture loses volume. Transfer the batter to a pastry bag fitted with a plain #11, ¹/₂-inch (11-mm to 12-mm) pastry tip.

Line baking sheets with parchment paper. Pipe disks about 1¹/₂ inches (3.5 cm) in diameter and ³/₄ inch (2 cm) apart on the lined baking sheets. Rap the baking sheets on a work surface covered with a clean kitchen towel to gently smooth out the disks. Set aside for at least 30 minutes at room temperature to allow a skin to form.

Preheat a convection oven to 350°F (180°C). Place the baking sheets in the oven. Bake for 12 minutes, quickly opening and closing the oven door twice during baking to release moisture. Remove the shells from the oven and slide them still on the parchment paper onto a work surface.

PREPARE THE ITALIAN MERINGUE. Add the egg whites to the bowl of a stand mixer fitted with the wire whisk. In a saucepan, boil the mineral water and and all but 1¼ teaspoons (5 g) of the granulated sugar. When the syrup starts to boil, wipe down the inside of the saucepan with a dampened pastry brush. As soon as the syrup reaches 239°F (115°C), begin beating the egg whites on high speed with the rest of the granulated sugar until the peaks are almost firm and droop slightly in the shape of a "bird's beak" when the whisk is lifted. When the syrup reaches 250°F (121°C), reduce the mixer speed to medium and slowly pour the syrup in a steady stream into the beaten egg whites, continuing to beat until the meringue has cooled.

PREPARE THE CRÈME ANGLAISE. In a saucepan, bring the milk to a boil. In a separate saucepan, whisk together the egg yolks and the granulated sugar until lightened. Slowly add the hot milk to the yolk–sugar mixture while whisking vigorously. Place the saucepan over low heat and cook to 185°F (85°C) while stirring continuously—rich in eggs, this cream has a tendency to stick to the bottom of the saucepan. Strain the cooked cream then transfer it to a stand mixer fitted with the wire whisk. Beat on medium speed until cooled.

PREPARE THE ROSE BUTTERCREAM. In a stand mixer, beat the butter on high speed for 5 minutes. Add the cooled crème anglaise, rose extract, and rose syrup. Beat again to combine.

Using a silicone spatula, fold in the 1½ cups (175 g) of Italian meringue a little at a time. Transfer the mixture to a pastry bag fitted with a plain #11, ½-inch (11-mm to 12-mm) pastry tip.

Turn half of the shells over with the flat sides up onto a new piece of parchment paper. Fill them with the rose buttercream. Close them with the rest of the shells, pressing down lightly.

Refrigerate the macarons for 24 hours. Remove them from the refrigerator 2 hours before eating them.

MAKES ABOUT 72 MACARONS
(OR ABOUT 144 SHELLS)
PREPARATION TIME: 5 MINUTES (5 DAYS IN ADVANCE, SEE "MACARON SHELLS STEP-BY-STEP" IN THE KITCHEN GUIDE)
COOKING TIME: ABOUT 25 MINUTES
RESTING TIME: 30 MINUTES
REFRIGERATION TIME: 24 HOURS

FOR THE ROSE MACARON SHELLS
3 cups (300 g) confectioners' sugar
2 cups plus 2 tablespoons (300 g) ground almonds
¾ teaspoon (3 g) liquid carmine red food color
7 large (220 g) "liquefied" egg whites, divided (see "Macaron Shells Step-by-Step" in the Kitchen Guide)
¼ cup plus 1 tablespoon (75 g) still mineral water
1½ cups (300 g) superfine granulated sugar

FOR THE ITALIAN MERINGUE
2 large (65 g) egg whites
2 tablespoons plus 1 teaspoon (35 g) still mineral water
⅔ cup (130 g) superfine granulated sugar, divided

FOR THE CRÈME ANGLAISE
⅓ cup plus 2 teaspoons (90 g) fresh whole milk
3½ large (70 g) egg yolks
3 tablespoons plus ½ teaspoon (40 g) superfine granulated sugar

FOR THE ROSE BUTTERCREAM
2 cups (450 g) fine French unsalted butter, preferably *beurre de la Viette*, room temperature
1 recipe Crème Anglaise (see above)
1¼ teaspoons (6 g) rose extract
1 tablespoon plus 2 teaspoons (30 g) rose syrup
1½ cups (175 g) Italian Meringue (see above)

Macaron Infiniment Citron

Sicilian lemons are my favorite. They are much juicier and more flavorful than other lemons. I imagined a lemon cream with a velvety texture, close to a lemon curd, flavored with fresh lemon zest and lemon juice. Cédric Casanova, a Sicilian from the shop La Tête dans les Olives, supplies me with the lemons.

MAKES ABOUT 72 MACARONS
(OR ABOUT 144 SHELLS)

PREPARATION TIME: 5 MINUTES (5 DAYS
IN ADVANCE, SEE "MACARON SHELLS
STEP-BY-STEP" IN THE KITCHEN GUIDE)
+ 30 MINUTES (2 DAYS IN ADVANCE) +
1 HOUR 30 MINUTES

COOKING TIME: ABOUT 12 MINUTES
(2 DAYS IN ADVANCE) + ABOUT
12 MINUTES

RESTING TIME: 30 MINUTES

REFRIGERATION TIME: 24 HOURS
(TWICE)

FOR THE LEMON CREAM
¼ cup (25 g) lemon zest (from 5
lemons)
1 cup plus 2 tablespoons
(220 g) superfine granulated sugar
4 large (200 g) eggs
½ cup plus 2 tablespoons
(160 g) freshly squeezed lemon
juice (from 2 lemons)
1¼ cups plus 1 tablespoon
(300 g) fine French unsalted butter,
preferably *beurre de la Viette*,
room temperature

PREPARE THE LEMON CREAM. Two days in advance, wash and dry the lemons. Using a microplane grater, zest the lemons over a bowl and measure the quantity of zest needed. Add the sugar to the bowl and rub it into the zest by pinching it with your fingers. Add the eggs and lemon juice then whisk to combine.

Cook to between 181°F (83°C) and 183°F (84°C) set over a bain-marie, whisking from time to time.

Place the bowl inside a larger bowl containing ice water and stir until the cream cools to 140°F (60°C).

Whisk in the butter in small pieces until incorporated then beat the cream for 10 minutes in a stand mixer fitted with the wire whisk. Cover the cream by gently pressing plastic wrap onto its surface. Refrigerate until the next day.

PREPARE THE LEMON MACARON SHELLS. The day before, sift together the confectioners' sugar and almonds.

Combine the food color with half of the "liquefied" egg whites. Pour this into the confectioners' sugar–almond mixture without mixing.

Add the remaining "liquefied" egg whites to the bowl of a stand mixer fitted with the wire whisk. In a sauce-pan, boil the mineral water and granulated sugar to 244°F (118°C). As soon as the syrup reaches 239°F (115°C), begin beating the egg whites on high speed.

When the syrup reaches 244°F (118°C), reduce the mixer speed to medium-high and pour the syrup in a steady stream down the inside edge of the bowl into the beaten egg whites. Beat the meringue until it cools to 122°F (50°C). Fold it with a silicone spat-ula into the confectioners' sugar–almond mixture until the mixture loses volume. Transfer the batter to a pastry bag fitted with a plain #11, ¹⁄₂-inch (11-mm to 12-mm) pastry tip.

Line baking sheets with parchment paper. Pipe disks about 1¹⁄₂ inches (3.5 cm) in diameter and ³⁄₄ inch (2 cm) apart on the lined baking sheets. Rap the bak-ing sheets on a work surface covered with a clean kitchen towel to gently smooth out the disks. Set aside for at least 30 minutes at room temperature to allow a skin to form.

Preheat a convection oven to 350°F (180°C). Place the baking sheets in the oven. Bake for 12 minutes, quickly opening and closing the oven door twice during baking to release moisture. Remove the shells from the oven and slide them still on the parchment paper onto a work surface.

Transfer the lemon cream to a pastry bag fitted with a plain #11, ¹⁄₂-inch (11-mm to 12-mm) pastry tip.

Turn half of the shells over with the flat sides up onto a new piece of parchment paper. Fill them with the lemon cream. Close them with the rest of the shells, pressing down lightly.

Refrigerate the macarons for 24 hours. Remove them from the refrigerator 2 hours before eating them.

FOR THE LEMON MACARON SHELLS
3 cups (300 g) confectioners' sugar
2 cups plus 2 tablespoons (300 g) ground almonds
1½ teaspoons (6 g) liquid lemon yellow food color
7 large (220 g) "liquefied" egg whites, divided (see "Macaron Shells Step-by-Step" in the Kitchen Guide)
¼ cup plus 1 tablespoon (75 g) still mineral water
1½ cups (300 g) superfine granulated sugar

I use sugar in the same way as salt—as a seasoning to reveal the nuances of other flavors and to contribute to the structure of the taste.

Macaron Moelleux Tiède

Here is another variation of the macaron that uses almond paste, giving it a flavor very close to that of an almond. This moist version is similar to the macarons found in Saint-Émilion. I highly recommend that you try these right out of the oven.

PREPARE THE SOFT MACARONS. Place the almond paste and a small amount of the egg whites in the bowl of a stand mixer fitted with the paddle attachment. Beat just until the almond paste is softened. Add a little more of the egg whites, if necessary, to help soften it.

Replace the paddle attachment with the wire whisk. Beat in the rest of the egg whites a little at a time. Continue beating for 10 minutes, stopping from time to time to scrape down the sides of the bowl and bring the mixture together with a silicone spatula or bowl scraper. Transfer the batter to a pastry bag fitted with a plain #10, ¼-inch (6–mm to 7–mm) pastry tip.

Line baking sheets with parchment paper. Pipe disks about 2½ inches (6 cm) in diameter and ¾ inch (2 cm) apart on the lined baking sheets. Dust the disks with confectioners' sugar. Let rest for 20 minutes.

Preheat a convection oven to 400°F (200°C) then dust the disks again with confectioners' sugar. Place the baking sheets in the oven. Bake for 7 minutes, quickly opening and closing the oven door once during baking to release moisture.

Remove the macarons from the oven and slide them still on the parchment paper onto a work surface. Serve immediately.

MAKES ABOUT 70 MACARONS

PREPARATION TIME: **5 MINUTES (5 DAYS IN ADVANCE, SEE "MACARON SHELLS STEP-BY-STEP" IN THE KITCHEN GUIDE) + 45 MINUTES**

RESTING TIME: **20 MINUTES**

COOKING TIME: **7 MINUTES**

FOR THE SOFT MACARONS
1⅔ pounds (750 g) plain almond paste (made with 60% almonds)
10 large (300 g) "liquefied" egg whites (see "Macaron Shells Step-by-Step" in the Kitchen Guide)

DECORATION
Confectioners' sugar, for dusting

Macaron Caramel à la Fleur de Sel

I love caramel when it has a strong flavor. For this recipe, I take sugar just to the point of burning it in order to showcase the deep flavors of caramel. You must watch the sugar very closely as it caramelizes.

PREPARE THE CARAMEL MACARON SHELLS. The day before, sift together the confectioners' sugar and almonds.

Combine the food color and the coffee extract with half of the "liquefied" egg whites. Pour this into the confectioners' sugar–almond mixture without mixing.

Add the remaining "liquefied" egg whites to the bowl of a stand mixer fitted with the wire whisk. In a saucepan, boil the mineral water and granulated sugar to 244°F (118°C). As soon as the syrup reaches 239°F (115°C), begin beating the egg whites on high speed.

When the syrup reaches 244°F (118°C), reduce the mixer speed to medium–high and pour the syrup in a steady stream down the inside edge of the bowl into the beaten egg whites. Beat the meringue until it cools to 122°F (50°C). Fold it with a silicone spatula into the confectioners' sugar–almond mixture until the mixture loses volume. Transfer the batter to a pastry bag fitted with a plain #11, ½-inch (11-mm to 12-mm) pastry tip.

Line baking sheets with parchment paper. Pipe disks about 1½ inches (3.5 cm) in diameter and ¾ inch (2 cm) apart on the lined baking sheets. Rap the baking sheets on a work surface covered with a clean kitchen towel to gently smooth out the disks. Set aside for at least 30 minutes at room temperature to allow a skin to form.

Preheat a convection oven to 350°F (180°C). Place the baking sheets in the oven. Bake for 12 minutes, quickly opening and closing the oven door twice during baking to release moisture. Remove the shells from the oven and slide them still on the parchment paper onto a work surface.

PREPARE THE SALTED-BUTTER CARAMEL. In a saucepan, bring the cream to a boil. In a separate heavy-bottomed saucepan placed over medium heat, melt ¼ cup (50 g) of the sugar. Add another ¼ cup (50 g) of the sugar then continue in the same way with the rest of the sugar. Cook just until the caramel develops a deep amber color. Off the heat, add the butter in small pieces and stir to combine using a silicone spatula. Stir in the hot cream in two parts. Place the saucepan back over the heat and cook the caramel to 226°F (108°C). Blend the caramel with an immersion blender, then pour it into a heat-resistant dish. Cover and refrigerate to cool.

PREPARE THE SALTED-BUTTER CARAMEL CREAM. Beat the butter for 10 minutes in the bowl of a stand mixer fitted with the wire whisk. Add the cooled salted-butter caramel and beat until very smooth. Transfer the cream to a pastry bag fitted with a plain #11, ½-inch (11-mm to 12-mm) pastry tip.

Turn half of the shells over with the flat sides up onto a new piece of parchment paper. Fill them with the salted-butter caramel cream. Close them with the rest of the shells, pressing down lightly.

Refrigerate the macarons for 24 hours. Remove them from the refrigerator 2 hours before eating them.

MAKES ABOUT 72 MACARONS (OR ABOUT 144 SHELLS)

PREPARATION TIME: **5 MINUTES (5 DAYS IN ADVANCE, SEE "MACARON SHELLS STEP-BY-STEP" IN THE KITCHEN GUIDE) + 1 HOUR 30 MINUTES**

COOKING TIME: **ABOUT 25 MINUTES**

RESTING TIME: **30 MINUTES**

REFRIGERATION TIME: **2 HOURS + 24 HOURS**

FOR THE CARAMEL MACARON SHELLS
3 cups (300 g) confectioners' sugar
2 cups plus 2 tablespoons (300 g) ground almonds
½ teaspoon (2 g) liquid yellow food color
1 tablespoon (15 g) coffee extract, preferably Trablit
7 large (220 g) "liquefied" egg whites, divided (see "Macaron Shells Step-by-Step" in the Kitchen Guide)
¼ cup plus 1 tablespoon (75 g) still mineral water
1½ cups (300 g) superfine granulated sugar

FOR THE SALTED-BUTTER CARAMEL
1½ cups minus 1 tablespoon (335 g) light whipping cream (32%–35% fat)
1½ cups (300 g) superfine granulated sugar
¼ cup plus 1¾ teaspoons (65 g) fine French butter, lightly salted, preferably *beurre de la Viette demi-sel*, room temperature

FOR THE SALTED-BUTTER CARAMEL CREAM
1¼ cups plus 1 teaspoon (290 g) fine French unsalted butter, preferably *beurre de la Viette*, room temperature
1 recipe Salted-Butter Caramel (see above)

Macaron Infiniment Praliné Noisette du Piémont

I have an extreme passion for the flavorful and sweet taste of hazelnuts from the Piedmont region of Italy. They motivated me to express their best flavor by toasting them and creating a macaron with the intense flavor of hazelnut praline.

PREPARE THE TOASTED HAZELNUTS. Two days in advance, spread the hazelnuts out on a baking sheet. Preheat the oven to 340°F (170°C).

Toast the hazelnuts for 15 minutes. Remove them from the oven and immediately transfer them to a sieve with large holes or to a colander. Roll them around to help remove their skins. Transfer the skinned hazelnuts to a plastic bag. Using a rolling pin, crush them into medium-size pieces. Set aside a scant ¼ cup (20 g) of the hazelnuts and place the rest back in the warm oven that has been turned off.

PREPARE THE TOASTED HAZELNUT PRALINE. Two days in advance, add the mineral water and sugar to a saucepan. Scrape the seeds out of the vanilla bean using a knife and add the seeds to the pan along with the vanilla bean pod. Bring the mixture to a boil. As soon as the syrup reaches 250°F (121°C), add the warm hazelnut pieces from the oven. Stir just until the syrup develops a sandy texture, then let it caramelize, stirring from time to time.

Pour the caramelized hazelnuts onto a baking sheet. Remove the vanilla bean pod and let the hazelnuts cool. Place them in a food processor and process them by pulsing them until fairly fine but not too fine: the praline should maintain a coarse texture.

MAKES ABOUT 72 MACARONS (OR ABOUT 144 SHELLS)

PREPARATION TIME: 5 MINUTES (5 DAYS IN ADVANCE, SEE "MACARON SHELLS STEP-BY-STEP" IN THE KITCHEN GUIDE) + 45 MINUTES (2 DAYS IN ADVANCE) + 1 HOUR 30 MINUTES

COOKING TIME: ABOUT 20 MINUTES (2 DAYS IN ADVANCE) + ABOUT 14 MINUTES

FREEZING TIME: 2 HOURS + 24 HOURS

RESTING TIME: 30 MINUTES

REFRIGERATION TIME: 1 HOUR (2 DAYS IN ADVANCE) + 24 HOURS

FOR THE TOASTED HAZELNUTS
2 cups (270 g) whole hazelnuts, preferably from Piedmont, with skins

FOR THE TOASTED HAZELNUT PRALINE
2 tablespoons plus 2 teaspoons (40 g) still mineral water
¾ cup (150 g) superfine granulated sugar
½ vanilla bean, halved lengthwise
1¾ cups (250 g) toasted, crushed hazelnuts (see above)

PREPARE THE HAZELNUT PRALINE SQUARES. Chop the chocolate using a serrated knife then melt it to between 113°F (45°C) and 122°F (50°C) on low heat, set over a bain-marie or in a microwave.

Stir in the store-bought hazelnut praline, hazelnut paste, and butter. Stir until thoroughly combined then add the ¼ cup (20 g) finely crushed hazelnuts and the crumbled cookies.

Transfer this mixture to a baking dish that has been lined with plastic wrap and, using an offset metal spatula, spread the praline into a thin, even layer about ⅛ inch (4 mm) thick. Refrigerate for 1 hour then freeze for 2 hours. Peel the plastic wrap from the hardened praline then cut into ½-inch (1.5-cm) squares. Wrap the squares and place them back in the freezer.

PREPARE THE PRALINE CREAM. Two days in advance, melt the cocoa butter over a bain-marie or in a microwave. Add it to the bowl of a stand mixer fitted with the paddle attachment, and beat together with the store-bought hazelnut praline and toasted hazelnut praline. Pour the mixture into a baking dish, cover it by gently pressing plastic wrap onto its surface, and refrigerate until the next day.

The day before, in the bowl of a stand mixer fitted with the paddle attachment, beat the butter for 5 minutes then add the chilled praline–cocoa butter mixture a little at a time.

PREPARE THE HAZELNUT PRALINE MACARON SHELLS. Sift together the confectioners' sugar, almonds, and ground hazelnuts. Add half the "liquefied" egg whites without mixing.

Add the remaining "liquefied" egg whites to the bowl of a stand mixer fitted with the wire whisk. In a saucepan, boil the mineral water and granulated sugar to 244°F (118°C). As soon as the syrup reaches 239°F (115°C), begin beating the egg whites on high speed.

When the syrup reaches 244°F (118°C), reduce the mixer speed to medium-high and pour the syrup in a steady stream down the inside edge of the bowl into the beaten egg whites. Beat the meringue until it cools to 122°F (50°C). Fold it with a silicone spatula into the confectioners' sugar–almond–hazelnut mixture until the mixture loses volume. Transfer the batter to a pastry bag fitted with a plain #11, ½-inch (11-mm to 12-mm) pastry tip.

Line baking sheets with parchment paper. Pipe disks about 1½ inches (3.5 cm) in diameter and ¾ inch (2 cm) apart on the lined baking sheets. Sprinkle them with the slivered hazelnuts. Rap the baking sheets on a work surface covered with a clean kitchen towel to gently smooth out the disks. Set aside for at least 30 minutes at room temperature to allow a skin to form.

Preheat a convection oven to 350°F (180°C). Place the baking sheets in the oven. Bake for 12 minutes, quickly opening and closing the oven door twice during baking to release moisture. Remove the shells from the oven and slide them still on the parchment paper onto a work surface.

Transfer the praline cream to a pastry bag fitted with a plain #11, ½-inch (11-mm to 12-mm) pastry tip.

Turn half the shells over with the flat sides up onto a new piece of parchment paper. Fill them with the praline cream then gently place a frozen praline square in the center of each. Pipe a small dab of cream on top of the praline square. Close them with the rest of the shells, pressing down lightly.

Refrigerate the macarons for 24 hours. Remove them from the refrigerator 2 hours before eating them.

FOR THE HAZELNUT PRALINE SQUARES
1½ ounces (45 g) Valrhona Jivara 40% cacao milk chocolate or any other 40% cacao milk chocolate
3 tablespoons plus 1 teaspoon (65 g) 60% hazelnut praline, preferably Valrhona
3½ ounces (100 g) hazelnut paste, preferably Valrhona
1 tablespoon plus 1 teaspoon (20 g) fine French unsalted butter, preferably *beurre de la Viette*, cut into small pieces
¼ cup (20 g) toasted, crushed hazelnuts (see above)
3 ounces (85 g) plain Gavottes crêpe cookies, crumbled
Note: *This will make more hazelnut praline squares than needed for 72 macarons.*

FOR THE PRALINE CREAM
1¾ ounces (50 g) cocoa butter, preferably Valrhona
½ cup plus 2 tablespoons (200 g) hazelnut praline, preferably Valrhona
7 ounces (200 g) Toasted Hazelnut Praline (see above)
½ cup plus 2½ tablespoons (150 g) fine French unsalted butter, preferably *beurre de la Viette*, room temperature

FOR THE PRALINE MACARON SHELLS
3 cups (300 g) confectioners' sugar
1 cup plus 1 tablespoon (150 g) ground almonds
1⅓ cups (150 g) ground hazelnuts
7 large (220 g) "liquefied" egg whites, divided (see "Macaron Shells Step-by-Step" in the Kitchen Guide)
¼ cup plus 1 tablespoon (75 g) still mineral water
1½ cups (300 g) superfine granulated sugar
Scant ½ cup (50 g) raw, slivered hazelnuts

Macaron Infiniment Pistache

Pistachios have a very subtle flavor. To accentuate their flavor and aroma, I add several drops of natural bitter almond extract to the ganache.

PREPARE THE PISTACHIO MACARON SHELLS. The day before, sift together the confectioners' sugar and almonds.

Combine the green and yellow food colors with half of the "liquefied" egg whites. Pour this into the confectioners' sugar–almond mixture without mixing.

Add the remaining "liquefied" egg whites to the bowl of a stand mixer fitted with the wire whisk. In a saucepan, boil the mineral water and granulated sugar to 244°F (118°C). As soon as the syrup reaches 239°F (115°C), begin beating the egg whites on high speed.

When the syrup reaches 244°F (118°C), reduce the mixer speed to medium-high and pour the syrup in a steady stream down the inside edge of the bowl into the beaten egg whites. Beat the meringue until it cools to 122°F (50°C). Fold it with a silicone spatula into the confectioners' sugar–almond mixture until the mixture loses volume. Transfer the batter to a pastry bag fitted with a plain #11, ½-inch (11-mm to 12-mm) pastry tip.

Line baking sheets with parchment paper. Pipe disks about 1½ inches (3.5 cm) in diameter and ¾ inch (2 cm) apart on the lined baking sheets. Rap the baking sheets on a work surface covered with a clean kitchen towel to gently smooth out the disks. Set aside for at least 30 minutes at room temperature to allow a skin to form.

Preheat a convection oven to 350°F (180°C). Place the baking sheets in the oven. Bake for 12 minutes, quickly opening and closing the oven door twice during baking to release moisture. Remove the shells from the oven and slide them still on the parchment paper onto a work surface.

PREPARE THE PISTACHIO GANACHE. Chop the white chocolate using a serrated knife then melt it to between 113°F (45°C) and 122°F (50°C) at low heat, set over a bain-marie or in a microwave. In a saucepan, bring the cream to a boil with the pistachio paste and the natural bitter almond oil, whisking from time to time. Pour the hot cream in thirds into the melted white chocolate, stirring after each addition starting in the center then in increasingly wider concentric circles toward the sides of the bowl. Using an immersion blender, blend the ganache until smooth.

Pour the ganache into a baking dish. Cover it by gently pressing plastic wrap onto its surface. Refrigerate for 6 hours, just until the ganache has developed a creamy consistency. Transfer the ganache to a pastry bag fitted with a plain #11, $^1/_2$-inch (11-mm to 12-mm) pastry tip.

Turn half of the shells over with the flat sides up onto a new piece of parchment paper. Fill them with the ganache. Close them with the rest of the shells, pressing down lightly.

Refrigerate the macarons for 24 hours. Remove them from the refrigerator 2 hours before eating them.

MAKES ABOUT 72 MACARONS (OR ABOUT 144 SHELLS)

PREPARATION TIME: 5 MINUTES (5 DAYS IN ADVANCE, SEE "MACARON SHELLS STEP-BY-STEP" IN THE KITCHEN GUIDE) + 1 HOUR 30 MINUTES

COOKING TIME: ABOUT 25 MINUTES

RESTING TIME: 30 MINUTES

REFRIGERATION TIME: 6 HOURS + 24 HOURS

FOR THE PISTACHIO MACARON SHELLS
3 cups (300 g) confectioners' sugar
2 cups plus 2 tablespoons (300 g) ground almonds
Scant ¼ teaspoon (0.7 g) liquid pistachio green food color
¼ teaspoon (1 g) liquid yellow food color
7 large (220 g) "liquefied" egg whites, divided (see "Macaron Shells Step-by-Step" in the Kitchen Guide)
¼ cup plus 1 tablespoon (75 g) still mineral water
1½ cups (300 g) superfine granulated sugar

FOR THE PISTACHIO GANACHE
10½ ounces (300 g) Valrhona Ivoire 35% white chocolate
1⅓ cups (300 g) light whipping cream (32%–35% fat)
1½ ounces (45 g) pure pistachio paste plus several drops natural bitter almond oil, or 1 ounce (25 g) pure pistachio paste plus ¾ ounce (20 g) almond-flavored pistachio paste

Macaron Moelleux Tiède à la Pistache

I encourage you to taste these macarons right out of the oven, as their texture is much softer than after they have cooled. While still warm, they have a wonderful flavor of toasted pistachios.

PREPARE THE SOFT MACARONS. Place the almond paste, pistachio paste, and a small amount of the egg whites in the bowl of a stand mixer fitted with the paddle attachment. Beat just until the mixture is softened. Add a little more of the egg whites, if necessary, to help soften it.

Replace the paddle attachment with the wire whisk. Beat in the rest of the egg whites a little at a time. Continue beating for 10 minutes, stopping from time to time to scrape down the sides of the bowl and bring the mixture together with a silicone spatula or bowl scraper. Transfer the batter to a pastry bag fitted with a plain #10, ¼-inch (6-mm to 7-mm) pastry tip.

Line baking sheets with parchment paper. Pipe disks measuring 2½ inches (6 cm) in diameter and ¾ inch (2 cm) apart on the lined baking sheets. Sprinkle them with the pistachios. Dust the disks with confectioners' sugar. Let rest for 20 minutes.

Preheat a convection oven to 400°F (200°C) then dust the disks again with confectioners' sugar. Place the baking sheets in the oven. Bake for 7 minutes, quickly opening and closing the oven door once during baking to release moisture.

Remove the macarons from the oven and slide them still on the parchment paper onto a work surface. Serve immediately.

MAKES ABOUT 70 MACARONS

PREPARATION TIME: **5 MINUTES (5 DAYS IN ADVANCE, SEE "MACARON SHELLS STEP-BY-STEP" IN THE KITCHEN GUIDE) + 45 MINUTES**

RESTING TIME: **20 MINUTES**

COOKING TIME: **7 MINUTES**

FOR THE SOFT MACARONS
1⅔ pounds (750 g) plain almond paste (made with 52% almonds)
3 ounces (80 g) pure pistachio paste, preferably Fugar
10 large (300 g) "liquefied" egg whites (see "Macaron Shells Step-by-Step" in the Kitchen Guide)

DECORATION
½ cup (70 g) Sicilian or Iranian pistachios, skins removed, chopped
Confectioners' sugar, for dusting

MY
"FÉTISH" FLAVOR
COMBINATIONS

Macaron Chloé

Chloé is a friend of mine who is passionate about chocolate but who detests the combination of chocolate and raspberry, which is why I wanted to rise to the challenge of creating this macaron and dedicate it to her. I worked to create a harmony between the acidity of the raspberries and the subtle bitterness and acidity of dark chocolate.

PREPARE THE CHOCOLATE MACARON SHELLS. Chop the cocoa paste using a serrated knife then melt it to between 113°F (45°C) and 122°F (50°C) set over a bain-marie or in a microwave.

Sift together the confectioners' sugar and almonds.

Combine the food color with half of the "liquefied" egg whites. Pour this into the confectioners' sugar–almond mixture without mixing.

Add the remaining "liquefied" egg whites to the bowl of a stand mixer fitted with the wire whisk. In a saucepan, boil the mineral water and granulated sugar to 244°F (118°C). As soon as the syrup reaches 239°F (115°C), begin beating the egg whites on high speed.

When the syrup reaches 244°F (118°C), reduce the mixer speed to medium-high and pour the syrup in a steady stream down the inside edge of the bowl into the beaten egg whites. Beat the meringue until it cools to 122°F (50°C). Fold about one-third of the meringue into the melted cocoa paste then add this mixture to the confections' sugar–almond mixture along with the rest of the meringue. Fold it with a silicone spatula until the mixture loses volume. Transfer the batter to a pastry bag fitted with a plain #11, ½-inch (11-mm to 12-mm) pastry tip.

THE DAY BEFORE, IF USING FRESH RASPBERRIES, PREHEAT THE OVEN TO 195°F (90°C). Spread the fresh raspberries for the filling onto a baking sheet lined with parchment paper, then place them in the oven. Leave them to dry for 2 hours, stirring every 30 minutes. Set them out to cool then place them in an airtight container until needed.

Line baking sheets with parchment paper. Pipe disks about 1½ inches (3.5 cm) in diameter and ¾ inch (2 cm) apart on the lined baking sheets. Rap the baking sheets on a work surface covered with a clean kitchen towel to gently smooth out the disks. Dust the disks with the cocoa. Set aside for at least 30 minutes at room temperature to allow a skin to form.

PREPARE THE RASPBERRY MACARON SHELLS. Sift together the confectioners' sugar and almonds.

Combine the food color with half of the "liquefied" egg whites. Pour this into the confectioners' sugar–almond mixture without mixing.

Add the remaining "liquefied" egg whites to the bowl of a stand mixer fitted with the wire whisk. In a saucepan, boil the mineral water and granulated sugar to 244°F (118°C). As soon as the syrup reaches 239°F (115°C), begin beating the egg whites on high speed.

When the syrup reaches 244°F (118°C), reduce the mixer speed to medium-high and pour the syrup in a steady stream down the inside edge of the bowl into the beaten egg whites. Beat the meringue until it cools to 122°F (50°C). Fold it with a silicone spatula into the confectioners' sugar–almond mixture until the mixture loses volume. Transfer the batter to a pastry bag fitted with a plain #11, ¹⁄₂-inch (11-mm to 12-mm) pastry tip.

Line baking sheets with parchment paper. Pipe disks about 1¹⁄₂ inches (3.5 cm) in diameter and ³⁄₄ inch (2 cm) apart on the lined baking sheets. Rap the baking sheets on a work surface covered with a clean kitchen towel to gently smooth out the disks. Set aside for at least 30 minutes at room temperature to allow a skin to form.

Preheat a convection oven to 350°F (180°C). Place the baking sheets in the oven. Bake for 12 minutes, quickly opening and closing the oven door twice during baking to release moisture. Remove the shells from the oven and slide them still on the parchment paper onto a work surface.

PREPARE THE CHOCOLATE-RASPBERRY GANACHE. Chop the chocolate using a serrated knife then melt it to between 113°F (45°C) and 122°F (50°C) set over a bain-marie or in a microwave.

If using whole raspberries, puree them using a food mill. Bring the raspberry puree to a boil in a saucepan. Remove it from the heat then pour it in thirds into the melted chocolate, stirring after each addition starting in the center then in increasingly wider concentric circles toward the sides of the bowl.

When the ganache has cooled to 140°F (60°C), stir in the butter in small pieces a little at a time until incorporated. Using an immersion blender, blend the ganache until smooth.

Pour the ganache into a baking dish. Cover it by gently pressing plastic wrap onto its surface. Refrigerate for 2 hours, just until the ganache has developed a creamy consistency. Transfer the ganache to a pastry bag fitted with a plain #11, ¹⁄₂-inch (11-mm to 12-mm) pastry tip.

Turn the chocolate shells over with the flat sides up onto a new piece of parchment paper. Fill them with the ganache then gently place a dried raspberry in the center. Pipe a small dab of ganache on top of the raspberry. Close them with the raspberry shells, pressing down lightly.

Refrigerate the macarons for 24 hours. Remove them from the refrigerator 2 hours before eating them.

MAKES ABOUT 72 MACARONS (OR ABOUT 144 SHELLS)
PREPARATION TIME: 5 MINUTES (5 DAYS IN ADVANCE, SEE "MACARON SHELLS STEP-BY-STEP" IN THE KITCHEN GUIDE) + 1 HOUR 30 MINUTES
COOKING TIME: ABOUT 2 HOURS + 20 MINUTES
RESTING TIME: 30 MINUTES (TWICE)
REFRIGERATION TIME: 2 HOURS + 24 HOURS

FOR THE CHOCOLATE MACARON SHELLS
2¹⁄₈ ounces (60 g) Valrhona 100% cocoa paste
1¹⁄₂ cups (150 g) confectioners' sugar
1 cup plus 1 tablespoon (150 g) ground almonds
4 drops / ¹⁄₁₆ teaspoon (0.25 g) liquid carmine red food color
3¹⁄₂ large (110 g) "liquefied" egg whites, divided (see "Macaron Shells Step-by-Step" in the Kitchen Guide)
3 tablespoons (43 g) still mineral water
³⁄₄ cup (150 g) superfine granulated sugar
1 cup plus 2 tablespoons (100 g) unsweetened cocoa, preferably Valrhona

FOR THE RASPBERRY MACARON SHELLS
1¹⁄₂ cups (150 g) confectioners' sugar
1 cup plus 1 tablespoon (150 g) ground almonds
Generous 1 teaspoon (5 g) liquid raspberry red food color
3¹⁄₂ large (110 g) "liquefied" egg whites, divided (see "Macaron Shells Step-by-Step" in the Kitchen Guide)
2 tablespoons plus 1³⁄₄ teaspoons (38 g) still mineral water
³⁄₄ cup (150 g) superfine granulated sugar
¹⁄₂ cup plus 1¹⁄₂ tablespoons (50 g) unsweetened cocoa, preferably Valrhona

FOR THE CHOCOLATE-RASPBERRY GANACHE
13 ounces (365 g) Valrhona Manjari 64% cacao dark chocolate
1²⁄₃ pints (550 g) fresh raspberries or 1²⁄₃ cups (360 g) raspberry puree
1¹⁄₄ cups plus 2 tablespoons (315 g) fine French unsalted butter, preferably *beurre de la Viette*, room temperature

FOR THE FILLING
Generous ¹⁄₂ pint (200 g) fresh raspberries or ¹⁄₄ cup (40 g) dried

Macaron Infiniment Café au Café Vert et au Café Bourbon Pointu de la Réunion

MAKES ABOUT 72 MACARONS
(OR ABOUT 144 SHELLS)

PREPARATION TIME: 5 MINUTES (5 DAYS
IN ADVANCE, SEE "MACARON SHELLS
STEP-BY-STEP" IN THE KITCHEN GUIDE)
+ 5 MINUTES (2 DAYS IN ADVANCE) +
1 HOUR 30 MINUTES

COOKING TIME: 3 TO 4 MINUTES
(2 DAYS IN ADVANCE) + ABOUT
20 MINUTES

INFUSION TIME: 24 HOURS (2 DAYS IN
ADVANCE) + 4 HOURS

RESTING TIME: 30 MINUTES (TWICE)

REFRIGERATION TIME: 12 HOURS +
6 HOURS + 2 HOURS + 24 HOURS

**FOR THE GREEN COFFEE
CREAM**
1⅓ cups (300 g) light whipping
cream (32%–35% fat)
¼ cup (15 g) green lapar rouge du
Brésil coffee beans, preferably
from l'Arbre à Café

**FOR THE COFFEE MACARON
SHELLS**
1½ cups (150 g) confectioners'
sugar
1 cup plus 1 tablespoon (150 g)
ground almonds
1 tablespoon (15 g) coffee extract,
preferably Trablit
3½ large (110 g) "liquefied" egg
whites, divided (see "Macaron
Shells Step-by-Step" in the Kitchen
Guide)
3 tablespoons (43 g) still mineral
water
¾ cup (150 g) superfine granulated
sugar

I combined two varieties of coffee with the single goal of sublimating each of them. Green coffee is a coffee that has not been roasted. With its fresh and vegetal flavor notes, this coffee marries naturally with the unique flavors of red fruits, musk, flowers, rhubarb, pineapples, rose, and spices of Bourbon pointu de la Réunion coffee from l'Arbre à Café.

PREPARE THE GREEN COFFEE CREAM. Two days in advance, in a saucepan, bring the cream to a boil with the green coffee beans. Reduce the heat and let simmer for 5 minutes. Set aside to cool to room temperature. Cover and refrigerate to infuse until the next day.

PREPARE THE COFFEE MACARON SHELLS. The day before, sift together the confectioners' sugar and almonds.

Combine the coffee extract with half of the "liquefied" egg whites. Pour this into the confectioners' sugar–almond mixture without mixing.

Add the remaining "liquefied" egg whites to the bowl of a stand mixer fitted with the wire whisk. In a saucepan, boil the mineral water and granulated sugar to 244°F (118°C). As soon as the syrup reaches 239°F (115°C), begin beating the egg whites on high speed.

When the syrup reaches 244°F (118°C), reduce the mixer speed to medium–high and pour the syrup in a steady stream down the inside edge of the bowl into the beaten egg whites. Beat the meringue until it cools to 122°F (50°C). Fold it with a silicone spatula into the confectioners' sugar–almond mixture until the mixture loses volume. Transfer the batter to a pastry bag fitted with a plain #11, ½-inch (11-mm to 12-mm) pastry tip.

Line baking sheets with parchment paper. Pipe disks about 1½ inches (3.5 cm) in diameter and ¾ inch (2 cm) apart on the lined baking sheets. Rap the baking sheets on a work surface covered with a clean kitchen towel to gently smooth out the disks. Set aside for at least 30 minutes at room temperature to allow a skin to form.

PREPARE THE GREEN COFFEE MACARON SHELLS. Sift together the confectioners' sugar and almonds.

Combine the green, brown, and yellow food colors with half of the "liquefied" egg whites. Pour this into the confectioners' sugar–almond mixture without mixing.

Add the remaining "liquefied" egg whites to the bowl of a stand mixer fitted with the wire whisk. In a saucepan, boil the mineral water and granulated sugar to 244°F (118°C). As soon as the syrup reaches 239°F (115°C), begin beating the egg whites on high speed.

When the syrup reaches 244°F (118°C), reduce the mixer speed to medium–high and pour the syrup in a steady stream down the inside edge of the bowl into the beaten egg whites. Beat the meringue until it cools to 122°F (50°C). Fold it with a silicone spatula into the confectioners' sugar–almond mixture until the mixture loses volume. Transfer the batter to a pastry bag fitted with a plain #11, ¹/₂-inch (11-mm to 12-mm) pastry tip.

Line baking sheets with parchment paper. Pipe disks about 1¹/₂ inches (3.5 cm) in diameter and ³/₄ inch (2 cm) apart on the lined baking sheets. Rap the baking sheets on a work surface covered with a clean kitchen towel to gently smooth out the disks. Set aside for at least 30 minutes at room temperature to allow a skin to form.

Preheat a convection oven to 350°F (180°C). Place the baking sheets in the oven. Bake for 12 minutes, quickly opening and closing the oven door twice during baking to release moisture. Remove the shells from the oven and slide them still on the parchment paper onto a work surface.

PREPARE THE COFFEE GANACHE. Place the coffee beans in a clean towel. Using a heavy saucepan, crush them into coarse pieces. In a saucepan, bring the cream to a boil. Add the coffee beans and stir to combine. Cover and set aside to infuse for 4 hours.

Chop the white chocolate using a serrated knife then melt it to between 113°F (45°C) and 122°F (50°C) set over a bain-marie or in a microwave.

Strain the cream and bring it to a boil in a saucepan. Pour the hot cream in thirds into the melted white chocolate, stirring after each addition starting in the center then in increasingly wider concentric circles toward the sides of the bowl. Using an immersion blender, blend the ganache until smooth.

Pour the ganache into a baking dish. Cover it by gently pressing plastic wrap onto its surface. Refrigerate for 6 hours, just until the ganache has developed a creamy consistency.

PREPARE THE GREEN COFFEE GANACHE. Strain the green coffee cream prepared the day before and heat it to about 140°F (60°C).

Chop the white chocolate using a serrated knife then melt it to between 113°F (45°C) and 122°F (50°C) set over a bain-marie or in a microwave.

Pour the hot cream in thirds into the melted white chocolate, stirring after each addition starting in the center then in increasingly wider concentric circles toward the sides of the bowl. Using an immersion blender, blend the ganache until smooth.

Pour the ganache into a baking dish. Cover it by gently pressing plastic wrap onto its surface. Refrigerate for 2 hours, just until the ganache has developed a creamy consistency.

Transfer the coffee ganache and the green coffee ganache to separate pastry bags fitted with plain #11, ¹/₂-inch (11-mm to 12-mm) pastry tips.

Turn the coffee shells over with the flat sides up onto a new piece of parchment paper. Fill them with the coffee ganache then pipe a dollop of green coffee ganache in the center. Close them with the green coffee macaron shells, pressing down lightly.

Refrigerate the macarons for 24 hours. Remove them from the refrigerator 2 hours before eating them.

FOR THE GREEN COFFEE MACARON SHELLS
1½ cups (150 g) confectioners' sugar
1 cup plus 1 tablespoon (150 g) ground almonds
8 drops / ⅛ teaspoon (0.5 g) liquid pistachio green food color
8 drops / ⅛ teaspoon (0.5 g) liquid chocolate brown food color
8 drops / ⅛ teaspoon (0.5 g) liquid yellow food color
3½ large (110 g) "liquefied" egg whites, divided (see "Macaron Shells Step-by-Step" in the Kitchen Guide)
2 tablespoons plus 1¾ teaspoons (38 g) still mineral water
¾ cup (150 g) superfine granulated sugar

FOR THE COFFEE GANACHE
¼ cup (16 g) Réunion Bourbon Pointu coffee beans
1 cup plus 2 tablespoons (260 g) light whipping cream (32%–35% fat)
8 ounces (225 g) Valrhona Ivoire 35% white chocolate

FOR THE GREEN COFFEE GANACHE
8 ounces (225 g) Green Coffee Cream (see above)
8 ounces (225 g) Valrhona Ivoire 35% white chocolate

Macaron Infiniment Mandarine

It is really the perfume of Sicilian mandarin oranges that I wanted to pay tribute to more than anything in this macaron. Their taste is incomparable. Their zest and pulp are much juicier than other mandarin oranges and their sweetness, bitterness, and slight acidity are in perfect harmony.

PREPARE THE SEMI-CANDIED MANDARIN ORANGES. Two days in advance, wash and dry the oranges. Cut off both rounded ends. Cut the oranges in half from top to bottom. Immerse them three times in boiling water for 20 seconds then leave them to boil for 2 minutes. Rinse them under cold water. Repeat these same steps twice more, then drain.

In a saucepan, bring the mineral water and the sugar to a boil. Place the oranges in the boiling syrup. Cover and let simmer very gently for 2 hours. Set aside to soak until the next day.

PREPARE THE MANDARIN CREAM. Two days in advance, wash and dry the oranges and the lemons. Using a microplane grater, zest them over a bowl and measure the quantities of zest needed. Add the sugar to the bowl and rub it into the zest by pinching it with your fingers. Whisk in the eggs, lemon juice, and orange juice and cook to between 181°F (83°C) and 183°F (84°C) set over a bain-marie, whisking from time to time. Place the bowl inside a larger bowl containing ice water and stir until the cream cools to 140°F (60°C). Whisk in the butter in small pieces until smooth, then beat the cream at medium speed for 10 minutes in a stand mixer fitted with the wire whisk. The cream will lighten in color and thicken in appearance. Cover the cream by gently pressing plastic wrap onto its surface. Refrigerate until the next day.

MAKES ABOUT 72 MACARONS (OR ABOUT 144 SHELLS)

PREPARATION TIME: 5 MINUTES (5 DAYS IN ADVANCE, SEE "MACARON SHELLS STEP-BY-STEP" IN THE KITCHEN GUIDE) + 30 MINUTES (2 DAYS IN ADVANCE) + 1 HOUR 30 MINUTES

COOKING TIME: ABOUT 2 HOURS (2 DAYS IN ADVANCE) + ABOUT 15 MINUTES

RESTING TIME: 30 MINUTES

REFRIGERATION TIME: 2 HOURS + 24 HOURS (TWICE)

FOR THE SEMI-CANDIED MANDARIN ORANGES
10 Sicilian mandarin oranges, preferably from La Tête dans les Olives
4¼ cups (1 kg) still mineral water
2½ cups (500 g) superfine granulated sugar

FOR THE MANDARIN CREAM
1 tablespoon plus 1 teaspoon (8 g) freshly grated Sicilian mandarin orange zest (from 2 oranges), preferably from La Tête dans les Olives
1 teaspoon (2 g) freshly grated lemon zest (from ½ lemon)
½ cup (100 g) superfine granulated sugar
3 large (160 g) eggs
3 tablespoons plus 1 teaspoon (50 g) freshly squeezed lemon juice (from 1 lemon)
⅓ cup minus 1 teaspoon (80 g) freshly squeezed Sicilian mandarin orange juice (from about ½ pound/ 250 g oranges), preferably from La Tête dans les Olives
1 cup plus 2½ tablespoons (260 g) fine French unsalted butter, preferably *beurre de la Viette*, room temperature

Savoir-faire is our heritage, handed down to us from our predecessors. We must preserve it, allow it to evolve, and pass it down.

**FOR THE MANDARIN
MACARON SHELLS**
3 cups (300 g) confectioners' sugar
2 cups plus 2 tablespoons (300 g)
ground almonds
**Generous 1½ teaspoons
(7 g)** liquid yellow food color
¼ teaspoon (1 g) liquid red food
color
7 large (220 g) "liquefied" egg
whites, divided (see "Macaron
Shells Step-by-Step" in the Kitchen
Guide)
¼ cup plus 1 tablespoon (75 g) still
mineral water
1½ cups (300 g) superfine
granulated sugar

**TO FINISH THE MANDARIN
CREAM**
5 ounces (140 g) cocoa butter,
preferably Valrhona
1⅓ pounds (612 g) Mandarin
Cream (see above)
½ cup (75 g) ground almonds

THE DAY BEFORE, PREPARE THE MANDARIN MACARON SHELLS. Sift together the confectioners' sugar and almonds.

Combine the yellow and red food colors with half of the "liquefied" egg whites. Pour this into the confectioners' sugar–almond mixture without mixing.

Add the remaining "liquefied" egg whites to the bowl of a stand mixer fitted with the wire whisk. In a saucepan, boil the mineral water and granulated sugar to 244°F (118°C). As soon as the syrup reaches 239°F (115°C), begin beating the egg whites on high speed.

When the syrup reaches 244°F (118°C), reduce the mixer speed to medium-high and pour the syrup in a steady stream down the inside edge of the bowl into the beaten egg whites. Beat the meringue until it cools to 122°F (50°C). Fold it with a silicone spatula into the confectioners' sugar–almond mixture until the mixture loses volume. Transfer the batter to a pastry bag fitted with a plain #11, ¹/₂-inch (11-mm to 12-mm) pastry tip.

Line baking sheets with parchment paper. Pipe disks about 1¹/₂ inches (3.5 cm) in diameter and ³/₄ inch (2 cm) apart on the lined baking sheets. Rap the baking sheets on a work surface covered with a clean kitchen towel to gently smooth out the disks. Set aside for at least 30 minutes at room temperature to allow a skin to form.

Preheat a convection oven to 350°F (180°C). Place the baking sheets in the oven. Bake for 12 minutes, quickly opening and closing the oven door twice during baking to release moisture. Remove the shells from the oven and slide them still on the parchment paper onto a work surface.

FINISH THE SEMI-CANDIED ORANGES. Drain the candied oranges for 1 hour in a sieve set over a bowl, then cut them into slightly smaller than ¹/₄-inch (5-mm) cubes and refrigerate until needed.

FINISH THE MANDARIN CREAM. Melt the cocoa butter at low heat over a bain-marie or in a microwave. Whisk the mandarin cream just until smooth, then whisk the melted cocoa butter into the mandarin cream a little at a time. Stir in the almonds. Transfer the cream to a pastry bag fitted with a plain #11, ¹/₂-inch (11-mm to 12-mm) pastry tip.

Turn half of the shells over with the flat sides up onto a new piece of parchment paper. Fill them with the mandarin cream. Place three cubes of the semi-candied oranges in the center. Pipe a small dab of mandarin cream on top. Close them with the rest of the shells, pressing down lightly.

Refrigerate the macarons for 24 hours. Remove them from the refrigerator 2 hours before eating them.

Macaron Mahogany

Mahogany is a type of precious wood. I love the sound of the name. Originally, I imagined a cake made with mango, caramel, coconut, and lychee, and later I developed a macaron with the same flavor profile. Filled with fresh mango seasoned with ginger and pepper, this macaron does not last long.

PREPARE THE COCONUT MACARON SHELLS. The day before, sift together the confectioners' sugar and almonds.

Stir the food color and the coffee extract into a third of the "liquefied" egg whites. Pour this into the confectioners' sugar–almond mixture along with 1¾ cups (150 g) of the coconut and the peanut oil without mixing.

Add the remaining "liquefied" egg whites to the bowl of a stand mixer fitted with the wire whisk. In a saucepan, boil the mineral water and granulated sugar to 244°F (118°C). As soon as the syrup reaches 239°F (115°C), begin beating the egg whites on high speed.

When the syrup reaches 244°F (118°C), reduce the mixer speed to medium-high and pour the syrup in a steady stream down the inside edge of the bowl into the beaten egg whites. Beat the meringue until it cools to 122°F (50°C). Fold it into the confectioners' sugar–almond–coconut-oil mixture until the mixture loses volume. Transfer the batter to a pastry bag fitted with a plain #11, ½-inch (11-mm to 12-mm) pastry tip.

Line baking sheets with parchment paper. Pipe disks about 1½ inches (3.5 cm) in diameter and ¾ inch (2 cm) apart on the lined baking sheets. Rap the baking sheets on a work surface covered with a clean kitchen towel to gently smooth out the disks. Lightly sprinkle the disks with the rest of the grated coconut. Set aside for at least 30 minutes at room temperature to allow a skin to form.

Preheat a convection oven to 350°F (180°C). Place the baking sheets in the oven. Bake for 12 minutes, quickly opening and closing the oven door twice during baking to release moisture. Remove the shells from the oven and slide them still on the parchment paper onto a work surface.

MAKES ABOUT 72 MACARONS
(OR ABOUT 144 SHELLS)
PREPARATION TIME: 5 MINUTES (5 DAYS
IN ADVANCE, SEE "MACARON SHELLS
STEP-BY-STEP" IN THE KITCHEN GUIDE)
+ 1 HOUR 40 MINUTES
COOKING TIME: ABOUT 35 MINUTES
RESTING TIME: 30 MINUTES
REFRIGERATION TIME: 2 HOURS +
24 HOURS

**FOR THE COCONUT
MACARON SHELLS**
3 cups (300 g) confectioners' sugar
2 cups plus 2 tablespoons (300 g)
ground almonds
½ teaspoon (2 g) liquid yellow
food color
2½ teaspoons (12 g) coffee extract,
preferably Trablit
9 large (270 g) "liquefied" egg
whites, divided (see "Macaron
Shells Step-by-Step" in the Kitchen
Guide)
2½ cups (220 g) grated coconut,
divided
⅓ cup (75 g) peanut oil
¼ cup plus 1 tablespoon (75 g) still
mineral water
**1¾ cups plus 2 tablespoons
(375 g)** superfine granulated sugar

FOR THE MANGO
2 very ripe fresh mangos, peeled
and cut into ½-inch (1.5-cm) cubes
**3 tablespoons plus 1 teaspoon
(50 g)** freshly squeezed lemon juice
(from 1 lemon)
Generous 1 teaspoon (5 g)
freshly grated ginger
Freshly ground Sarawak black
pepper

**FOR THE SALTED-BUTTER
CARAMEL**
**1½ cups minus 1 tablespoon
(335 g)** light whipping cream
(32%–35% fat)
1½ cups (300 g) superfine
granulated sugar
**¼ cup plus 1¾ teaspoons
(65 g)** fine French butter, lightly
salted, preferably *beurre de la
Viette demi-sel*

**FOR THE SALTED-BUTTER
CARAMEL CREAM**
1¼ cups plus 1 teaspoon (290 g)
fine French unsalted butter,
preferably *beurre de la Viette*,
room temperature
1 recipe Salted-Butter Caramel
(see above)

PREPARE THE MANGO. Stir the mango together with the lemon juice and ginger. Season with the pepper, about three turns of the peppermill. Stir to combine, then refrigerate until needed.

PREPARE THE SALTED-BUTTER CARAMEL. In a saucepan, bring the cream to a boil. In a separate heavy-bottomed saucepan placed over medium heat, melt ¼ cup (50 g) of the sugar. Add another ¼ cup (50 g) of the sugar then continue in the same way with the rest of the sugar. Cook just until the caramel develops a deep amber color. Off the heat, add the butter in small pieces and stir to combine using a silicone spatula. Stir in the hot cream in two parts. Place the saucepan back over the heat and cook the caramel to 226°F (108°C). Blend the caramel with an immersion blender, then pour it into a heat-resistant baking dish. Cover and refrigerate to cool.

PREPARE THE SALTED-BUTTER CARAMEL CREAM. Beat the butter for 10 minutes in the bowl of a stand mixer fitted with the wire whisk. Add the cooled salted-butter caramel and beat until very smooth. Transfer the cream to a pastry bag fitted with a plain #11, ½-inch (11-mm to 12-mm) pastry tip.

Turn half of the shells over with the flat sides up onto a new piece of parchment paper. Fill them with the salted-butter caramel cream. Place three mango cubes in the center. Pipe a small dab of the cream on top of the cubes. Close them with the rest of the shells, pressing down lightly.

Refrigerate the macarons for 24 hours. Remove them from the refrigerator 2 hours before eating them.

MY STYLE
IS
TASTE!

Macaron au Chocolat et Whisky Pur Malt

I tasted this Japanese single malt whisky, Chichibu the First, in a restaurant called Le Baratin in Paris. It is a peaty, smoky whisky with a high alcohol content. You must allow all of the alcohol to evaporate before adding it to the ganache so that only the flavor remains.

When the syrup reaches 244°F (118°C), reduce the mixer speed to medium-high and pour the syrup in a steady stream down the inside edge of the bowl into the beaten egg whites. Beat the meringue until it cools to 122°F (50°C). Fold it with a silicone spatula into the confectioners' sugar–almond mixture until the mixture loses volume. Transfer the batter to a pastry bag fitted with a plain #11, $^1/_2$-inch (11-mm to 12-mm) pastry tip.

Line baking sheets with parchment paper. Pipe disks about $1^1/_2$ inches (3.5 cm) in diameter and $^3/_4$ inch (2 cm) apart on the lined baking sheets. Rap the baking sheets on a work surface covered with a clean kitchen towel to gently smooth out the disks. Using a tea infuser, sprinkle them with the gold flake. Set aside for at least 30 minutes at room temperature to allow a skin to form.

Preheat a convection oven to 350°F (180°C). Place the baking sheets in the oven. Bake for 12 minutes, quickly opening and closing the oven door twice during baking to release moisture. Remove the shells from the oven and slide them still on the parchment paper onto a work surface.

PREPARE THE GOLD MACARON SHELLS. The day before, sift together the confectioners' sugar and almonds.

Combine the food color and coffee extract with half of the "liquefied" egg whites. Pour this into the confectioners' sugar–almond mixture without mixing.

Add the remaining "liquefied" egg whites to the bowl of a stand mixer fitted with the wire whisk. In a saucepan, boil the mineral water and granulated sugar to 244°F (118°C). As soon as the syrup reaches 239°F (115°C), begin beating the egg whites on high speed.

PREPARE THE CHOCOLATE-WHISKY GANACHE. In a very large saucepan, heat the whisky to about 104°F (40°C). Remove the saucepan from the heat then very carefully ignite the whisky with a torch until all of the alcohol has burned off. Set the whisky aside to cool.

Chop the chocolate and the cocoa paste using a serrated knife then melt them to between 113°F (45°C) and 122°F (50°C) set over a bain-marie or in a microwave.

In a saucepan, bring the cream and the reduced whisky to a boil. Pour the hot mixture in thirds into the melted chocolate, stirring after each addition starting in the center then in increasingly wider concentric circles toward the sides of the bowl. Using an immersion blender, blend the ganache until smooth.

Add the butter in small pieces. Blend again until smooth. Pour the ganache into a baking dish. Cover it by gently pressing plastic wrap onto its surface. Refrigerate for 2 hours, just until the ganache has developed a creamy consistency. Transfer the ganache to a pastry bag fitted with a plain #11, ½-inch (11-mm to 12-mm) pastry tip.

Turn half of the shells over with the flat sides up onto a new piece of parchment paper. Fill them with the ganache. Close them with the rest of the shells, pressing down lightly.

Refrigerate the macarons for 24 hours. Remove them from the refrigerator 2 hours before eating them.

MAKES ABOUT 72 MACARONS (OR ABOUT 144 SHELLS)

PREPARATION TIME: 5 MINUTES (5 DAYS IN ADVANCE, SEE "MACARON SHELLS STEP-BY-STEP" IN THE KITCHEN GUIDE) + 1 HOUR 30 MINUTES

COOKING TIME: ABOUT 25 MINUTES

RESTING TIME: 30 MINUTES

REFRIGERATION TIME: 2 HOURS + 24 HOURS

FOR THE GOLD MACARON SHELLS
3 cups (300 g) confectioners' sugar
2 cups plus 2 tablespoons (300 g) ground almonds
½ teaspoon (2 g) liquid yellow food color
1 tablespoon (15 g) coffee extract, preferably Trablit
7 large (220 g) "liquefied" egg whites, divided (see "Macaron Shells Step-by-Step" in the Kitchen Guide)
¼ cup plus 1 tablespoon (75 g) still mineral water
1½ cups (300 g) superfine granulated sugar
Edible gold flake for sprinkling

FOR THE CHOCOLATE-WHISKY GANACHE
1½ cups plus 1 tablespoon (350 g) Chichibu the First single malt whisky or other fine single malt whisky (to make ⅔ cup/135 g whisky reduction)
11¾ ounces (335 g) Valrhona Araguani 72% cacao dark chocolate
1¼ ounces (35 g) Valrhona 100% cocoa paste
1 cup (235 g) light whipping cream (32%–35% fat)
½ cup (115 g) fine French unsalted butter, preferably *beurre de la Viette*, room temperature

Macaron Agapé

Agapé! The name for a very special and unconditional love, carefully chosen for this macaron with its spices of Christmas enhanced with the luscious flavors and soft acidity of a lemon cream. I suggest you make your own gingerbread, as there is nothing better.

MAKES ABOUT 72 MACARONS
(OR ABOUT 144 SHELLS)

PREPARATION TIME: 5 MINUTES (5 DAYS
IN ADVANCE, SEE "MACARON SHELLS
STEP-BY-STEP" IN THE KITCHEN GUIDE)
+ 30 MINUTES (2 DAYS IN ADVANCE) +
1 HOUR 40 MINUTES

COOKING TIME: 1 HOUR 20 MINUTES
(2 DAYS IN ADVANCE) + ABOUT
15 MINUTES

RESTING TIME: 30 MINUTES +
30 MINUTES

REFRIGERATION TIME: 24 HOURS
(TWICE)

○

FOR THE GINGERBREAD
½ cup (45 g) all-purpose flour
3 tablespoons plus 1 teaspoon
(30 g) potato starch
1½ cups (150 g) rye flour
3 teaspoons (15 g) baking soda
2 tablespoon plus 1 teaspoon
(15 g) gingerbread spice
¼ cup plus 2 tablespoons
(90 g) fine French unsalted butter,
preferably *beurre de la Viette*,
room temperature
1 tablespoons plus 2 teaspoons
(25 g) light brown sugar
3½ tablespoons (70 g) glucose
syrup or corn syrup
⅔ cup (225 g) all-flower honey
¾ cup (225 g) orange marmalade
from a jar
½ teaspoon (3 g) fleur de sel sea
salt, preferably *fleur de sel de
Guérande*
2½ large (125 g) eggs
Butter and flour to grease the
loaf pan

→

PREPARE THE GINGERBREAD. Two days in advance, sift together the all-purpose flour, potato starch, rye flour, baking soda, and gingerbread spice. In a stand mixer fitted with the paddle attachment, beat the butter, brown sugar, syrup, honey, marmalade, and sea salt on high speed. Add the eggs and beat for another 2 minutes. Beat in the flour mixture just until the batter is smooth.

Preheat a convection oven to 325°F (160°C). Grease an 8¼-inch- (21-cm-) long loaf pan with the butter then dust it with the flour. Pour in the cake batter then place the pan in the oven and bake for 40 minutes. Unmold the cake and let it cool before wrapping it in plastic wrap. Store at room temperature.

PREPARE THE LEMON CREAM. Two days in advance, wash and dry the lemons. Using a microplane grater, zest the lemons over a bowl and measure the quantity of zest needed. Add the sugar to the bowl and rub it into the zest by pinching it with your fingers. Add the eggs and the lemon juice then whisk to combine. Cook to between 181°F (83°C) and 183°F (84°C) on medium heat, set over a bain-marie, whisking from time to time. Place the bowl inside a larger bowl containing ice water and stir until the cream cools to 140°F (60°C). Using a whisk, stir in the butter in small pieces until incorporated. Beat the cream for 10 minutes in a stand mixer fitted with the wire whisk. Cover the cream by gently pressing plastic wrap onto its surface. Refrigerate until the next day.

PREPARE THE CARAMEL MACARON SHELLS. Sift together the confectioners' sugar and almonds.

Combine the food color and the coffee extract with half of the "liquefied" egg whites. Pour this into the confectioners' sugar–almond mixture without mixing.

Add the remaining "liquefied" egg whites to the bowl of a stand mixer fitted with the wire whisk. In a saucepan, boil the mineral water and granulated sugar to 244°F (118°C). As soon as the syrup reaches 239°F (115°C), begin beating the egg whites on high speed.

When the syrup reaches 244°F (118°C), reduce the mixer speed to medium–high and pour the syrup in a steady stream down the inside edge of the bowl into the beaten egg whites. Beat the meringue until it cools to 122°F (50°C). Fold it with a silicone spatula into the confectioners' sugar–almond mixture until the mixture loses volume. Transfer the batter to a pastry bag fitted with a plain #11, ¹/₂–inch (11–mm to 12–mm) pastry tip.

Line baking sheets with parchment paper. Pipe disks about 1¹/₂ inches (3.5 cm) in diameter and ³/₄ inch (2 cm) apart on the lined baking sheets. Rap the baking sheets on a work surface covered with a clean kitchen towel to gently smooth out the disks. Set aside for at least 30 minutes at room temperature to allow a skin to form.

Preheat a convection oven to 350°F (180°C). Place the baking sheets in the oven. Bake for 12 minutes, quickly opening and closing the oven door twice during baking to release moisture. Remove the shells from the oven and slide them still on the parchment paper onto a work surface.

Slice the gingerbread then cut it up into ¹/₂–inch (1.5–cm) cubes.

Transfer the lemon cream to a pastry bag fitted with a plain #11, ¹/₂–inch (11–mm to 12–mm) pastry tip. Turn the lemon shells over with the flat side up onto a new piece of parchment paper. Fill them with the lemon cream. Gently place a cube of gingerbread in the center. Pipe a dab of the lemon cream on top of the gingerbread. Close them with the caramel macaron shells, pressing down lightly.

Refrigerate the macarons for 24 hours. Remove them from the refrigerator 2 hours before eating them.

PREPARE THE LEMON MACARON SHELLS. The day before, sift together the confectioners' sugar and almonds.

Combine the food color with half of the "liquefied" egg whites. Pour this into the confectioners' sugar–almond mixture without mixing.

Add the remaining "liquefied" egg whites to the bowl of a stand mixer fitted with the wire whisk. In a saucepan, boil the mineral water and granulated sugar to 244°F (118°C). As soon as the syrup reaches 239°F (115°C), begin beating the egg whites on high speed.

When the syrup reaches 244°F (118°C), reduce the mixer speed to medium–high and pour the syrup in a steady stream down the inside edge of the bowl into the beaten egg whites. Beat the meringue until it cools to 122°F (50°C). Fold it with a silicone spatula into the confectioners' sugar–almond mixture until the mixture loses volume. Transfer the batter to a pastry bag fitted with a plain #11, ¹/₂–inch (11–mm to 12–mm) pastry tip.

Line baking sheets with parchment paper. Pipe disks about 1¹/₂ inches (3.5 cm) in diameter and ³/₄ inch (2 cm) apart on the lined baking sheets. Rap the baking sheets on a work surface covered with a clean kitchen towel to gently smooth out the disks. Set aside for at least 30 minutes at room temperature to allow a skin to form.

FOR THE LEMON CREAM
¼ cup (25 g) lemon zest (from 5 lemons)
1 cup plus 2 tablespoons (220 g) superfine granulated sugar
4 large (200 g) eggs
½ cup plus 2 tablespoons (160 g) freshly squeezed lemon juice (from 2 lemons)
1¼ cups plus 1 tablespoon (300 g) fine French unsalted butter, preferably *beurre de la Viette*, room temperature

FOR THE LEMON MACARON SHELLS
1½ cups (150 g) confectioners' sugar
1 cup plus 1 tablespoon (150 g) ground almonds
¾ teaspoon (3 g) liquid yellow food color
3½ large (110 g) "liquefied" egg whites, divided (see "Macaron Shells Step-by-Step" in the Kitchen Guide)
2 tablespoons plus 1¾ teaspoons (38 g) still mineral water
¾ cup (150 g) superfine granulated sugar

FOR THE CARAMEL MACARON SHELLS
1½ cups (150 g) confectioners' sugar
1 cup plus 1 tablespoon (150 g) ground almonds
¼ teaspoon (1 g) liquid yellow food color
1¾ teaspoons (7.5 g) coffee extract, preferably Trablit
3½ large (110 g) "liquefied" egg whites, divided (see "Macaron Shells Step-by-Step" in the Kitchen Guide)
3 tablespoons (43 g) still mineral water
¾ cup (150 g) superfine granulated sugar

Macaron PX

MAKES ABOUT 72 MACARONS
(OR ABOUT 144 SHELLS)
PREPARATION TIME: 5 MINUTES (5 DAYS
IN ADVANCE, SEE "MACARON SHELLS
STEP-BY-STEP" IN THE KITCHEN GUIDE)
+ 3 MINUTES (2 DAYS IN ADVANCE) +
1 HOUR 30 MINUTES
MACERATION TIME: 12 HOURS
DRAINING TIME: 12 HOURS
COOKING TIME: ABOUT 25 MINUTES
RESTING TIME: 30 MINUTES
REFRIGERATION TIME: 12 HOURS
(TWICE) + 2 HOURS + 24 HOURS

FOR THE PX RAISINS
¼ cup plus 3 tablespoons
(100 g) PX sherry (Pedro Ximénez
Triana)
⅔ cup (100 g) golden raisins

**FOR THE PX MACARON
SHELLS**
3 cups (300 g) confectioners' sugar
2 cups plus 2 tablespoons (300 g)
ground almonds
Generous 1 teaspoon (5 g) liquid
chocolate brown food color
7 large (220 g) "liquefied" egg
whites, divided (see "Macaron
Shells Step-by-Step" in the Kitchen
Guide)
¼ cup plus 1 tablespoon (75 g) still
mineral water
1½ cups (300 g) superfine
granulated sugar

During a lunch with Philippe Poulachon from Byzance Group, I tasted the Spanish white grape variety Pedro Ximénez Triana, known simply as PX. It had a strong flavor of sun-dried grapes. I had the idea to develop a macaron filled with golden raisins marinated in PX.

PREPARE THE PX RAISINS. Two days in advance, heat the PX to 140°F (60°C) then pour it over the raisins. Refrigerate for 12 hours to macerate. The next day, drain the raisins then refrigerate them again for 12 hours.

PREPARE THE PX MACARON SHELLS. The day before, sift together the confectioners' sugar and almonds.

Combine the food color with half of the "liquefied" egg whites. Pour this into the confectioners' sugar–almond mixture without mixing.

Add the remaining "liquefied" egg whites to the bowl of a stand mixer fitted with the wire whisk. In a saucepan, boil the mineral water and granulated sugar to 244°F (118°C). As soon as the syrup reaches 239°F (115°C), begin beating the egg whites on high speed.

When the syrup reaches 244°F (118°C), reduce the mixer speed to medium–high and pour the syrup in a steady stream down the inside edge of the bowl into the beaten egg whites. Beat the meringue until it cools to 122°F (50°C). Fold it with a silicone spatula into the confectioners' sugar–almond mixture until the mixture loses volume. Transfer the batter to a pastry bag fitted with a plain #11, ½-inch (11-mm to 12-mm) pastry tip.

Line baking sheets with parchment paper. Pipe disks about 1½ inches (3.5 cm) in diameter and ¾ inch (2 cm) apart on the lined baking sheets. Rap the baking sheets on a work surface covered with a clean kitchen towel to gently smooth out the disks. Set aside for at least 30 minutes at room temperature to allow a skin to form.

Preheat a convection oven to 350°F (180°C). Place the baking sheets in the oven. Bake for 12 minutes, quickly opening and closing the oven door twice during baking to release moisture. Remove the shells from the oven and slide them still on the parchment paper onto a work surface.

PREPARE THE PX CREAM. Chop the white chocolate using a serrated knife then melt it to between 113°F (45°C) and 122°F (50°C) set over a bain-marie or in a microwave.

In a saucepan, bring the cream to a boil. Pour the hot cream in thirds into the melted white chocolate, stirring after each addition starting in the center then in increasingly wider concentric circles toward the sides of the bowl. Heat the PX to 104°F (40°C) then incorporate it in the same way into the white chocolate–cream mixture. Using an immersion blender, blend the cream until smooth.

Pour the PX cream into a baking dish. Cover it by gently pressing plastic wrap onto its surface. Refrigerate for 2 hours, just until the cream has developed a creamy consistency.

Transfer the PX cream to a pastry bag fitted with a plain #11, ½-inch (11-mm to 12-mm) pastry tip.

Turn half of the shells over with the flat sides up onto a new piece of parchment paper. Fill them with the cream. Gently place two or three PX raisins in the center. Pipe a dab of cream on top of the raisins. Close them with the rest of the shells, pressing down lightly.

Refrigerate the macarons for 24 hours. Remove them from the refrigerator 2 hours before eating them.

FOR THE PX CREAM
13½ ounces **(385 g)** Valrhona Ivoire 35% white chocolate
½ cup minus 2¼ teaspoons **(105 g)** light whipping cream (32%–35% fat)
1 cup (215 g) PX sherry (Pedro Ximénez Triana)

Taste is the only thing that matters in my creations.

Macaron Caraquillo

In Catalonia, I enjoy carajillos, which are traditional drinks made of coffee flavored with anise liqueur. And so I imagined this macaron, which combines the chocolate notes of the Iapar rouge du Brésil coffee and the strong aroma of a bittersweet 61% cacao dark chocolate, accented with a touch of anise liqueur.

PREPARE THE CHOCOLATE MACARON SHELLS.
The day before, chop the cocoa paste using a serrated knife then melt it to between 113°F (45°C) and 122°F (50°C) set over a bain-marie or in a microwave.

Sift together the confectioners' sugar and almonds.

Combine the food color with half of the "liquefied" egg whites. Pour this into the confectioners' sugar–almond mixture without mixing.

Add the remaining "liquefied" egg whites to the bowl of a stand mixer fitted with the wire whisk. In a sauce-pan, boil the mineral water and granulated sugar to 244°F (118°C). As soon as the syrup reaches 239°F (115°C), begin beating the egg whites on high speed.

When the syrup reaches 244°F (118°C), reduce the mixer speed to medium-high and pour the syrup in a steady stream down the inside edge of the bowl into the beaten egg whites. Beat the meringue until it cools to 122°F (50°C). Fold about one-third of the meringue into the melted cocoa paste then add this mixture to the confections' sugar–almond mixture along with the rest of the meringue. Fold it with a sil-icone spatula until the mixture loses volume. Trans-fer the batter to a pastry bag fitted with a plain #11. ½-inch (11-mm to 12-mm) pastry tip.

PREPARE THE COFFEE-ANISE GANACHE. Chop the chocolate using a serrated knife then melt it to between 113°F (45°C) and 122°F (50°C) set over a bain-marie or in a microwave.

In a saucepan, bring the cream and coffee to a boil. Remove from the heat then cover and let infuse for 10 minutes. Strain the cream through a fine-mesh sieve.

Pour the hot cream in thirds into the melted chocolate, stirring after each addition starting in the center then in increasingly wider concentric circles toward the sides of the bowl. Stir in the butter in small pieces, then stir in the Ricard. Using an immersion blender, blend the ganache until smooth.

Line baking sheets with parchment paper. Pipe disks about 1½ inches (3.5 cm) in diameter and ¾ inch (2 cm) apart on the lined baking sheets. Rap the baking sheets on a work surface covered with a clean kitchen towel to gently smooth out the disks. Lightly dust the disks with silver dust. Set aside for at least 30 minutes at room temperature to allow a skin to form.

Preheat a convection oven to 350°F (180°C). Place the baking sheets in the oven. Bake for 12 minutes, quickly opening and closing the oven door twice during baking to release moisture. Remove the shells from the oven and slide them still on the parchment paper onto a work surface.

Pour the ganache into a baking dish. Cover it by gently pressing plastic wrap onto its surface. Refrigerate for 2 hours, just until the ganache has developed a creamy consistency. Transfer the ganache to a pastry bag fitted with a plain #11, ½-inch (11-mm to 12-mm) pastry tip.

Turn half of the shells over with the flat sides up onto a new piece of parchment paper. Fill them with the ganache. Close them with the rest of the shells, pressing down lightly.

Refrigerate the macarons for 24 hours. Remove them from the refrigerator 2 hours before eating them.

MAKES ABOUT 72 MACARONS (OR ABOUT 144 SHELLS)

PREPARATION TIME: 5 MINUTES (5 DAYS IN ADVANCE, SEE "MACARON SHELLS STEP-BY-STEP" IN THE KITCHEN GUIDE) + 1 HOUR 30 MINUTES

COOKING TIME: ABOUT 15 MINUTES

INFUSION TIME: 10 MINUTES

RESTING TIME: 30 MINUTES

REFRIGERATION TIME: 2 HOURS + 24 HOURS

FOR THE CHOCOLATE MACARON SHELLS
4¼ ounces (120 g) Valrhona 100% cocoa paste
3 cups (300 g) confectioners' sugar
2 cups plus 2 tablespoons (300 g) ground almonds
8 drops / ⅛ teaspoon (0.5 g) liquid carmine red food color
7 large (220 g) "liquefied" egg whites, divided (see "Macaron Shells Step-by-Step" in the Kitchen Guide)
¼ cup plus 1 tablespoon (75 g) still mineral water
1½ cups (300 g) superfine granulated sugar
Edible glittering (or "pearl") silver dust, for sprinkling

FOR THE COFFEE-ANISE GANACHE
14 ounces (400 g) Valrhona Extra-bitter 61% cacao dark chocolate
1⅓ cups plus 1⅓ tablespoons (320 g) light whipping cream (32%–35% fat)
3 tablespoons plus 1 teaspoon (20 g) ground lapar rouge du Brésil coffee, preferably from l'Arbre à Café
¼ cup plus ¾ teaspoon (60 g) fine French unsalted butter, preferably *beurre de la Viette*, room temperature
1 tablespoon plus 1 teaspoon (20 g) Ricard or other anise liqueur

Macaron Crème Brûlée

When I first experienced the crème brûlée, I loved the contrast of the silky vanilla cream with the crunchy, lightly caramelized sugar coating. I created this macaron to marry the smooth texture of my Infiniment vanille ganache with a light crunch from finely broken pieces of salted-butter caramel.

MAKES ABOUT 72 MACARONS
(OR ABOUT 144 SHELLS)

PREPARATION TIME: **5 MINUTES (5 DAYS IN ADVANCE, SEE "MACARON SHELLS STEP-BY-STEP" IN THE KITCHEN GUIDE) + 2 HOURS**

COOKING TIME: **ABOUT 30 MINUTES**

INFUSION TIME: **30 MINUTES**

RESTING TIME: **30 MINUTES (TWICE)**

REFRIGERATION TIME: **4 HOURS + 24 HOURS**

**FOR THE SALTED-BUTTER
CARAMEL SHARDS**
2½ tablespoons (50 g) glucose
syrup or corn syrup
¼ cup (50 g) superfine granulated
sugar
**3 tablespoons plus 1¾ teaspoons
(50 g)** fine French butter, lightly
salted

PREPARE THE SALTED-BUTTER CARAMEL SHARDS. The day before, in a heavy-bottomed saucepan, heat the syrup and sugar until caramelized to a dark amber color. Add the butter while stirring continuously.

Bring the caramel back to a boil then pour it onto a baking sheet lined with parchment paper. Tilt the baking sheet to spread the caramel into a thin layer. Cover the caramel with a second piece of parchment paper. Using a rolling pin, roll the caramel between the two sheets to spread it thinly. Let harden before breaking it into pieces using the rolling pin. Briefly process the broken caramel pieces in a food processor to create small shards. Set aside at room temperature and keep dry.

PREPARE THE VANILLA MACARON SHELLS. Sift together the confectioners' sugar, almonds, and vanilla powder.

Pour half of the "liquefied" egg whites into the confectioners' sugar–almond–vanilla mixture without mixing.

Add the remaining "liquefied" egg whites to the bowl of a stand mixer fitted with the wire whisk. In a saucepan, boil the mineral water and granulated sugar to 244°F (118°C). As soon as the syrup reaches 239°F (115°C), begin beating the egg whites on high speed.

When the syrup reaches 244°F (118°C), reduce the mixer speed to medium–high and pour the syrup in a steady stream down the inside edge of the bowl into the beaten egg whites. Beat the meringue until it cools to 122°F (50°C). Fold it with a silicone spatula into the confectioners' sugar–almond mixture until the mixture loses volume. Transfer the batter to a pastry bag fitted with a plain #11, 1/2-inch (11-mm to 12-mm) pastry tip.

Line baking sheets with parchment paper. Pipe disks about 1½ inches (3.5 cm) in diameter and ¾ inch (2 cm) apart on the lined baking sheets. Rap the baking sheets on a work surface covered with a clean kitchen towel to gently smooth out the disks. Set aside for at least 30 minutes at room temperature to allow a skin to form.

PREPARE THE CARAMEL MACARON SHELLS. Sift together the confectioners' sugar and almonds.

Combine the food color and coffee extract with half of the "liquefied" egg whites. Pour this into the confectioners' sugar–almond mixture without mixing.

Add the remaining "liquefied" egg whites to the bowl of a stand mixer fitted with the wire whisk. In a saucepan, boil the mineral water and granulated sugar to 244°F (118°C). As soon as the syrup reaches 239°F (115°C), begin beating the egg whites on high speed.

When the syrup reaches 244°F (118°C), reduce the mixer speed to medium–high and pour the syrup in a steady stream down the inside edge of the bowl into the beaten egg whites. Beat the meringue until it cools to 122°F (50°C). Fold it with a silicone spatula into the confectioners' sugar–almond mixture until the mixture loses volume. Transfer the batter to a pastry bag fitted with a plain #11, 1/2-inch (11-mm to 12-mm) pastry tip.

Line baking sheets with parchment paper. Pipe disks about 1½ inches (3.5 cm) in diameter and ¾ inch (2 cm) apart on the lined baking sheets. Rap the baking sheets on a work surface covered with a clean kitchen towel to gently smooth out the disks. Set aside for at least 30 minutes at room temperature to allow a skin to form.

Preheat a convection oven to 350°F (180°C). Place the baking sheets in the oven. Bake for 12 minutes, quickly opening and closing the oven door twice during baking to release moisture. Remove the shells from the oven and slide them still on the parchment paper onto a work surface.

PREPARE THE VANILLA GANACHE. Add the cream to a saucepan. Scrape the seeds out of the vanilla beans using a knife. Add the seeds and the vanilla bean pods to the cream and bring to a boil. Remove from the heat then cover and let infuse for at least 30 minutes.

Chop the white chocolate using a serrated knife then melt it to between 113°F (45°C) and 122°F (50°C) set over a bain-marie or in a microwave.

Strain the infused cream through a fine-mesh sieve then bring it back to a boil. Pour the hot cream in thirds into the melted white chocolate, stirring after each addition starting in the center then in increasingly wider concentric circles toward the sides of the bowl.

Pour the ganache into a baking dish. Cover it by gently pressing plastic wrap onto its surface. Refrigerate for 4 hours, just until the ganache has developed a creamy consistency. Stir the salted-butter caramel shards into the ganache then transfer the ganache to a pastry bag fitted with a plain #11, ½-inch (11-mm to 12-mm) pastry tip.

Turn the vanilla macaron shells over with the flat sides up onto a new piece of parchment paper. Fill them with the ganache. Close them with the caramel macaron shells, pressing down lightly.

Refrigerate the macarons for 24 hours. Remove them from the refrigerator 2 hours before eating them.

FOR THE VANILLA MACARON SHELLS
1½ cups (150 g) confectioners' sugar
1 cup plus 1 tablespoon (150 g) ground almonds
Scant 1 teaspoon (1.5 g) vanilla powder
3½ large (110 g) "liquefied" egg whites, divided (see "Macaron Shells Step-by-Step" in the Kitchen Guide)
3 tablespoons (43 g) still mineral water
¾ cup (150 g) superfine granulated sugar

FOR THE CARAMEL MACARON SHELLS
1½ cups (150 g) confectioners' sugar
1 cup plus 1 tablespoon (150 g) ground almonds
¼ teaspoon (1 g) liquid yellow food color
1¾ teaspoons (7.5 g) coffee extract, preferably Trablit
3½ large (110 g) "liquefied" egg whites, divided (see "Macaron Shells Step-by-Step" in the Kitchen Guide)
2 tablespoons plus 1¾ teaspoons (38 g) still mineral water
¾ cup (150 g) superfine granulated sugar

FOR THE VANILLA GANACHE
1½ cups (345 g) light whipping cream (32%–35% fat)
2 Tahitian vanilla beans, halved lengthwise
2 Madagascar vanilla beans, halved lengthwise
2 Mexican vanilla beans, halved lengthwise
13½ ounces (385 g) Valrhona Ivoire 35% white chocolate
1 recipe Salted-Butter Caramel Shards (see page 99)

Macaron Chocolat et Vanille

The combination of chocolate and vanilla in chocolate bars, candies, and couverture chocolates is a long tradition. I wanted to push the relationship of these two ingredients further, so I searched for ingredients that would create a macaron with a strong flavor.

PREPARE THE VANILLA MACARON SHELLS. The day before, sift together the confectioners' sugar, almonds, and vanilla powder.

Pour half of the "liquefied" egg whites into the confectioners' sugar–almond–vanilla mixture without mixing.

Add the remaining "liquefied" egg whites to the bowl of a stand mixer fitted with the wire whisk. In a saucepan, boil the mineral water and granulated sugar to 244°F (118°C). As soon as the syrup reaches 239°F (115°C), begin beating the egg whites on high speed.

When the syrup reaches 244°F (118°C), reduce the mixer speed to medium–high and pour the syrup in a steady stream down the inside edge of the bowl into the beaten egg whites. Beat the meringue until it cools to 122°F (50°C). Fold it into the confectioners' sugar–almond–vanilla mixture until the mixture loses volume. Transfer the batter to a pastry bag fitted with a plain #11, ½-inch (11-mm to 12-mm) pastry tip.

Line baking sheets with parchment paper. Pipe disks about 1½ inches (3.5 cm) in diameter and ¾ inch (2 cm) apart on the lined baking sheets. Rap the baking sheets on a work surface covered with a clean kitchen towel to gently smooth out the disks. Dust the disks with vanilla powder. Set aside for at least 30 minutes at room temperature to allow a skin to form.

Preheat a convection oven to 350°F (180°C). Place the baking sheets in the oven. Bake for 12 minutes, quickly opening and closing the oven door twice during baking to release moisture. Remove the shells from the oven and slide them still on the parchment paper onto a work surface.

PREPARE THE CHOCOLATE AND VANILLA GANACHE. Add the cream to a saucepan. Scrape the seeds out of the vanilla beans using a knife. Add the seeds and the vanilla bean pods to the cream and bring to a boil. Remove from the heat then cover and let infuse for at least 30 minutes.

Chop the milk and dark chocolate using a serrated knife then melt them together to between 113°F (45°C) and 122°F (50°C) set over a bain-marie or in a microwave.

Strain the infused cream through a fine-mesh sieve then bring it back to a boil. Pour the hot cream in thirds into the melted chocolate, stirring after each addition starting in the center then in increasingly wider concentric circles toward the sides of the bowl. Stir in the butter in pieces. Using an immersion blender, blend the ganache until smooth.

Pour the ganache into a baking dish. Cover it by gently pressing plastic wrap onto its surface. Refrigerate for 2 hours, just until the ganache has developed a creamy consistency. Transfer the ganache to a pastry bag fitted with a plain #11, ½-inch (11-mm to 12-mm) pastry tip.

Turn half of the shells over with the flat sides up onto a new piece of parchment paper. Fill them with the ganache. Close them with the rest of the shells, pressing down lightly.

Refrigerate the macarons for 24 hours. Remove them from the refrigerator 2 hours before eating them.

MAKES ABOUT 72 MACARONS (OR ABOUT 144 SHELLS)

PREPARATION TIME: **5 MINUTES (5 DAYS IN ADVANCE, SEE "MACARON SHELLS STEP-BY-STEP" IN THE KITCHEN GUIDE) + 1 HOUR 30 MINUTES**

COOKING TIME: **ABOUT 15 MINUTES**

INFUSION TIME: **30 MINUTES**

RESTING TIME: **30 MINUTES**

REFRIGERATION TIME: **2 HOURS + 24 HOURS**

FOR THE VANILLA MACARON SHELLS
3 cups (300 g) confectioners' sugar
2 cups plus 2 tablespoons (300 g) ground almonds
1 teaspoon (2 g) vanilla powder, plus more for sprinkling
7 large (220 g) "liquefied" egg whites, divided (see "Macaron Shells Step-by-Step" in the Kitchen Guide)
¼ cup plus 1 tablespoon (75 g) still mineral water
1½ cups (300 g) superfine granulated sugar

FOR THE CHOCOLATE AND VANILLA GANACHE
1¾ cups (400 g) light whipping cream (32%–35% fat)
5 Mexican vanilla beans, halved lengthwise
5 Madagascar vanilla beans, halved lengthwise
5 Tahitian vanilla beans, halved lengthwise
8 ounces (225 g) Valrhona Jivara 40% cacao milk chocolate
5¾ ounces (160 g) Valrhona Extra-bitter 61% cacao dark chocolate
2 tablespoons plus 1 teaspoon (35 g) fine French unsalted butter, preferably *beurre de la Viette*, room temperature

Macaron Coing à la Rose

While exploring the garden at my boarding school, l'Institut de Champagnat in Issenheim, France, I was walking along an orchard of quince that emitted an aroma of ripe yellow fruits. It was when I tasted cooked quince that I discovered the delicate flavor of rose; this flavor combination became obvious to me.

PREPARE THE TINTED SUGAR. The day before, preheat the oven to 140°F (60°C). Put on disposable gloves. Rub the yellow food color into the coarse sugar using your fingertips. Spread the sugar out on a baking sheet. Place the baking sheet in the oven for 30 minutes to dry the sugar. Set aside to cool to room temperature.

PREPARE THE MACARON SHELLS. Sift together the confectioners' sugar and almonds.

Combine the yellow and red food colors with half of the "liquefied" egg whites. Pour this into the confectioners' sugar–almond mixture without mixing.

Add the remaining "liquefied" egg whites to the bowl of a stand mixer fitted with the wire whisk. In a saucepan, boil the mineral water and granulated sugar to 244°F (118°C). As soon as the syrup reaches 239°F (115°C), begin beating the egg whites on high speed.

When the syrup reaches 244°F (118°C), reduce the mixer speed to medium-high and pour the syrup in a steady stream down the inside edge of the bowl into the beaten egg whites. Beat the meringue until it cools to 122°F (50°C). Fold it with a silicone spatula into the confectioners' sugar–almond mixture until the mixture loses volume. Transfer the batter to a pastry bag fitted with a plain #11, ¹/₂–inch (11-mm to 12-mm) pastry tip.

Line baking sheets with parchment paper. Pipe disks about 1¹/₂ inches (3.5 cm) in diameter and ³/₄ inch (2 cm) apart on the lined baking sheets. Rap the baking sheets on a work surface covered with a clean kitchen towel to gently smooth out the disks. Sprinkle the disks with the tinted sugar. Set aside for at least 30 minutes at room temperature to allow a skin to form.

Preheat a convection oven to 350°F (180°C). Place the baking sheets in the oven. Bake for 12 minutes, quickly opening and closing the oven door twice during baking to release moisture. Remove the shells from the oven and slide them still on the parchment paper onto a work surface.

PREPARE THE ROSE-FLAVORED QUINCE GANACHE.
Steam the quinces for 15 minutes then process them
in a blender or food processor to create a smooth
puree. Add the puree and the lemon juice to a saucepan and heat through.

Chop the white chocolate using a serrated knife then
melt it to between 113°F (45°C) and 122°F (50°C) set
over a bain-marie or in a microwave.

In a saucepan, bring the cream and the warm quince
puree to a boil. Pour the hot mixture in thirds into the
melted white chocolate, stirring after each addition
starting in the center then in increasingly wider concentric circles toward the sides of the bowl. Stir in the
rose syrup and the rose extract. Using an immersion
blender, blend the ganache until smooth.

Pour the ganache into a baking dish. Cover it by gently pressing plastic wrap onto its surface. Refrigerate
for 4 hours, just until the ganache has developed a
creamy consistency. Transfer the ganache to a pastry
bag fitted with a plain #11, ¹⁄₂-inch (11-mm to 12-mm)
pastry tip.

Turn half of the shells over with the flat sides up
onto a new piece of parchment paper. Fill them with
the ganache. Close them with the rest of the shells,
pressing down lightly.

Refrigerate the macarons for 24 hours. Remove them
from the refrigerator 2 hours before eating them.

MAKES ABOUT 72 MACARONS
(OR ABOUT 144 SHELLS)
PREPARATION TIME: **5 MINUTES (5 DAYS
IN ADVANCE, SEE "MACARON SHELLS
STEP-BY-STEP" IN THE KITCHEN GUIDE)
+ 2 HOURS**
COOKING TIME: **ABOUT 1 HOUR
30 MINUTES**
RESTING TIME: **30 MINUTES**
REFRIGERATION TIME: **4 HOURS +
24 HOURS**

FOR THE TINTED SUGAR
Scant ¾ **teaspoon (2.5 g)** liquid
yellow food color
1¼ cups (250 g) coarse sugar
Note: *This will make more tinted
sugar than is needed for one batch
of macarons.*

FOR THE MACARON SHELLS
3 cups (300 g) confectioners' sugar
2 cups plus 2 tablespoons (300 g)
ground almonds
Scant ¾ **teaspoon (2.5 g)** liquid
yellow food color
¼ teaspoon (1 g) liquid red food
color
7 large (220 g) "liquefied" egg
whites, divided (see "Macaron
Shells Step-by-Step" in the Kitchen
Guide)
¼ cup plus 1 tablespoon (75 g) still
mineral water
1½ cups (300 g) superfine
granulated sugar
Tinted Sugar (see above)

**FOR THE ROSE-FLAVORED
QUINCE GANACHE**
1⅓ pounds (600 g) quince (about
4 quinces, to make 1 cup/230 g
quince puree), peeled and cubed
Scant **2 tablespoons (25 g)** freshly
squeezed lemon juice (from ½
lemon)
13½ ounces (385 g) Valrhona Ivoire
35% white chocolate
**¼ cup plus 2 tablespoons
(90 g)** light whipping cream
(32%–35% fat)
1 tablespoon (20 g) rose syrup
¼ teaspoon (1 g) rose extract

Macaron Dépaysé

This macaron is called dépaysé ("out of one's element") because its inspiration is Japanese. I combined Uji matcha green tea, which is a powder made from jade tea with a deliciously herbaceous and lightly bitter flavor, with that of the smoothness of azukis (Japanese red beans) that I season with Sarawak black pepper, lime zest, rice vinegar, and fresh ginger.

PREPARE THE DÉPAYSÉ MACARON SHELLS. The day before, sift together the confectioners' sugar and almonds.

Combine both the green food colors with half of the "liquefied" egg whites. Pour this into the confectioners' sugar–almond mixture without mixing.

Add the remaining "liquefied" egg whites to the bowl of a stand mixer fitted with the wire whisk. In a saucepan, boil the mineral water and granulated sugar to 244°F (118°C). As soon as the syrup reaches 239°F (115°C), begin beating the egg whites on high speed.

When the syrup reaches 244°F (118°C), reduce the mixer speed to medium-high and pour the syrup in a steady stream down the inside edge of the bowl into the beaten egg whites. Beat the meringue until it cools to 122°F (50°C). Fold it with a silicone spatula into the confectioners' sugar–almond mixture until the mixture loses volume. Transfer the batter to a pastry bag fitted with a plain #11, ½-inch (11-mm to 12-mm) pastry tip.

Line baking sheets with parchment paper. Pipe disks about 1½ inches (3.5 cm) in diameter and ¾ inch (2 cm) apart on the lined baking sheets. Rap the baking sheets on a work surface covered with a clean kitchen towel to gently smooth out the disks. Using a tea infuser, lightly dust the shells with the green tea powder. Set aside for at least 30 minutes at room temperature to allow a skin to form.

MAKES ABOUT 72 MACARONS
(OR ABOUT 144 SHELLS)
PREPARATION TIME: **5 MINUTES (5 DAYS
IN ADVANCE, SEE "MACARON SHELLS
STEP-BY-STEP" IN THE KITCHEN GUIDE)
+ 2 HOURS**
COOKING TIME: **ABOUT 25 MINUTES**
RESTING TIME: **30 MINUTES**
REFRIGERATION TIME: **4 HOURS +
24 HOURS**

FOR THE DÉPAYSÉ MACARON SHELLS

3 cups (300 g) confectioners' sugar
2 cups plus 2 tablespoons (300 g) ground almonds
8 drops / ⅛ teaspoon (0.5 g) liquid mint green food color
8 drops / ⅛ teaspoon (0.5 g) liquid pistachio green food color
7 large (220 g) "liquefied" egg whites, divided (see "Macaron Shells Step-by-Step" in the Kitchen Guide)
¼ cup plus 1 tablespoon (75 g) still mineral water
1½ cups (300 g) superfine granulated sugar
Uji matcha green tea powder, for sprinkling

FOR THE RED BEAN COMPOTE

2 (6 g) gelatin leaves or **2 teaspoons (6 g)** unflavored powdered gelatin
15¾ ounces (450 g) precooked Japanese red beans, preferably Morinaga Yude Azuki beans from Kioko
1 tablespoon plus 1 teaspoon (3 g) freshly grated lime zest (from 1 lime)
⅓ teaspoon (2 g) freshly grated ginger
1 tablespoon plus 1 teaspoon (20 g) rice vinegar
Scant ⅛ teaspoon (0.25 g) freshly ground Sarawak black pepper

FOR THE GREEN TEA CREAM

13½ ounces (385 g) Valrhona Ivoire 35% white chocolate
1¾ cups plus 1⅓ tablespoons (425 g) light whipping cream (32%–35% fat)
¼ cup plus 1 tablespoon (30 g) Uji matcha green tea powder, preferably Cannon

---

Preheat a convection oven to 350°F (180°C). Place the baking sheets in the oven. Bake for 12 minutes, quickly opening and closing the oven door twice during baking to release moisture. Remove the shells from the oven and slide them still on the parchment paper onto a work surface.

PREPARE THE RED BEAN COMPOTE. If using gelatin sheets, separate them and place them in cold water to soak for 20 minutes. If using powdered gelatin, sprinkle it over 3 tablespoons (44 g) of cold water, stir to moisten, then let it soften for 5 minutes. Gently heat 4 ounces (113 g) of the beans. Off the heat, stir in the gelatin sheets that have been squeezed of their excess liquid, or add the softened powdered gelatin. Stir in the rest of the beans, the lime zest, ginger, vinegar, and pepper. Let cool.

PREPARE THE GREEN TEA CREAM. Chop the white chocolate using a serrated knife then melt it to between 113°F (45°C) and 122°F (50°C) set over a bain-marie or in a microwave.

In a saucepan, bring the cream to a boil. Let cool to 140°F (60°C) then stir in the green tea powder. Vigorously whisk the cream then pour it in thirds into the melted white chocolate, stirring after each addition starting in the center then in increasingly wider concentric circles toward the sides of the bowl. Using an immersion blender, blend the cream until smooth.

Pour the green tea cream into a baking dish. Cover it by gently pressing plastic wrap onto its surface. Refrigerate for 4 hours, just until the cream has developed a creamy consistency. Transfer the green tea cream and the red bean compote to separate pastry bags fitted with a plain #11, ½-inch (11-mm to 12-mm) pastry tip.

Turn half of the shells over with the flat sides up onto a new piece of parchment paper. Fill them with the green tea cream then pipe a dollop of red bean compote in the center. Close them with the rest of the shells, pressing down lightly.

Refrigerate the macarons for 24 hours. Remove them from the refrigerator 2 hours before eating them.

Macaron Fortunella

*The kumquat is part of the
Fortunella botanical family.
This little oval citrus fruit has a
particularly unique flavor—it's both
sweet and bitter. I chose to combine
it with a subtle touch of anise,
which suppresses the bitterness
and prolongs the fruit's taste.*

PREPARE THE CANDIED KUMQUATS. Three days in advance, rinse and dry the kumquats. Cut them lengthwise in half and scrape out the seeds. Place the kumquats in a bowl. In a saucepan, bring the mineral water, sugar, and star anise to a boil. Pour the boiling liquid over the kumquats then refrigerate them to macerate for 24 hours.

Two days in advance, remove the star anise from the candied kumquats, then drain the kumquats and cut about twenty of them into coarse pieces. Place them in a sieve set over a bowl, then place the bowl in the refrigerator for 24 hours to drain.

PREPARE THE KUMQUAT COMPOTE. In a blender or food processor, process the rest of the kumquats with the lemon juice, marmalade, and pepper. Refrigerate for 24 hours.

PREPARE THE TINTED SUGAR. The day before, preheat the oven to 140°F (60°C). Put on disposable gloves. Rub the gold dust into the sugar. Spread the sugar out onto a baking sheet. Place the baking sheet in the oven for 30 minutes to dry the sugar. Set aside to cool to room temperature.

PREPARE THE FORTUNELLA MACARON SHELLS. Sift together the confectioners' sugar and almonds.

Combine the yellow and red food color with half of the "liquefied" egg whites. Pour this into the confectioners' sugar–almond mixture without mixing.

Add the remaining "liquefied" egg whites to the bowl of a stand mixer fitted with the wire whisk. In a saucepan, boil the mineral water and granulated sugar to 244°F (118°C). As soon as the syrup reaches 239°F (115°C), begin beating the egg whites on high speed.

When the syrup reaches 244°F (118°C), reduce the mixer speed to medium–high and pour the syrup in a steady stream down the inside edge of the bowl into the beaten egg whites. Beat the meringue until it cools to 122°F (50°C). Fold it with a silicone spatula into the confectioners' sugar–almond mixture until the mixture loses volume. Transfer the batter to a pastry bag fitted with a plain #11, ½-inch (11-mm to 12-mm) pastry tip.

Line baking sheets with parchment paper. Pipe disks about 1½ inches (3.5 cm) in diameter and ¾ inch (2 cm) apart on the lined baking sheets. Rap the baking sheets on a work surface covered with a clean kitchen towel to gently smooth out the disks. Sprinkle the disks with the tinted sugar. Set aside for at least 30 minutes at room temperature to allow a skin to form.

Preheat a convection oven to 350°F (180°C). Place the baking sheets in the oven. Bake for 12 minutes, quickly opening and closing the oven door twice during baking to release moisture. Remove the shells from the oven and slide them still on the parchment paper onto a work surface.

PREPARE THE KUMQUAT CREAM. Heat the kumquat compote to 140°F (60°C). Chop the white chocolate using a serrated knife then melt it to between 113°F (45°C) and 122°F (50°C) set over a bain-marie or in a microwave.

Pour the hot compote in thirds into the melted white chocolate, stirring after each addition starting in the center then in increasingly wider concentric circles toward the sides of the bowl. Using an immersion blender, blend the cream until smooth.

Pour the kumquat cream into a baking dish. Cover it by gently pressing plastic wrap onto its surface. Refrigerate for 2 hours, just until the cream has developed a creamy consistency. Transfer the cream to a pastry bag fitted with a plain #11, ½-inch (11-mm to 12-mm) pastry tip.

Turn half of the shells over with the flat sides up onto a new piece of parchment paper. Fill them with the kumquat cream. Place three pieces of candied kumquat in the center. Pipe a dab of cream on top of the candied kumquat pieces. Close them with the rest of the shells, pressing down lightly.

Refrigerate the macarons for 24 hours. Remove them from the refrigerator 2 hours before eating them.

MAKES ABOUT 72 MACARONS (OR ABOUT 144 SHELLS)
PREPARATION TIME: 5 MINUTES (5 DAYS IN ADVANCE, SEE "MACARON SHELLS STEP-BY-STEP" IN THE KITCHEN GUIDE) + 20 MINUTES (3 DAYS IN ADVANCE) + 20 MINUTES (2 DAYS IN ADVANCE) + 1 HOUR 30 MINUTES
MACERATION TIME: 24 HOURS
DRAINING TIME: 24 HOURS
COOKING TIME: 5 MINUTES (3 DAYS IN ADVANCE) + 30 MINUTES (2 DAYS IN ADVANCE) + ABOUT 25 MINUTES
RESTING TIME: 30 MINUTES
REFRIGERATION TIME: 2 HOURS + 24 HOURS (TWICE)

FOR THE CANDIED KUMQUATS
1½ pounds (700 g) fresh kumquats
3¾ cups plus 1 tablespoon (900 g) still mineral water
2¼ cups (450 g) superfine granulated sugar
2 (5 g) star anise

FOR THE KUMQUAT COMPOTE
11 ounces (310 g) Candied Kumquats (see above)
2 tablespoons (30 g) freshly squeezed lemon juice (from ½ lemon)
¼ cup plus 2 tablespoons (125 g) orange marmalade from a jar
⅓ teaspoon (1 g) freshly ground Sarawak black pepper

FOR THE TINTED SUGAR
2½ teaspoons (2.5 g) edible gold dust
1¼ cups (250 g) coarse sugar
Note: *This will make more tinted sugar than is needed for one batch of macarons.*

FOR THE FORTUNELLA MACARON SHELLS
3 cups (300 g) confectioners' sugar
2 cups plus 2 tablespoons (300 g) ground almonds
Scant 1 teaspoon (3.5 g) liquid yellow food color
8 drops / ⅛ teaspoon (0.5 g) liquid red food color
7 large (220 g) "liquefied" egg whites, divided (see "Macaron Shells Step-by-Step" in the Kitchen Guide)
¼ cup plus 1 tablespoon (75 g) still mineral water
1½ cups (300 g) superfine granulated sugar

FOR THE KUMQUAT CREAM
1 pound (460 g) Kumquat Compote (see above)
13½ ounces (385 g) Valrhona Ivoire 35% white chocolate

Macaron Huile de Noisette et Asperge Vert

MAKES ABOUT 72 MACARONS
(OR ABOUT 144 SHELLS)

PREPARATION TIME: 5 MINUTES (5 DAYS
IN ADVANCE, SEE "MACARON SHELLS
STEP-BY-STEP" IN THE KITCHEN GUIDE)
+ 2 HOURS

COOKING TIME: ABOUT 20 MINUTES

RESTING TIME: 30 MINUTES (TWICE)

REFRIGERATION TIME: 2 HOURS +
24 HOURS

○

**FOR THE GREEN MACARON
SHELLS**
1½ cups (150 g) confectioners'
sugar
1 cup plus 1 tablespoon (150 g)
ground almonds
Scant 1 teaspoon (3.5 g) liquid
olive green food color
3½ large (110 g) "liquefied" egg
whites, divided (see "Macaron
Shells Step-by-Step" in the Kitchen
Guide)
3 tablespoons plus 1 teaspoon
(48 g) still mineral water
¾ cup (150 g) superfine granulated
sugar

*Emmanuel Renaut,
three-Michelin-starred
chef in Megève, France,
was the inspiration
for this macaron.
After having tasted a
hazelnut and green
asparagus financier
at his restaurant as a
starter, I had the idea
to create a macaron
that contains the
subtlety of hazelnut oil
in the cream along with
the delicate bitterness
of green asparagus.*

PREPARE THE GREEN MACARON SHELLS. The day before, sift together the confectioners' sugar and almonds.

Combine the food color with half of the "liquefied" egg whites. Pour this into the confectioners' sugar–almond mixture without mixing.

Add the remaining "liquefied" egg whites to the bowl of a stand mixer fitted with the wire whisk. In a saucepan, boil the mineral water and granulated sugar to 244°F (118°C). As soon as the syrup reaches 239°F (115°C), begin beating the egg whites on high speed.

When the syrup reaches 244°F (118°C), reduce the mixer speed to medium-high and pour the syrup in a steady stream down the inside edge of the bowl into the beaten egg whites. Beat the meringue until it cools to 122°F (50°C). Fold it with a silicone spatula into the confectioners' sugar–almond mixture until the mixture loses volume. Transfer the batter to a pastry bag fitted with a plain #11, ½-inch (11-mm to 12-mm) pastry tip.

Line baking sheets with parchment paper. Pipe disks about 1½ inches (3.5 cm) in diameter and ¾ inch (2 cm) apart on the lined baking sheets. Rap the baking sheets on a work surface covered with a clean kitchen towel to gently smooth out the disks. Set aside for at least 30 minutes at room temperature to allow a skin to form.

PREPARE THE PLAIN MACARON SHELLS. Sift together the confectioners' sugar and almonds.

Pour half of the "liquefied" egg whites into the confectioners' sugar–almond mixture without mixing.

Add the remaining "liquefied" egg whites to the bowl of a stand mixer fitted with the wire whisk. In a saucepan, boil the mineral water and granulated sugar to 244°F (118°C). As soon as the syrup reaches 239°F (115°C), begin beating the egg whites on high speed.

When the syrup reaches 244°F (118°C), reduce the mixer speed to medium-high and pour the syrup in a steady stream down the inside edge of the bowl into the beaten egg whites. Beat the meringue until it cools to 122°F (50°C). Fold it with a silicone spatula into the confectioners' sugar–almond mixture until the mixture loses volume. Transfer the batter to a pastry bag fitted with a plain #11, ½-inch (11-mm to 12-mm) pastry tip.

Line baking sheets with parchment paper. Pipe disks about 1½ inches (3.5 cm) in diameter and ¾ inch (2 cm) apart on the lined baking sheets. Rap the baking sheets on a work surface covered with a clean kitchen towel to gently smooth out the disks. Set aside for at least 30 minutes at room temperature to allow a skin to form.

Preheat a convection oven to 350°F (180°C). Place the baking sheets in the oven. Bake for 12 minutes, quickly opening and closing the oven door twice during baking to release moisture. Remove the shells from the oven and slide them still on the parchment paper onto a work surface.

PREPARE THE HAZELNUT OIL CREAM. Chop the white chocolate using a serrated knife then melt it to between 113°F (45°C) and 122°F (50°C) set over a bain-marie or in a microwave.

In a saucepan, bring the cream to a boil. Pour the hot cream in thirds into the melted white chocolate, stirring after each addition starting in the center then in increasingly wider concentric circles toward the sides of the bowl. Using an immersion blender, blend the cream until smooth.

Heat the hazelnut oil to between 95°F (35°C) and 104°F (40°C). As soon as the chocolate–cream mixture falls below 122°F (50°C), stir in the hot hazelnut oil in thirds. Using an immersion blender, blend the cream until smooth.

Pour the hazelnut oil cream into a baking dish. Cover it by gently pressing plastic wrap onto its surface. Refrigerate for 2 hours, just until the cream has developed a creamy consistency. Transfer the hazelnut oil cream to a pastry bag fitted with a plain #11, ½-inch (11-mm to 12-mm) pastry tip.

PREPARE THE ASPARAGUS ROUNDS. Place ice cubes in a large bowl. Break off the base of the asparagus stems to a length of between 1½ to 2 inches (4 to 5 cm). Do not peel the stems. Cut the stems into rounds measuring about ¼ inch (5 mm). Add the sugar, salt, and enough water to cover the asparagus to a saucepan. Bring it to a boil. Immerse the asparagus in the boiling water for 45 seconds. Immediately remove them to the bowl of ice to stop the cooking process. Drain them again, then place them on paper towels to dry.

Turn the green macaron shells over with the flat sides up onto a new piece of parchment paper. Fill them with the hazelnut oil cream then place three or four asparagus rounds in the center. Pipe a dab of cream on top of the rounds. Close them with the plain macaron shells, pressing down lightly.

Refrigerate the macarons for 24 hours. Remove them from the refrigerator 2 hours before eating them.

FOR THE PLAIN MACARON SHELLS
1½ cups (150 g) confectioners' sugar
1 cup plus 1 tablespoon (150 g) ground almonds
3½ large (110 g) "liquefied" egg whites, divided (see "Macaron Shells Step-by-Step" in the Kitchen Guide)
2 tablespoons plus 1¾ teaspoons (38 g) still mineral water
¾ cup (150 g) superfine granulated sugar

FOR THE HAZELNUT OIL CREAM
10½ ounces (300 g) Valrhona Ivoire 35% white chocolate
½ cup plus 1⅓ tablespoons (135 g) light whipping cream (32%–35% fat)
1 cup plus 2 teaspoons (200 g) hazelnut oil, preferably from Huilerie Beaujolaise

FOR THE ASPARAGUS ROUNDS
10½ ounces (300 g) green asparagus spears
¼ cup (50 g) superfine granulated sugar
1 tablespoon plus 1 teaspoon (20 g) salt

Macaron Huile d'Olive à la Mandarine

Olivier Baussan, founder of Première Pression Provence, presses whole fresh mandarin oranges and olives together to obtain a highly aromatic oil. I decided to use this delicate and aromatic oil in the cream of this macaron and heightened its flavor by adding mandarin compote.

PREPARE THE ORANGE MACARON SHELLS. The day before, sift together the confectioners' sugar and almonds.

Combine the yellow and red food color with half of the "liquefied" egg whites. Pour this into the confectioners' sugar–almond mixture without mixing.

Add the remaining "liquefied" egg whites to the bowl of a stand mixer fitted with the wire whisk. In a saucepan, boil the mineral water and granulated sugar to 244°F (118°C). As soon as the syrup reaches 239°F (115°C), begin beating the egg whites on high speed.

When the syrup reaches 244°F (118°C), reduce the mixer speed to medium–high and pour the syrup in a steady stream down the inside edge of the bowl into the beaten egg whites. Beat the meringue until it cools to 122°F (50°C). Fold it with a silicone spatula into the confectioners' sugar–almond mixture until the mixture loses volume. Transfer the batter to a pastry bag fitted with a plain #11, ½-inch (11-mm to 12-mm) pastry tip.

Line baking sheets with parchment paper. Pipe disks about 1½ inches (3.5 cm) in diameter and ¾ inch (2 cm) apart on the lined baking sheets. Rap the baking sheets on a work surface covered with a clean kitchen towel to gently smooth out the disks. Set aside for at least 30 minutes at room temperature to allow a skin to form.

PREPARE THE GREEN MACARON SHELLS. Sift together the confectioners' sugar and almonds.

Combine the green food color with half of the "liquefied" egg whites. Pour this into the confectioners' sugar–almond mixture without mixing.

Add the remaining "liquefied" egg whites to the bowl of a stand mixer fitted with the wire whisk. In a saucepan, boil the mineral water and granulated sugar to 244°F (118°C). As soon as the syrup reaches 239°F (115°C), begin beating the egg whites on high speed.

When the syrup reaches 244°F (118°C), reduce the mixer speed to medium-high and pour the syrup in a steady stream down the inside edge of the bowl into the beaten egg whites. Beat the meringue until it cools to 122°F (50°C). Fold it with a silicone spatula into the confectioners' sugar–almond mixture until the mixture loses volume. Transfer the batter to a pastry bag fitted with a plain #11, ¹/₂-inch (11-mm to 12-mm) pastry tip.

Line baking sheets with parchment paper. Pipe disks about 1¹/₂ inches (3.5 cm) in diameter and ³/₄ inch (2 cm) apart on the lined baking sheets. Rap the baking sheets on a work surface covered with a clean kitchen towel to gently smooth out the disks. Set aside for at least 30 minutes at room temperature to allow a skin to form.

Preheat a convection oven to 350°F (180°C). Place the baking sheets in the oven. Bake for 12 minutes, quickly opening and closing the oven door twice during baking to release moisture. Remove the shells from the oven and slide them still on the parchment paper onto a work surface.

PREPARE THE MANDARIN COMPOTE. Wash and dry the mandarin oranges. Using a microplane grater, zest the oranges and measure the quantity of zest needed. Press the oranges to collect the juice and remove the flesh. Measure the quantity of the juice and flesh needed then add this to the zest. Using an immersion blender, puree the mixture thoroughly. Combine the agar–agar with the sugar. In a saucepan, bring the marmalade and the agar–sugar mixture to a boil. Boil for 1 minute, stirring frequently. Remove from the heat then stir in the puree a little at a time. Let cool. Transfer the mandarin compote to a pastry bag fitted with a plain #11, ¹/₂-inch (11-mm to 12-mm) pastry tip.

PREPARE THE MANDARIN OLIVE OIL CREAM. Chop the white chocolate using a serrated knife then melt it to between 113°F (45°C) and 122°F (50°C) set over a bain-marie or in a microwave.

In a saucepan, bring the cream to a boil. Pour the hot cream in thirds into the melted white chocolate, stirring after each addition starting in the center then in increasingly wider concentric circles toward the sides of the bowl. Using an immersion blender, blend the cream until smooth. As soon as the cream falls below 122°F (50°C), stir in the mandarin olive oil in thirds until smooth.

Pour the cream into a baking dish. Cover it by gently pressing plastic wrap onto its surface. Refrigerate for 4 hours, just until the cream has developed a creamy consistency. Transfer the cream to a pastry bag fitted with a plain #11, ¹/₂-inch (11-mm to 12-mm) pastry tip.

Turn the orange macaron shells over with the flat sides up onto a new piece of parchment paper. Fill them with the mandarin olive oil cream then pipe a dollop of mandarin compote in the center. Pipe a dab of cream on top of the compote. Close them with the green macaron shells, pressing down lightly.

Refrigerate the macarons for 24 hours. Remove them from the refrigerator 2 hours before eating them.

MAKES ABOUT 72 MACARONS (OR ABOUT 144 SHELLS)

PREPARATION TIME: 5 MINUTES (5 DAYS IN ADVANCE, SEE "MACARON SHELLS STEP-BY-STEP" IN THE KITCHEN GUIDE) + 1 HOUR 50 MINUTES

COOKING TIME: ABOUT 20 MINUTES

RESTING TIME: 30 MINUTES (TWICE)

REFRIGERATION TIME: 4 HOURS + 24 HOURS

FOR THE ORANGE MACARON SHELLS
1½ cups (150 g) confectioners' sugar
1 cup plus 1 tablespoon (150 g) ground almonds
Scant 1 teaspoon (3.5 g) liquid yellow food color
¼ teaspoon (1 g) liquid red food color
3½ large (110 g) "liquefied" egg whites, divided (see "Macaron Shells Step-by-Step" in the Kitchen Guide)
3 tablespoons (43 g) still mineral water
¾ cup (150 g) superfine granulated sugar

FOR THE GREEN MACARON SHELLS
1½ cups (150 g) confectioners' sugar
1 cup plus 1 tablespoon (150 g) ground almonds
¼ teaspoon (1 g) liquid olive green food color
3½ large (110 g) "liquefied" egg whites, divided (see "Macaron Shells Step-by-Step" in the Kitchen Guide)
2 tablespoons plus 1¾ teaspoons (38 g) still mineral water
¾ cup (150 g) superfine granulated sugar

FOR THE MANDARIN COMPOTE
2 teaspoons (4 g) freshly grated mandarin orange zest (from 1 orange)
1⅓ cups (335 g) freshly squeezed mandarin orange juice and flesh (from 4 oranges)
2 teaspoons (5 g) agar-agar
2½ teaspoons (10 g) superfine granulated sugar
¼ cup plus 1⅓ tablespoons (105 g) orange marmalade from a jar

FOR THE MANDARIN OLIVE OIL CREAM
8 ounces (225 g) Valrhona Ivoire 35% white chocolate
⅓ cup plus 1½ tablespoons (100 g) light whipping cream (32%–35% fat)
⅔ cup (150 g) mandarin olive oil, preferably from Première Pression Provence

Macaron Fragola

In Italy, strawberries (fragola) are traditionally served with a drizzle of balsamic vinegar. I transformed this unusual combination by working with the acidity and syrupy texture of 25-year-old balsamic vinegar and the natural acidity and refreshing flavor of strawberries.

MAKES ABOUT 72 MACARONS
(OR ABOUT 144 SHELLS)

PREPARATION TIME: **5 MINUTES (5 DAYS IN ADVANCE, SEE "MACARON SHELLS STEP-BY-STEP" IN THE KITCHEN GUIDE) + 1 HOUR 30 MINUTES**

COOKING TIME: **ABOUT 55 MINUTES**

RESTING TIME: **30 MINUTES**

REFRIGERATION TIME: **4 HOURS + 24 HOURS**

FOR THE TINTED SUGAR
Scant ¾ teaspoon **(2.5 g)** liquid red food color
1¼ cups **(250 g)** coarse sugar
Note: *This will make more tinted sugar than is needed for one batch of macarons.*

FOR THE MACARON SHELLS
3 cups **(300 g)** confectioners' sugar
2 cups plus 2 tablespoons **(300 g)** ground almonds
7 large (220 g) "liquefied" egg whites, divided (see "Macaron Shells Step-by-Step" in the Kitchen Guide)
¼ cup plus 1 tablespoon **(75 g)** still mineral water
1½ cups **(300 g)** superfine granulated sugar
Tinted Sugar (see above)

PREPARE THE TINTED SUGAR. The day before, preheat the oven to 140°F (60°C). Put on disposable gloves. Rub the food color into the coarse sugar using your fingertips. Spread the sugar out on a baking sheet. Place the baking sheets in the oven for 30 minutes to dry the sugar. Set aside to cool to room temperature.

PREPARE THE MACARON SHELLS. Sift the confectioners' sugar and almonds together in a bowl.

Pour half of the "liquefied" egg whites into the confectioners' sugar–almond mixture without mixing.

Add the remaining "liquefied" egg whites to the bowl of a stand mixer fitted with the wire whisk. In a saucepan, boil the mineral water and granulated sugar to 244°F (118°C). As soon as the syrup reaches 239°F (115°C), begin beating the egg whites on high speed.

When the syrup reaches 244°F (118°C), reduce the mixer speed to medium-high and pour the syrup in a steady stream down the inside edge of the bowl into the beaten egg whites. Beat the meringue until it cools to 122°F (50°C). Fold it with a silicone spatula into the confectioners' sugar–almond mixture until the mixture loses volume. Transfer the batter to a pastry bag fitted with a plain #11, ¹/₂-inch (11-mm to 12-mm) pastry tip.

Line baking sheets with parchment paper. Pipe disks about 1¹/₂ inches (3.5 cm) in diameter and ³/₄ inch (2 cm) apart on the lined baking sheets. Rap the baking sheets on a work surface covered with a clean kitchen towel to gently smooth out the disks. Sprinkle the disks with the tinted sugar. Set aside for at least 30 minutes at room temperature to allow a skin to form.

Preheat a convection oven to 350°F (180°C). Place the baking sheets in the oven. Bake for 12 minutes, quickly opening and closing the oven door twice during baking to release moisture. Remove the shells from the oven and slide them still on the parchment paper onto a work surface.

PREPARE THE BALSAMIC VINEGAR CREAM. Chop the white chocolate and the cocoa butter using a serrated knife then melt them in separate bowls to between 113°F (45°C) and 122°F (50°C) set over a bain-marie or in a microwave.

In a saucepan, bring the cream to a boil. Pour the hot cream in thirds into the melted white chocolate, stirring after each addition starting in the center then in increasingly wider concentric circles toward the sides of the bowl. When cooled, stir in the melted cocoa butter then the vinegar. Using an immersion blender, blend the cream until smooth.

Pour the cream into a baking dish. Cover it by gently pressing plastic wrap onto its surface. Refrigerate for 4 hours, just until the cream has developed a creamy consistency. Transfer the balsamic vinegar cream to a pastry bag fitted with a plain #11, ½-inch (11-mm to 12-mm) pastry tip.

PREPARE THE STRAWBERRY COMPOTE. Rinse and gently dry the strawberries. Remove any stems. Using a food mill, puree the strawberries; you should have about 1¾ cups (400 g) of puree. Add half of the puree to a saucepan and heat it through. Combine the sugar with the agar-agar. Add this mixture to the warm puree then bring to a boil for 2 minutes, stirring frequently. Stir in the rest of the strawberry puree and the lemon juice a little at a time. Stir to thoroughly combine then set aside to cool. Transfer the compote to a pastry bag fitted with a plain #11, ½-inch (11-mm to 12-mm) pastry tip.

Turn half of the shells over with the flat sides up onto a new piece of parchment paper. Fill them with the balsamic vinegar cream then pipe a dollop of strawberry compote in the center. Pipe a small dab of the cream on the compote, then close them with the rest of the shells, pressing down lightly.

Refrigerate the macarons for 24 hours. Remove them from the refrigerator 2 hours before eating them.

FOR THE STRAWBERRY COMPOTE
1½ pints (500 g) strawberries, preferably wild Mara, Ciflorette, or Gariguette
Scant ¼ cup (45 g) superfine granulated sugar
1 teaspoon (5 g) agar-agar
Scant 2 tablespoons (25 g) freshly squeezed lemon juice (from ½ lemon)

FOR THE BALSAMIC VINEGAR CREAM
8¾ ounces (250 g) Valrhona Ivoire 35% white chocolate
1¾ ounces (50 g) cocoa butter, preferably Valrhona
½ cup plus 2⅓ tablespoons (150 g) light whipping cream (32%–35% fat)
¼ cup (60 g) 25-year-old balsamic vinegar or any premium, aged balsamic vinegar

Macaron Imagine

This macaron, completely inspired by Japanese elements, has two different bitter tastes, the first from Uji matcha green tea and the second from black sesame seeds. The flavors marry surprisingly well and become harmonious in the cream with a crunchy center of crisp black sesame seed and puffed rice.

PREPARE THE GREEN IMAGINE MACARON SHELLS. The day before, sift together the confectioners' sugar and almonds.

Combine the food color with half of the "liquefied" egg whites. Pour this into the confectioners' sugar–almond mixture without mixing.

Add the remaining "liquefied" egg whites to the bowl of a stand mixer fitted with the wire whisk. In a saucepan, boil the mineral water and granulated sugar to 244°F (118°C). As soon as the syrup reaches 239°F (115°C), begin beating the egg whites on high speed.

When the syrup reaches 244°F (118°C), reduce the mixer speed to medium–high and pour the syrup in a steady stream down the inside edge of the bowl into the beaten egg whites. Beat the meringue until it cools to 122°F (50°C). Fold it with a silicone spatula into the confectioners' sugar–almond mixture until the mixture loses volume. Transfer the batter to a pastry bag fitted with a plain #11, ¹/₂–inch (11–mm to 12–mm) pastry tip.

Line baking sheets with parchment paper. Pipe disks about 1¹/₂ inches (3.5 cm) in diameter and ³/₄ inch (2 cm) apart on the lined baking sheets. Rap the baking sheets on a work surface covered with a clean kitchen towel to gently smooth out the disks. Set aside for at least 30 minutes at room temperature to allow a skin to form.

PREPARE THE WHITE IMAGINE MACARON SHELLS. Sift together the confectioners' sugar and almonds.

Pour half of the "liquefied" egg whites into the confectioners' sugar–almond mixture without mixing.

Add the remaining "liquefied" egg whites to the bowl of a stand mixer fitted with the wire whisk. In a saucepan, boil the mineral water and granulated sugar to 244°F (118°C). As soon as the syrup reaches 239°F (115°C), begin beating the egg whites on high speed.

When the syrup reaches 244°F (118°C), reduce the mixer speed to medium–high and pour the syrup in a steady stream down the inside edge of the bowl into the beaten egg whites. Beat the meringue until it cools to 122°F (50°C). Fold it with a silicone spatula into the confectioners' sugar–almond mixture until the mixture loses volume. Transfer the batter to a pastry bag fitted with a plain #11, ¹/₂-inch (11-mm to 12-mm) pastry tip.

Line baking sheets with parchment paper. Pipe disks about 1¹/₂ inches (3.5 cm) in diameter and ³/₄ inch (2 cm) apart on the lined baking sheets. Rap the baking sheets on a work surface covered with a clean kitchen towel to gently smooth out the disks. Sprinkle the disks with golden sesame seeds. Set aside for at least 30 minutes at room temperature to allow a skin to form.

Preheat a convection oven to 350°F (180°C). Place the baking sheets in the oven. Bake for 12 minutes, quickly opening and closing the oven door twice during baking to release moisture. Remove the shells from the oven and slide them still on the parchment paper onto a work surface.

PREPARE THE BLACK SESAME CRUNCH. Chop the white chocolate and the cocoa butter using a serrated knife then melt them together along with the butter to between 113°F (45°C) and 122°F (50°C) set over a bain-marie or in a microwave.

Add the black sesame paste and the almond praline and stir to combine. Carefully stir in the golden sesame seeds and puffed rice.

Pour the mixture into a baking dish lined with plastic wrap. Gently press a second piece of plastic wrap onto its surface. Refrigerate for 30 minutes.

Remove the crunch layer from the refrigerator then carefully peel away both pieces of plastic wrap. Cut the layer into ¹/₂-inch (1.5-cm) squares. Place the squares in a container and freeze.

PREPARE THE GREEN TEA CREAM. Chop the white chocolate using a serrated knife then melt it to between 113°F (45°C) and 122°F (50°C) set over a bain-marie or in a microwave.

In a saucepan, bring the cream to a boil. Let it cool to 140°F (60°C), then stir in the green tea powder. Vigorously whisk the cream then pour it in thirds into the melted chocolate, stirring after each addition starting in the center then in increasingly wider concentric circles toward the sides of the bowl. Using an immersion blender, blend the cream until smooth.

Pour the green tea cream into a baking dish. Cover it by gently pressing plastic wrap onto its surface. Refrigerate for 4 hours, just until the cream has developed a creamy consistency. Transfer the green tea cream to a pastry bag fitted with a plain #11, ¹/₂-inch (11-mm to 12-mm) pastry tip.

Turn the green Imagine shells over with the flat sides up onto a new piece of parchment paper. Fill them with the green tea cream then carefully place a black sesame crunch square in the center. Pipe a dab of cream on top of the square. Close them with the white Imagine macaron shells, pressing down lightly.

Refrigerate the macarons for 24 hours. Remove them from the refrigerator 2 hours before eating them.

MAKES ABOUT 72 MACARONS (OR ABOUT 144 SHELLS)

PREPARATION TIME: 5 MINUTES (5 DAYS IN ADVANCE, SEE "MACARON SHELLS STEP-BY-STEP" IN THE KITCHEN GUIDE) + 2 HOURS 15 MINUTES

COOKING TIME: ABOUT 20 MINUTES

RESTING TIME: 30 MINUTES (TWICE)

REFRIGERATION TIME: 30 MINUTES + 4 HOURS + 24 HOURS

FOR THE GREEN IMAGINE MACARON SHELLS
1½ cups **(150 g)** confectioners' sugar
1 cup plus 1 tablespoon **(150 g)** ground almonds
¼ teaspoon **(1 g)** liquid olive green food color
3½ large **(110 g)** "liquefied" egg whites, divided (see "Macaron Shells Step-by-Step" in the Kitchen Guide)
3 tablespoons **(43 g)** still mineral water
¾ cup **(150 g)** superfine granulated sugar

FOR THE WHITE IMAGINE MACARON SHELLS
1½ cups **(150 g)** confectioners' sugar
1 cup plus 1 tablespoon **(150 g)** ground almonds
3½ large **(110 g)** "liquefied" egg whites, divided (see "Macaron Shells Step-by-Step" in the Kitchen Guide)
2 tablespoons plus 1¾ teaspoons **(38 g)** still mineral water
¾ cup **(150 g)** superfine granulated sugar
Golden sesame seeds, for sprinkling

FOR THE BLACK SESAME CRUNCH
1¾ ounces **(50 g)** Valrhona Ivoire 35% white chocolate
⅓ ounce **(10 g)** cocoa butter, preferably Valrhona
1 tablespoon plus 1 teaspoon **(20 g)** fine French unsalted butter, preferably *beurre de la Viette*
5¾ ounces **(160 g)** black sesame paste, preferably from Kioko Paris
1 tablespoon **(20 g)** almond praline (made with 60% almonds), preferably Valrhona
Scant ¼ cup **(20 g)** golden sesame seeds, preferably from Thiercelin
2⅛ ounces **(60 g)** puffed rice, preferably Kellogg's Rice Krispies

FOR THE GREEN TEA CREAM
8¾ ounces **(250 g)** Valrhona Ivoire 35% white chocolate
1 cup plus 3 tablespoons **(275 g)** light whipping cream (32%–35% fat)
3 tablespoons plus 1 teaspoon **(20 g)** Uji matcha green tea powder

Macaron
Indulgence

I love fresh garden peas and I have a habit of seasoning them with fresh mint. In order to accentuate the freshness of this macaron, I added a little mint liqueur into the cream. My advice is to not let the mint leaves infuse for more than 10 minutes; any longer and their flavor changes, diminishing their freshness and strength.

PREPARE THE FRESH MINT CREAM. The day before, chop the white chocolate and the cocoa butter using a serrated knife then melt them together to between 113°F (45°C) and 122°F (50°C) set over a bain-marie or in a microwave.

In a saucepan, bring the cream to a boil. Remove from the heat then add the mint leaves. Cover and let infuse for 10 minutes.

Strain the infused cream. Remove the mint leaves and finely chop them. Pour the hot cream in thirds into the melted chocolate-cocoa butter mixture, stirring after each addition starting in the center then in increasingly wider concentric circles toward the sides of the bowl. Add the chopped mint and peppermint liqueur. Using an immersion blender, blend the cream until smooth.

Pour the fresh mint cream into a baking dish. Cover it by gently pressing plastic wrap onto its surface. Refrigerate for 6 hours. Transfer the fresh mint cream to a pastry bag fitted with a plain #11, ½-inch (11-mm to 12-mm) pastry tip.

MAKES ABOUT 72 MACARONS
(OR ABOUT 144 SHELLS)
PREPARATION TIME: 5 MINUTES (5 DAYS IN ADVANCE, SEE "MACARON SHELLS STEP-BY-STEP" IN THE KITCHEN GUIDE) + 1 HOUR 50 MINUTES
COOKING TIME: ABOUT 20 MINUTES
INFUSION TIME: 10 MINUTES
RESTING TIME: 30 MINUTES (TWICE)
REFRIGERATION TIME: 6 HOURS + 24 HOURS

FOR THE FRESH MINT CREAM
10½ ounces (300 g) Valrhona Ivoire 35% white chocolate
About ½ ounce (17 g) cocoa butter, preferably Valrhona
1⅓ cups (300 g) light whipping cream (32%–35% fat)
¼ cup (10 g) fresh mint leaves, roughly chopped
1 tablespoon (15 g) Get 27 peppermint liqueur

PREPARE THE MINT GREEN MACARON SHELLS. Sift together the confectioners' sugar and almonds.

Combine the food color with half of the "liquefied" egg whites. Pour this into the confectioners' sugar–almond mixture without mixing.

Add the remaining "liquefied" egg whites to the bowl of a stand mixer fitted with the wire whisk. In a saucepan, boil the mineral water and granulated sugar to 244°F (118°C). As soon as the syrup reaches 239°F (115°C), begin beating the egg whites on high speed.

When the syrup reaches 244°F (118°C), reduce the mixer speed to medium-high and pour the syrup in a steady stream down the inside edge of the bowl into the beaten egg whites. Beat the meringue until it cools to 122°F (50°C). Fold it with a silicone spatula into the confectioners' sugar–almond mixture until the mixture loses volume. Transfer the batter to a pastry bag fitted with a plain #11, ¹⁄₂-inch (11-mm to 12-mm) pastry tip.

PREPARE THE PISTACHIO GREEN MACARON SHELLS. Sift together the confectioners' sugar and almonds.

Combine the food color with half of the "liquefied" egg whites. Pour this into the confectioners' sugar–almond mixture without mixing.

Add the remaining "liquefied" egg whites to the bowl of a stand mixer fitted with the wire whisk. In a saucepan, boil the mineral water and granulated sugar to 244°F (118°C). As soon as the syrup reaches 239°F (115°C), begin beating the egg whites on high speed.

When the syrup reaches 244°F (118°C), reduce the mixer speed to medium-high and pour the syrup in a steady stream down the inside edge of the bowl into the beaten egg whites. Beat the meringue until it cools to 122°F (50°C). Fold it with a silicone spatula into the confectioners' sugar–almond mixture until the mixture loses volume. Transfer the batter to a pastry bag fitted with a plain #11, ¹⁄₂-inch (11-mm to 12-mm) pastry tip.

Line baking sheets with parchment paper. Pipe disks about 1¹⁄₂ inches (3.5 cm) in diameter and ³⁄₄ inch (2 cm) apart on the lined baking sheets. Rap the baking sheets on a work surface covered with a clean kitchen towel to gently smooth out the disks. Set aside for at least 30 minutes at room temperature to allow a skin to form.

Line baking sheets with parchment paper. Pipe disks about 1¹⁄₂ inches (3.5 cm) in diameter and ³⁄₄ inch (2 cm) apart on the lined baking sheets. Rap the baking sheets on a work surface covered with a clean kitchen towel to gently smooth out the disks. Set aside for at least 30 minutes at room temperature to allow a skin to form.

Preheat a convection oven to 350°F (180°C). Place the baking sheets in the oven. Bake for 12 minutes, quickly opening and closing the oven door twice during baking to release moisture. Remove the shells from the oven and slide them still on the parchment paper onto a work surface.

PREPARE THE SUGARED PEAS. Fill a bowl with ice water. In a saucepan, bring the mineral water, sugar, and salt to a boil. Add the peas and cook for about 4 minutes. Drain, then immerse the peas immediately in the ice water. Drain them again, then transfer them to paper towels to dry.

Turn the pistachio green shells over with the flat sides up onto a new piece of parchment paper. Fill them with the fresh mint cream then place five peas in the center. Pipe a dab of the cream on top. Close them with the mint green macaron shells, pressing down lightly.

Refrigerate the macarons for 24 hours. Remove them from the refrigerator 2 hours before eating them.

FOR THE PISTACHIO GREEN MACARON SHELLS
1½ cups (150 g) confectioners' sugar
1 cup plus 1 tablespoon (150 g) ground almonds
½ teaspoon (2 g) liquid pistachio green food color
3½ large (110 g) "liquefied" egg whites, divided (see "Macaron Shells Step-by-Step" in the Kitchen Guide)
3 tablespoons (43 g) still mineral water
¾ cup (150 g) superfine granulated sugar

FOR THE MINT GREEN MACARON SHELLS
1½ cups (150 g) confectioners' sugar
1 cup plus 1 tablespoon (150 g) ground almonds
½ teaspoon (2 g) liquid mint green food color
3½ large (110 g) "liquefied" egg whites, divided (see "Macaron Shells Step-by-Step" in the Kitchen Guide)
2 tablespoons plus 1¾ teaspoons (38 g) still mineral water
¾ cup (150 g) superfine granulated sugar

FOR THE SUGARED PEAS
2 cups plus 2 tablespoons (500 g) still mineral water
3 tablespoons plus ½ teaspoon (40 g) superfine granulated sugar
1 pinch salt
2 cups (250 g) fresh or frozen shelled peas

Creativity is both the origin and the result of different dreams.

Macaron Magnifique

In Japan, when the rhizome of the wasabi grows deep in the ground, it has a sweet taste. This unusual characteristic motivated me to work with it. In 1998, I made my first attempt with a grapefruit and wasabi sorbet in a dessert called Émotion *and a plated dessert called* Entre. *Combined in this macaron with the fresh sweetness of strawberry, the wasabi is magnificent.*

PREPARE THE TINTED ALMONDS. The day before, put on disposable gloves. Rub the food color into the almonds with your fingertips then beat them in the bowl of a stand mixer fitted with the paddle attachment. Set aside.

PREPARE THE MAGNIFICENT MACARON SHELLS. Sift together the confectioners' sugar and almonds.

Dilute the titanium dioxide powder in the warm water then stir it into half of the "liquefied" egg whites. Pour this into the confectioners' sugar–almond mixture without mixing.

Add the remaining "liquefied" egg whites to the bowl of a stand mixer fitted with the wire whisk. In a saucepan, boil the mineral water and granulated sugar to 244°F (118°C). As soon as the syrup reaches 239°F (115°C), begin beating the egg whites on high speed.

When the syrup reaches 244°F (118°C), reduce the mixer speed to medium-high and pour the syrup in a steady stream down the inside edge of the bowl into the beaten egg whites. Beat the meringue until it cools to 122°F (50°C). Fold it with a silicone spatula into the confectioners' sugar–almond mixture until the mixture loses volume. Transfer the batter to a pastry bag fitted with a plain #11, ¹/₂-inch (11-mm to 12-mm) pastry tip.

Line baking sheets with parchment paper. Pipe disks about 1¹/₂ inches (3.5 cm) in diameter and ³/₄ inch (2 cm) apart on the lined baking sheets. Rap the baking sheets on a work surface covered with a clean kitchen towel to gently smooth out the tops of the disks. Sprinkle the disks with the tinted almonds. Set aside for at least 30 minutes at room temperature to allow a skin to form.

Preheat a convection oven to 350°F (180°C). Place the baking sheets in the oven. Bake for 12 minutes, quickly opening and closing the oven door twice during baking to release moisture. Remove the shells from the oven and slide them still on the parchment paper onto a work surface.

PREPARE THE STRAWBERRY COMPOTE. Rinse and gently dry the strawberries. Remove any stems. Using a food mill, puree the strawberries; you should have about 1⅛ pounds (500 g) of puree. Add half of the puree to a saucepan and heat it through. Combine the sugar with the agar-agar. Add this mixture to the warm puree then bring it to a boil for 2 minutes, stirring frequently. Stir in the rest of the strawberry puree and the lemon juice a little at a time. Stir to combine, then set aside to cool. Transfer the compote to a pastry bag fitted with a plain #11, ¹/₂-inch (11-mm to 12-mm) pastry tip.

PREPARE THE WASABI CREAM. Peel the wasabi and finely grate it using a sharkskin wasabi grater or a microplane grater.

Chop the white chocolate using a serrated knife then melt it and the cocoa butter together to between 113°F (45°C) and 122°F (50°C) set over a bain-marie or in a microwave.

Add the yuzu juice and the cream to separate saucepans. Heat the yuzu juice to 113°F (45°C) and bring the cream to a boil. Pour the hot cream then the warm yuzu juice in thirds into the melted white chocolate–cocoa butter mixture stirring after each addition starting in the center then in increasingly wider concentric circles toward the sides of the bowl. Add the wasabi. Using an immersion blender, blend the cream until smooth.

Pour the wasabi cream into a baking dish. Cover it by gently pressing plastic wrap onto its surface. Refrigerate for 4 hours, just until the cream has developed a creamy consistency. Transfer the wasabi cream to a pastry bag fitted with a plain #11, ¹/₂-inch (11-mm to 12-mm) pastry tip.

Turn half of the shells over with the flat sides up onto a new piece of parchment paper. Fill them with the wasabi cream then pipe a small dollop of strawberry compote in the center. Pipe a small dab of the cream on top of the strawberry compote. Close them with the rest of the shells, pressing down lightly.

Refrigerate the macarons for 24 hours. Remove them from the refrigerator 2 hours before eating them.

MAKES ABOUT 72 MACARONS (OR ABOUT 144 SHELLS)

PREPARATION TIME: 5 MINUTES (5 DAYS IN ADVANCE, SEE "MACARON SHELLS STEP-BY-STEP" IN THE KITCHEN GUIDE) + 2 HOURS

COOKING TIME: ABOUT 30 MINUTES

RESTING TIME: 30 MINUTES

REFRIGERATION TIME: 4 HOURS + 24 HOURS

○

FOR THE TINTED ALMONDS
Generous 2 teaspoons (10 g) liquid strawberry red food color
1½ cups minus 1 tablespoon (200 g) ground blanched almonds

◯◯

FOR THE MAGNIFICENT MACARON SHELLS
3 cups (300 g) confectioners' sugar
2 cups plus 2 tablespoons (300 g) ground almonds
2⅔ teaspoons (16 g) titanium dioxide powder
1¾ teaspoons (8 g) warm water
7 large (220 g) "liquefied" egg whites, divided (see "Macaron Shells Step-by-Step" in the Kitchen Guide)
¼ cup plus 1 tablespoon (75 g) still mineral water
1½ cups (300 g) superfine granulated sugar
Tinted Almonds (see above)

◯◯◯

FOR THE STRAWBERRY COMPOTE
1½ pints plus ½ cup (620 g) strawberries, preferably wild Mara, Ciflorette, or Gariguette
¼ cup plus 2½ teaspoons (60 g) superfine granulated sugar
Scant 2 teaspoons (3.5 g) agar-agar
2 tablespoons (30 g) freshly squeezed lemon juice (from ½ lemon)

◯◯◯

FOR THE WASABI CREAM
½ ounce (15 g) fresh wasabi stem, preferably from Issé Workshop
8¾ ounces (250 g) Valrhona Ivoire 35% white chocolate
½ ounce (15 g) cocoa butter, preferably Valrhona
2 tablespoons (25 g) sweetened yuzu juice
¾ cup plus 2 tablespoons (200 g) light whipping cream (32%–35% fat)

Macaron Yuzu

I love the incredible flavor of yuzu. Rare and highly prized, this little Asian citrus fruit has a fruity and floral flavor that simultaneously evokes the flavors of mandarin orange, lime zest, and lemon juice. To accentuate the flavor of this macaron, I added candied yuzu from Kochi to the yuzu cream.

PREPARE THE TINTED SUGAR. The day before, preheat the oven to 140°F (60°C). Put on disposable gloves. Rub the food color into the coarse sugar using your fingertips. Spread the sugar out on a baking sheet. Place the baking sheet in the oven for 30 minutes to dry the sugar. Set aside to cool to room temperature.

PREPARE THE PLAIN MACARON SHELLS. Sift together the confectioners' sugar and almonds.

Dilute the titanium dioxide powder in the warm water then stir it into half of the "liquefied" egg whites. Pour this into the confectioners' sugar–almond mixture without mixing.

Add the remaining "liquefied" egg whites to the bowl of a stand mixer fitted with the wire whisk. In a saucepan, boil the mineral water and granulated sugar to 244°F (118°C). As soon as the syrup reaches 239°F (115°C), begin beating the egg whites on high speed.

When the syrup reaches 244°F (118°C), reduce the mixer speed to medium–high and pour the syrup in a steady stream down the inside edge of the bowl into the beaten egg whites. Beat the meringue until it cools to 122°F (50°C). Fold it with a silicone spatula into the confectioners' sugar–almond mixture until the mixture loses volume. Transfer the batter to a pastry bag fitted with a plain #11, ½-inch (11-mm to 12-mm) pastry tip.

Line baking sheets with parchment paper. Pipe disks about 1½ inches (3.5 cm) in diameter and ¾ inch (2 cm) apart on the lined baking sheets. Rap the baking sheets on a work surface covered with a clean kitchen towel to gently smooth out the disks. Sprinkle the disks with the tinted sugar. Set aside for at least 30 minutes at room temperature to allow a skin to form.

Preheat a convection oven to 350°F (180°C). Place the baking sheets in the oven. Bake for 12 minutes, quickly opening and closing the oven door twice during baking to release moisture. Remove the shells from the oven and slide them still on the parchment paper onto a work surface.

MAKES ABOUT 72 MACARONS
(OR ABOUT 144 SHELLS)
PREPARATION TIME: **5 MINUTES (5 DAYS
IN ADVANCE, SEE "MACARON SHELLS
STEP-BY-STEP" IN THE KITCHEN GUIDE)**
+ 1 HOUR 30 MINUTES
COOKING TIME: **ABOUT 1 HOUR**
RESTING TIME: **30 MINUTES**
REFRIGERATION TIME: **4 HOURS +
24 HOURS**

FOR THE TINTED SUGAR
Scant ¾ teaspoon (2.5 g) liquid yellow food color
1¼ cups (250 g) coarse sugar
Note: *This will make more tinted sugar than is needed for one batch of macarons.*

FOR THE PLAIN MACARON SHELLS
3 cups (300 g) confectioners' sugar
2 cups plus 2 tablespoons (300 g) ground almonds
2⅔ teaspoons (16 g) titanium dioxide powder
1¾ teaspoons (8 g) warm water
7 large (220 g) "liquefied" egg whites, divided (see "Macaron Shells Step-by-Step" in the Kitchen Guide)
¼ cup plus 1 tablespoon (75 g) still mineral water
1½ cups (300 g) superfine granulated sugar
Tinted Sugar (see above)

→ PREPARE THE YUZU CREAM. Chop the white chocolate using a serrated knife then melt it to between 113°F (45°C) and 122°F (50°C) set over a bain-marie or in a microwave.

In a saucepan, heat the yuzu juice to 122°F (50°C). In a separate saucepan, bring the cream and yuzu zest to a boil. Pour the hot cream and the yuzu juice in thirds into the melted white chocolate, stirring after each addition starting in the center then in increasingly wider concentric circles toward the sides of the bowl. Using an immersion blender, blend the cream until smooth.

Pour the yuzu cream into a baking dish. Cover it by gently pressing plastic wrap onto its surface. Refrigerate for 4 hours, just until the cream has developed a creamy consistency. Transfer the yuzu cream and the pureed yuzu to separate pastry bags fitted with a plain #11, ½-inch (11-mm to 12-mm) pastry tip.

Turn half of the shells over with the flat sides up onto a new piece of parchment paper. Fill them with the yuzu cream then pipe a dollop of candied yuzu in the center. Pipe a dab of the cream on top. Close them with the rest of the shells, pressing down lightly.

Refrigerate the macarons for 24 hours. Remove them from the refrigerator 2 hours before eating them.

FOR THE YUZU CREAM
11¾ ounces (335 g) Valrhona Ivoire 35% white chocolate
¼ cup plus 1 tablespoon (65 g) pure unsweetened yuzu juice, preferably from Issé Workshop
½ cup plus 1 tablespoon (130 g) light whipping cream (32%–35% fat)
⅛ ounce (4 g) powdered yuzu zest, preferably from Issé Workshop

FOR THE FILLING
15 ounces (430 g) pureed candied Kochi yuzu, preferably from Nishikidori Market

None of my creations yields to the temptation of technical exploit or show— my only guide is the taste!

Macaron Pomme Verte à l'Angélique de Montagne

Lovage has a strong flavor of wild celery. It's often called mountain angelica or wild celery. By combining lovage with the acidity of green apple, its strong flavor becomes fresh and delicate, reminiscent of pine needles.

PREPARE THE GREEN MACARON SHELLS. The day before, sift together the confectioners' sugar and almonds.

Combine the food color with half of the "liquefied" egg whites. Pour this into the confectioners' sugar–almond mixture without mixing.

Add the remaining "liquefied" egg whites to the bowl of a stand mixer fitted with the wire whisk. In a saucepan, boil the mineral water and granulated sugar to 244°F (118°C). As soon as the syrup reaches 239°F (115°C), begin beating the egg whites on high speed.

When the syrup reaches 244°F (118°C), reduce the mixer speed to medium–high and pour the syrup in a steady stream down the inside edge of the bowl into the beaten egg whites. Beat the meringue until it cools to 122°F (50°C). Fold it with a silicone spatula into the confectioners' sugar–almond mixture until the mixture loses volume. Transfer the batter to a pastry bag fitted with a plain #11, ½-inch (11–mm to 12–mm) pastry tip.

Line baking sheets with parchment paper. Pipe disks about 1½ inches (3.5 cm) in diameter and ¾ inch (2 cm) apart on the lined baking sheets. Rap the baking sheets on a work surface covered with a clean kitchen towel to gently smooth out the disks. Sprinkle them with gold flake. Set aside for at least 30 minutes at room temperature to allow a skin to form.

Preheat a convection oven to 350°F (180°C). Place the baking sheets in the oven. Bake for 12 minutes, quickly opening and closing the oven door twice during baking to release moisture. Remove the shells from the oven and slide them still on the parchment paper onto a work surface.

PREPARE THE LOVAGE JUICE. Fill a bowl with ice water. Immerse the lovage leaves in a saucepan of boiling water. Drain, then submerge them in the ice water. In a saucepan, heat the mineral water and the sugar to 140°F (60°C). Drain the lovage leaves then place them in the saucepan and blend using an immersion blender.

PREPARE THE LOVAGE CREAM. Rinse the green apples, unpeeled, then remove their seeds and cut them into large pieces and process them through a juicer. Collect both the pulp and the juice and stir them together then measure the quantity needed.

Chop the white chocolate and cocoa butter using a serrated knife then melt them together to between 113°F (45°C) and 122°F (50°C) set over a bain-marie or in a microwave.

In a saucepan, bring the green apple pulp and juice and the lemon juice to a boil. Pour the hot mixture in two parts into the melted white chocolate–cocoa butter mixture, stirring after each addition starting in the center then in increasingly wider concentric circles toward the sides of the bowl. Heat the lovage juice to 104°F (40°C). Add the heated juice to the chocolate mixture and stir again to combine. Using an immersion blender, blend the cream until smooth.

Pour the lovage cream into a baking dish. Cover it by gently pressing plastic wrap onto its surface. Refrigerate for 6 hours, just until the cream has developed a creamy consistency. Transfer the green apple lovage cream to a pastry bag fitted with a plain #11, ½-inch (11-mm to 12-mm) pastry tip.

PREPARE THE GREEN APPLES. Sprinkle the apple cubes with the lemon juice and pepper.

Turn half of the shells over with the flat sides up onto a new piece of parchment paper. Fill them with the lovage cream. Gently place three cubes of green apple in the center then pipe a small dab of the cream on top of the cubes. Close them with the rest of the shells, pressing down lightly.

Refrigerate the macarons for 24 hours. Remove them from the refrigerator 2 hours before eating them.

MAKES ABOUT 72 MACARONS (OR ABOUT 144 SHELLS)

PREPARATION TIME: 5 MINUTES (5 DAYS IN ADVANCE, SEE "MACARON SHELLS STEP-BY-STEP" IN THE KITCHEN GUIDE) + 2 HOURS 15 MINUTES

COOKING TIME: ABOUT 30 MINUTES

RESTING TIME: 30 MINUTES

REFRIGERATION TIME: 6 HOURS + 24 HOURS

FOR THE GREEN MACARON SHELLS
3 cups (300 g) confectioners' sugar
2 cups plus 2 tablespoons (300 g) ground almonds
1 teaspoon (4 g) liquid pistachio green food color
7 large (220 g) "liquefied" egg whites, divided (see "Macaron Shells Step-by-Step" in the Kitchen Guide)
¼ cup plus 1 tablespoon (75 g) still mineral water
1½ cups (300 g) superfine granulated sugar
Edible gold flake, preferably from Degami, for sprinkling

FOR THE LOVAGE JUICE
½ cup (20 g) lovage leaves
⅓ cup plus 1½ tablespoons (100 g) still mineral water
1 tablespoon plus ¾ teaspoon (16 g) superfine granulated sugar

FOR THE LOVAGE CREAM
2 Granny Smith apples (to make ¾ cup plus 1 tablespoon/ 185 g fresh puree), or use Boiron brand green apple puree
1 pound (465 g) Valrhona Ivoire 35% white chocolate
½ ounce (15 g) cocoa butter, preferably Valrhona
2 tablespoons (35 g) freshly squeezed lemon juice (from ½ lemon)
¼ cup plus 1 tablespoon (80 g) Lovage Juice (see above)

FOR THE GREEN APPLES
1 large (160 g) Granny Smith apple, quartered and cut into ¼-inch (5-mm) cubes
Generous 1 tablespoon (20 g) freshly squeezed lemon juice (from ½ lemon)
⅓ teaspoon (1 g) freshly ground Sarawak black pepper

Macaron Yasamine

Combining the sweet creaminess of mango, which is lightly acidic, with the soft floral nature of jasmine creates a flavor with a clear Asian influence. Yasamine macaron takes all of the characteristics associated with candied grapefruit and enriches it with a touch of bitterness from the jasmine tea.

MAKES ABOUT 72 MACARONS
(OR ABOUT 144 SHELLS)

PREPARATION TIME: 5 MINUTES (5 DAYS
IN ADVANCE, SEE "MACARON SHELLS
STEP-BY-STEP" IN THE KITCHEN GUIDE)
+ 30 MINUTES (2 DAYS IN ADVANCE) +
1 HOUR 30 MINUTES

COOKING TIME: 1 HOUR 40 MINUTES
(2 DAYS IN ADVANCE) + ABOUT 25
MINUTES

INFUSION TIME: 3 MINUTES

MACERATION TIME: 24 HOURS

DRAINING TIME: 1 HOUR

RESTING TIME: 30 MINUTES

REFRIGERATION TIME: 2 HOURS +
24 HOURS

○

FOR THE CANDIED
GRAPEFRUIT
2 unwaxed grapefruits
10 crushed Sawarak black
peppercorns
4¼ cups (1 L) still mineral water
2½ cups (500 g) superfine
granulated sugar
¼ cup (62 g) freshly squeezed
lemon juice (from 1 lemon)
1 star anise
1 vanilla bean, halved lengthwise

PREPARE THE CANDIED GRAPEFRUIT. Two days in advance, wash and dry the grapefruit. Cut off both rounded ends to create a flat top and bottom. Set the grapefruit on a flat end and, using a knife, slice down the grapefruit all the way around from top to bottom to remove the rind in large strips. Leave about $^3/_8$ inch (1 cm) of the pulp attached to each strip.

Place the strips of rind in a saucepan of boiling water. When the water reaches a boil again, cook the strips for 2 minutes then drain. Rinse them under cold water. Repeat these steps twice, boiling and draining the strips, then set the strips aside to dry.

Place the peppercorns in a saucepan along with the mineral water, sugar, lemon juice, and star anise. Scrape the seeds out of the vanilla bean using a knife. Add the seeds and the vanilla bean pod to the pan. Bring to a boil over low heat. Add the strips of grapefruit rind. Cover three-quarters of the top of the saucepan. Simmer very gently for 1 hour 30 minutes.

Transfer to a bowl and let cool. Cover and refrigerate until the next day.

The day before, drain the strips for 1 hour in a sieve set over a bowl. Cut them into $^1/_8$-inch (3-mm) cubes.

→ PREPARE THE YASAMINE MACARON SHELLS. Mix together the crispy flakes and silver dust and set aside. Sift together the confectioners' sugar and almonds.

Dilute the titanium dioxide powder in the warm water then stir it into half of the "liquefied" egg whites. Pour this into the confectioners' sugar–almond mixture without mixing.

Add the remaining "liquefied" egg whites to the bowl of a stand mixer fitted with the wire whisk. In a saucepan, boil the mineral water and granulated sugar to 244°F (118°C). As soon as the syrup reaches 239°F (115°C), begin beating the egg whites on high speed.

When the syrup reaches 244°F (118°C), reduce the mixer speed to medium-high and pour the syrup in a steady stream down the inside edge of the bowl into the beaten egg whites. Beat the meringue until it cools to 122°F (50°C). Fold it with a silicone spatula into the confectioners' sugar–almond mixture until the mixture loses volume. Transfer the batter to a pastry bag fitted with a plain #11, ½-inch (11-mm to 12-mm) pastry tip.

Line baking sheets with parchment paper. Pipe disks about 1½ inches (3.5 cm) in diameter and ¾ inch (2 cm) apart on the lined baking sheets. Rap the baking sheets on a work surface covered with a clean kitchen towel to gently smooth out the disks. Sprinkle them with the mixture of crispy flakes and silver dust. Set aside for at least 30 minutes at room temperature to allow a skin to form.

Preheat a convection oven to 350°F (180°C). Place the baking sheets in the oven. Bake for 12 minutes, quickly opening and closing the oven door twice during baking to release moisture. Remove the shells from the oven and slide them still on the parchment paper onto a work surface.

PREPARE THE JASMINE AND GRAPEFRUIT CREAM. Chop the white chocolate using a serrated knife then melt it to between 113°F (45°C) and 122°F (50°C) set over a bain-marie or in a microwave.

In a saucepan, heat the cream to 167°F (75°C). Add the tea and let it infuse for 3 minutes, but no longer.

Strain the cream then pour it in thirds into the melted white chocolate, stirring after each addition starting in the center then in increasingly wider concentric circles toward the sides of the bowl. Using an immersion blender, blend the cream until smooth. Finely chop the candied grapefruit. Add it to the cream and stir to combine.

Pour the jasmine and grapefruit cream into a baking dish. Cover it by gently pressing plastic wrap onto its surface. Refrigerate for 2 hours, just until the cream has developed a creamy consistency.

**FOR THE YASAMINE
MACARON SHELLS**
Valrhona Éclats d'Or crispy flakes
or crumbled plain Gavottes crêpe
cookies
Edible silver dust, preferably from
Merck, for sprinkling
3 cups (300 g) confectioners' sugar
2 cups plus 2 tablespoons (300 g)
ground almonds
2⅔ teaspoons (16 g) titanium
dioxide powder
1¾ teaspoons (8 g) warm water
7 large (220 g) "liquefied" egg
whites, divided (see "Macaron
Shells Step-by-Step" in the Kitchen
Guide)
¼ cup plus 1 tablespoon (75 g) still
mineral water
1½ cups (300 g) superfine
granulated sugar

**FOR THE JASMINE AND
GRAPEFRUIT CREAM**
8¾ ounces (250 g) Valrhona Ivoire
35% white chocolate
**1 cup plus 3 tablespoons
(275 g)** light whipping cream
(32%–35% fat)
¾ ounce (20 g) Chinese jasmine
jade pearls green tea, preferably
Cannon
2⅛ ounces (60 g) Candied
Grapefruit (see page 151)

FOR THE MANGO COMPOTE
**1 tablespoon plus 1¾ teaspoons
(20 g)** superfine granulated sugar
1 teaspoon (5 g) agar-agar
1¾ cups (390 g) mango puree
3 tablespoons (40 g) freshly
squeezed lemon juice (from
1 lemon)

PREPARE THE MANGO COMPOTE. Combine the sugar with the agar-agar. Add the mango puree and lemon juice then bring to a boil, stirring frequently. Let boil for 1 minute. Remove from the heat to cool.

Transfer the jasmine and grapefruit cream and the mango compote to separate pastry bags fitted with plain #11, ½-inch (11-mm to 12-mm) pastry tips.

Turn half of the shells over with the flat sides up onto a new piece of parchment paper. Fill them with the jasmine and grapefruit cream then pipe a small dollop of mango compote in the center. Pipe a small dab of the cream on top of the mango compote. Close them with the rest of the shells, pressing down lightly.

Refrigerate the macarons for 24 hours. Remove them from the refrigerator 2 hours before eating them.

Macaron Réglisse Violette

I work very little with licorice because its flavor is difficult to manage. All the same, I have fond memories of Zan licorice tablets flavored with violet that were sold in my family bakery. This combination gave me the idea to combine licorice with violet in a macaron.

MAKES ABOUT 72 MACARONS
(OR ABOUT 144 SHELLS)

PREPARATION TIME: **5 MINUTES (5 DAYS
IN ADVANCE, SEE "MACARON SHELLS
STEP-BY-STEP" IN THE KITCHEN GUIDE)
+ 1 HOUR 30 MINUTES**

COOKING TIME: **ABOUT 30 MINUTES**

RESTING TIME: **30 MINUTES (TWICE)**

REFRIGERATION TIME: **2 HOURS +
24 HOURS**

FOR THE BLACK MACARON SHELLS
1½ cups (150 g) confectioners' sugar
1 cup plus 1 tablespoon (150 g) ground almonds
Generous 2 teaspoons (10 g) liquid charcoal black food color
3½ large (110 g) "liquefied" egg whites, divided (see "Macaron Shells Step-by-Step" in the Kitchen Guide)
3 tablespoons (43 g) still mineral water
¾ cup (150 g) superfine granulated sugar

PREPARE THE BLACK MACARON SHELLS. The day before, sift together the confectioners' sugar and almonds.

Combine the food color with half of the "liquefied" egg whites. Pour this into the confectioners' sugar–almond mixture without mixing.

Add the remaining "liquefied" egg whites to the bowl of a stand mixer fitted with the wire whisk. In a saucepan, boil the mineral water and granulated sugar to 244°F (118°C). As soon as the syrup reaches 239°F (115°C), begin beating the egg whites on high speed.

When the syrup reaches 244°F (118°C), reduce the mixer speed to medium-high and pour the syrup in a steady stream down the inside edge of the bowl into the beaten egg whites. Beat the meringue until it cools to 122°F (50°C). Fold it with a silicone spatula into the confectioners' sugar–almond mixture until the mixture loses volume. Transfer the batter to a pastry bag fitted with a plain #11, ½-inch (11-mm to 12-mm) pastry tip.

Line baking sheets with parchment paper. Pipe disks about 1½ inches (3.5 cm) in diameter and ¾ inch (2 cm) apart on the lined baking sheets. Rap the baking sheets on a work surface covered with a clean kitchen towel to gently smooth out the disks. Set aside for at least 30 minutes at room temperature to allow a skin to form.

PREPARE THE CASSIS MACARON SHELLS. Sift together the confectioners' sugar and almonds.

Combine the food color with half of the "liquefied" egg whites. Pour this into the confectioners' sugar–almond mixture without mixing.

Add the remaining "liquefied" egg whites to the bowl of a stand mixer fitted with the wire whisk. In a saucepan, boil the mineral water and granulated sugar to 244°F (118°C). As soon as the syrup reaches 239°F (115°C), begin beating the egg whites on high speed.

When the syrup reaches 244°F (118°C), reduce the mixer speed to medium-high and pour the syrup in a steady stream down the inside edge of the bowl into the beaten egg whites. Beat the meringue until it cools to 122°F (50°C). Fold it with a silicone spatula into the confectioners' sugar–almond mixture until the mixture loses volume. Transfer the batter to a pastry bag fitted with a plain #11, ¹/₂-inch (11-mm to 12-mm) pastry tip.

Line baking sheets with parchment paper. Pipe disks about 1¹/₂ inches (3.5 cm) in diameter and ³/₄ inch (2 cm) apart on the lined baking sheets. Rap the baking sheets on a work surface covered with a clean kitchen towel to gently smooth out the disks. Set aside for at least 30 minutes at room temperature to allow a skin to form.

Preheat a convection oven to 350°F (180°C). Place the baking sheets in the oven. Bake for 12 minutes, quickly opening and closing the oven door twice during baking to release moisture. Remove the shells from the oven and slide them still on the parchment paper onto a work surface.

PREPARE THE VIOLET LICORICE CREAM. Chop the white chocolate using a serrated knife then melt it to between 113°F (45°C) and 122°F (50°C) set over a bain-marie or in a microwave.

In a saucepan, bring the cream to a boil. Pour the hot cream in thirds into the melted white chocolate, stirring after each addition starting in the center then in increasingly wider concentric circles toward the sides of the bowl. Stir in the violet essence and licorice. Using an immersion blender, blend the cream until smooth.

Pour the violet licorice cream into a baking dish. Cover it by gently pressing plastic wrap onto its surface. Refrigerate for 2 hours, just until the cream has developed a creamy consistency. Transfer the violet licorice cream to a pastry bag fitted with a plain #11, ¹/₂-inch (11-mm to 12-mm) pastry tip.

Turn the black macaron shells over with the flat sides up onto a new piece of parchment paper. Fill them with the violet licorice cream. Close them with the cassis macaron shells, pressing down lightly.

Refrigerate the macarons for 24 hours. Remove them from the refrigerator 2 hours before eating them.

FOR THE CASSIS MACARON SHELLS

1½ cups (150 g) confectioners' sugar
1 cup plus 1 tablespoon (150 g) ground almonds
½ teaspoon (2 g) liquid dark violet food color
3½ large (110 g) "liquefied" egg whites, divided (see "Macaron Shells Step-by-Step" in the Kitchen Guide)
2 tablespoons plus 1¾⅛ teaspoons (38 g) still mineral water
¾ cup (150 g) superfine granulated sugar

FOR THE VIOLET LICORICE CREAM

1¼ pounds (525 g) Valrhona Ivoire 35% white chocolate
2 cups minus 1 tablespoon (450 g) light whipping cream (32%–35% fat)
10 drops / generous ⅛ teaspoon (0.6 g) violet essence flavoring
Scant 1 tablespoon (5 g) ground licorice root

Macaron au Citron Caviar

Finger limes are small, rare, and unusual citrus fruit that are sought after by top chefs for their incredible texture and small translucent pearls that explode in the mouth and release a bright, lemony aroma. I filled the center of these yuzu and lemon macarons with gelée made from these surprising tiny pearls.

MAKES ABOUT 72 MACARONS
(OR ABOUT 144 SHELLS)

PREPARATION TIME: **5 MINUTES (5 DAYS IN ADVANCE, SEE "MACARON SHELLS STEP-BY-STEP" IN THE KITCHEN GUIDE) + 1 HOUR 30 MINUTES**

COOKING TIME: **ABOUT 25 MINUTES**

RESTING TIME: **30 MINUTES**

REFRIGERATION TIME: **4 HOURS + 24 HOURS (TWICE)**

○

FOR THE CITRUS MACARON SHELLS
3 cups (300 g) confectioners' sugar
2 cups plus 2 tablespoons (300 g) ground almonds
1½ teaspoons (6 g) liquid lemon yellow food color
7 large (220 g) "liquefied" egg whites, divided (see "Macaron Shells Step-by-Step" in the Kitchen Guide)
¼ cup plus 1 tablespoon (75 g) still mineral water
1½ cups (300 g) superfine granulated sugar

PREPARE THE CITRUS MACARON SHELLS. The day before, sift together the confectioners' sugar and almonds.

Combine the food color with half of the "liquefied" egg whites. Pour this into the confectioners' sugar–almond mixture without mixing.

Add the remaining "liquefied" egg whites to the bowl of a stand mixer fitted with the wire whisk. In a saucepan, boil the mineral water and granulated sugar to 244°F (118°C). As soon as the syrup reaches 239°F (115°C), begin beating the egg whites on high speed.

When the syrup reaches 244°F (118°C), reduce the mixer speed to medium-high and pour the syrup in a steady stream down the inside edge of the bowl into the beaten egg whites. Beat the meringue until it cools to 122°F (50°C). Fold it with a silicone spatula into the confectioners' sugar–almond mixture until the mixture loses volume. Transfer the batter to a pastry bag fitted with a plain #11, ½-inch (11-mm to 12-mm) pastry tip.

Line baking sheets with parchment paper. Pipe disks about 1½ inches (3.5 cm) in diameter and ¾ inch (2 cm) apart on the lined baking sheets. Rap the baking sheets on a work surface covered with a clean kitchen towel to gently smooth out the disks. Set aside for at least 30 minutes at room temperature to allow a skin to form.

Preheat a convection oven to 350°F (180°C). Place the baking sheets in the oven. Bake for 12 minutes, quickly opening and closing the oven door twice during baking to release moisture. Remove the shells from the oven and slide them still on the parchment paper onto a work surface.

→

PREPARE THE CITRUS CAVIAR *GELÉE*. Cut the finger limes in half lengthwise. Remove the pearls and set them aside. In a saucepan, combine the sugar with the agar-agar. Add the mineral water and bring to a boil while whisking. Remove from the heat and let cool for 5 minutes. Add the finger lime pearls and stir to combine. Add the mixture to an airtight container and refrigerate for 12 hours.

Just before using, pour the citrus caviar *gelée* into a large bowl and stir until smooth. Transfer the *gelée* and the yuzu and lemon cream to separate pastry bags fitted with plain #11, ½-inch (11-mm to 12-mm) pastry tips.

Turn half of the shells over with the flat sides up onto a new piece of parchment paper. Fill them with the yuzu and lemon cream then pipe a dollop of the *gelée* in the center. Pipe a dab of the cream on top of the *gelée*. Close them with the rest of the shells, pressing down lightly.

Refrigerate the macarons for 24 hours. Remove them from the refrigerator 2 hours before eating them.

PREPARE THE YUZU AND LEMON CREAM. Chop the white chocolate using a serrated knife then melt it to between 113°F (45°C) and 122°F (50°C) set over a bain-marie or in a microwave.

In a saucepan, heat the yuzu juice to 122°F (50°C). In a separate saucepan, heat the cream with the lemon zest to 122°F (50°C). Pour the hot cream then the warm yuzu juice in thirds into the melted white chocolate, stirring after each addition starting in the center then in increasingly wider concentric circles toward the sides of the bowl. Using an immersion blender, blend the cream until smooth.

Pour the yuzu and lemon cream into a baking dish. Cover it by gently pressing plastic wrap onto its surface. Refrigerate for 4 hours, just until the cream has developed a creamy consistency.

FOR THE YUZU AND LEMON CREAM
1⅛ pounds (500 g) Valrhona Ivoire 35% white chocolate
1 cup minus 2 teaspoons (200 g) pure unsweetened yuzu juice, preferably from Issé Workshop
¾ cup plus 2 tablespoons (200 g) light whipping cream (32%–35% fat)
3 teaspoons (6 g) freshly grated lemon zest (from 1 lemon)

FOR THE CITRUS CAVIAR
GELÉE
10½ ounces (300 g) finger limes (citrus caviar) to obtain 3½ ounces (100 g) pulp
2½ teaspoons (10 g) superfine granulated sugar
1 teaspoon (2 g) agar-agar
½ cup plus 2 teaspoons (125 g) still mineral water

THE "VELOUTÉS" COLLECTION

Macaron Velouté Ispahan

Ispahan is the most iconic flavor combination of Pierre Hermé Paris. The Macaron Velouté Ispahan is a journey of the senses derived from the harmonious creaminess of an explosive trio of fruity and floral flavors: the first is sweet and floral like a bouquet of roses, the second is from lychees with their luscious sweetness, and the last from tart raspberry.

MAKES ABOUT 72 MACARONS
(OR ABOUT 144 SHELLS)

PREPARATION TIME: **5 MINUTES (5 DAYS IN ADVANCE, SEE "MACARON SHELLS STEP-BY-STEP" IN THE KITCHEN GUIDE) + 1 HOUR 50 MINUTES**

COOKING TIME: **2 HOURS + 30 MINUTES**

RESTING TIME: **30 MINUTES (TWICE)**

REFRIGERATION TIME: **4 HOURS + 24 HOURS**

FOR THE DRIED FRUIT
14 ounces (400 g) canned lychee in syrup, or 7 ounces (200 g) drained or fresh lychee
Generous ½ pint (200 g) fresh raspberries, or about ¼ cup plus 1 tablespoon (40 g) dried

FOR THE WHITE MACARON SHELLS
1½ cups (150 g) confectioners' sugar
1 cup plus 1 tablespoon (150 g) ground almonds
1⅓ teaspoons (8 g) titanium dioxide powder
1 teaspoon (4 g) warm water
3½ large (110 g) "liquefied" egg whites, divided (see "Macaron Shells Step-by-Step" in the Kitchen Guide)
2 tablespoons plus 1¾ teaspoons (38 g) still mineral water
¾ cup (150 g) superfine granulated sugar

PREPARE THE DRIED FRUIT. The day before, preheat the oven to 195°F (90°C). Chop the lychees into small pieces and place them on paper towels. If using fresh raspberries, spread them onto a baking sheet lined with parchment paper. Spread the lychees onto a second baking sheet lined with parchment paper. Place the baking sheets in the oven. Leave them to dry for 2 hours, stirring the fruit every 30 minutes. Let cool.

PREPARE THE WHITE MACARON SHELLS. Sift together the confectioners' sugar and almonds.

Dilute the titanium dioxide powder in the warm water then stir it into half of the "liquefied" egg whites. Pour this into the confectioners' sugar–almond mixture without mixing.

Add the remaining "liquefied" egg whites to the bowl of a stand mixer fitted with the wire whisk. In a saucepan, boil the mineral water and granulated sugar to 244°F (118°C). As soon as the syrup reaches 239°F (115°C), begin beating the egg whites on high speed.

When the syrup reaches 244°F (118°C), reduce the mixer speed to medium–high and pour the syrup in a steady stream down the inside edge of the bowl into the beaten egg whites. Beat the meringue until it cools to 122°F (50°C). Fold it with a silicone spatula into the confectioners' sugar–almond mixture until the mixture loses volume. Transfer the batter to a pastry bag fitted with a plain #11, ½-inch (11-mm to 12-mm) pastry tip.

Line baking sheets with parchment paper. Pipe disks about 1½ inches (3.5 cm) in diameter and ¾ inch (2 cm) apart on the lined baking sheets. Rap the baking sheets on a work surface covered with a clean kitchen towel to gently smooth out the disks. Set aside for at least 30 minutes at room temperature to allow a skin to form.

PREPARE THE ROSE MACARON SHELLS. Sift together the confectioners' sugar and almonds.

Combine the food color with half of the "liquefied" egg whites. Pour this into the confectioners' sugar–almond mixture without mixing.

Add the remaining "liquefied" egg whites to the bowl of a stand mixer fitted with the wire whisk. In a saucepan, boil the mineral water and granulated sugar to 244°F (118°C). As soon as the syrup reaches 239°F (115°C), begin beating the egg whites on high speed.

When the syrup reaches 244°F (118°C), reduce the mixer speed to medium–high and pour the syrup in a steady stream down the inside edge of the bowl into the beaten egg whites. Beat the meringue until it cools to 122°F (50°C). Fold it with a silicone spatula into the confectioners' sugar–almond mixture until the mixture loses volume. Transfer the batter to a pastry bag fitted with a plain #11, ¹⁄₂–inch (11-mm to 12-mm) pastry tip.

Line baking sheets with parchment paper. Pipe disks about 1¹⁄₂ inches (3.5 cm) in diameter and ³⁄₄ inch (2 cm) apart on the lined baking sheets. Rap the baking sheets on a work surface covered with a clean kitchen towel to gently smooth out the disks. Using a tea infuser, lightly dust half of each disk with the ruby red dust. Set aside for at least 30 minutes at room temperature to allow a skin to form.

Preheat a convection oven to 350°F (180°C). Place the baking sheets in the oven. Bake for 12 minutes, quickly opening and closing the oven door twice during baking to release moisture. Remove the shells from the oven and slide them still on the parchment paper onto a work surface.

PREPARE THE ROSE GANACHE. Chop the white chocolate using a serrated knife then melt it to between 113°F (45°C) and 122°F (50°C) set over a bain-marie or in a microwave.

In a saucepan, combine the yogurt, yogurt powder, and powdered milk. Heat to 140°F (60°C) while stirring. Pour the hot mixture in thirds into the melted white chocolate, stirring after each addition starting in the center then in increasingly wider concentric circles toward the sides of the bowl. Add the rose extract. Using an immersion blender, blend the ganache until smooth.

Pour the ganache into a baking dish. Cover it by gently pressing plastic wrap onto its surface. Refrigerate for 4 hours, just until the ganache has developed a creamy consistency. Transfer the ganache to a pastry bag fitted with a plain #11, ¹⁄₂–inch (11-mm to 12-mm) pastry tip.

Turn the white macaron shells over with the flat sides up onto a new piece of parchment paper. Fill them with the ganache. Place a piece of dried raspberry and lychee in the center, pressing them gently into the ganache. Pipe a small dab of ganache on top of the fruit. Close them with the rose macaron shells, pressing down lightly.

Refrigerate the macarons for 24 hours. Remove them from the refrigerator 2 hours before eating them.

FOR THE ROSE MACARON SHELLS
1½ cups (150 g) confectioners' sugar
1 cup plus 1 tablespoon (150 g) ground almonds
Scant ½ teaspoon (1.5 g) liquid carmine red food color
3½ large (110 g) "liquefied" egg whites, divided (see "Macaron Shells Step-by-Step" in the Kitchen Guide)
2 tablespoons plus 1¾ teaspoons (38 g) still mineral water
¾ cup (150 g) superfine granulated sugar
Edible ruby red dust, for sprinkling

FOR THE ROSE GANACHE
14 ounces (400 g) Valrhona Ivoire 35% white chocolate
1½ cups (350 g) plain stirred yogurt
3⅔ ounces (105 g) Sosa powdered Mediterranean acid yogurt
3 tablespoons (25 g) powdered milk
Generous 1 teaspoon (5 g) rose extract

Macaron Velouté Banane

I love the milky, creamy consistency that one experiences with various types of yogurt, except those with zero percent fat. I wanted to reveal this same texture in a macaron by designing a silky yogurt cream with the perfect balance of acidity and creaminess and by incorporating semi-dried banana in the center.

PREPARE THE SEMI-DRIED BANANAS. The day before, preheat the oven to 176°F (80°C). Peel the bananas then cut them lengthwise in half. Sprinkle them with the lemon juice. Place them on a baking sheet lined with parchment paper then place the baking sheet in the oven and leave them to partially dry, about 2 hours; the bananas are ready when they are mostly but not entirely dry. Set them aside to cool then cut them into small pieces measuring about $\frac{1}{8}$ inch (3 to 4 mm). Set aside to cool to room temperature.

PREPARE THE WHITE MACARON SHELLS. Sift the confectioners' sugar and almonds together in a bowl.

Dilute the titanium dioxide powder in the warm water then stir it into half of the "liquefied" egg whites. Pour this into the confectioners' sugar–almond mixture without mixing.

Add the remaining "liquefied" egg whites to the bowl of a stand mixer fitted with the wire whisk. In a saucepan, boil the mineral water and granulated sugar to 244°F (118°C). As soon as the syrup reaches 239°F (115°C), begin beating the egg whites on high speed.

When the syrup reaches 244°F (118°C), reduce the mixer speed to medium-high and pour the syrup in a steady stream down the inside edge of the bowl into the beaten egg whites. Beat the meringue until it cools to 122°F (50°C). Fold it with a silicone spatula into the confectioners' sugar–almond mixture until the mixture loses volume. Transfer the batter to a pastry bag fitted with a plain #11, $\frac{1}{2}$-inch (11-mm to 12-mm) pastry tip.

Line baking sheets with parchment paper. Pipe disks about 1$\frac{1}{2}$ inches (3.5 cm) in diameter and $\frac{3}{4}$ inch (2 cm) apart on the lined baking sheets. Rap the baking sheets on a work surface covered with a clean kitchen towel to gently smooth out the disks. Set aside for at least 30 minutes at room temperature to allow a skin to form.

PREPARE THE BANANA MACARON SHELLS. Sift the confectioners' sugar and almonds together in a bowl.

Combine the yellow and red food colors with half of the "liquefied" egg whites. Pour this into the confectioners' sugar–almond mixture without mixing.

Add the remaining "liquefied" egg whites to the bowl of a stand mixer fitted with the wire whisk. In a saucepan, boil the mineral water and granulated sugar to 244°F (118°C). As soon as the syrup reaches 239°F (115°C), begin beating the egg whites on high speed.

When the syrup reaches 244°F (118°C), reduce the mixer speed to medium–high and pour the syrup in a steady stream down the inside edge of the bowl into the beaten egg whites. Beat the meringue until it cools to 122°F (50°C). Fold it with a silicone spatula into the confectioners' sugar–almond mixture until the mixture loses volume. Transfer the batter to a pastry bag fitted with a plain #11, ½-inch (11-mm to 12-mm) pastry tip.

Line baking sheets with parchment paper. Pipe disks about 1½ inches (3.5 cm) in diameter and ¾ inch (2 cm) apart on the lined baking sheets. Rap the baking sheets on a work surface covered with a clean kitchen towel to gently smooth out the disks. Lightly dust the disks with the cocoa. Set aside for at least 30 minutes at room temperature to allow a skin to form.

Preheat a convection oven to 350°F (180°C). Place the baking sheets in the oven. Bake for 12 minutes, quickly opening and closing the oven door twice during baking to release moisture. Remove the shells from the oven and slide them still on the parchment paper onto a work surface.

PREPARE THE YOGURT GANACHE. Chop the white chocolate using a serrated knife then melt it to between 113°F (45°C) and 122°F (50°C) set over a bain-marie or in a microwave.

In a saucepan, combine the yogurt, yogurt powder, and powdered milk. Heat to 140°F (60°C) while stirring. Pour the hot mixture in thirds into the melted white chocolate, stirring after each addition starting in the center then in increasingly wider concentric circles toward the sides of the bowl. Using an immersion blender, blend the ganache until smooth.

Pour the ganache into a baking dish. Cover it by gently pressing plastic wrap onto its surface. Refrigerate for 4 hours, just until the ganache has developed a creamy consistency. Transfer the ganache to a pastry bag fitted with a plain #11, ½-inch (11-mm to 12-mm) pastry tip.

Turn the white macaron shells over with the flat sides up onto a new piece of parchment paper. Fill them with the yogurt ganache then place three or four pieces of semi-dried banana in the center of the ganache. Pipe a dab of the ganache onto the banana pieces. Close them with the banana macaron shells, pressing down lightly.

Refrigerate the macarons for 24 hours. Remove them from the refrigerator 2 hours before eating them.

MAKES ABOUT 72 MACARONS (OR ABOUT 144 SHELLS)

PREPARATION TIME: 5 MINUTES (5 DAYS IN ADVANCE, SEE "MACARON SHELLS STEP-BY-STEP" IN THE KITCHEN GUIDE) + 1 HOUR 50 MINUTES

COOKING TIME: ABOUT 2 HOURS + 20 MINUTES

RESTING TIME: 30 MINUTES (TWICE)

REFRIGERATION TIME: 4 HOURS + 24 HOURS

FOR THE SEMI-DRIED BANANAS
4 ripe bananas
Generous 1 tablespoon (20 g) freshly squeezed lemon juice (from ½ lemon)

FOR THE WHITE MACARON SHELLS
1½ cups (150 g) confectioners' sugar
1 cup plus 1 tablespoon (150 g) ground almonds
1⅓ teaspoons (8 g) titanium dioxide powder
1 teaspoon (4 g) warm water
3½ large (110 g) "liquefied" egg whites, divided (see "Macaron Shells Step-by-Step" in the Kitchen Guide)
3 tablespoons (43 g) still mineral water
¾ cup (150 g) superfine granulated sugar

FOR THE BANANA MACARON SHELLS
1½ cups (150 g) confectioners' sugar
1 cup plus 1 tablespoon (150 g) ground almonds
Generous 1 teaspoon (5 g) liquid lemon yellow food color
Scant ½ teaspoon (1.5 g) liquid carmine red food color
3½ large (110 g) "liquefied" egg whites, divided (see "Macaron Shells Step-by-Step" in the Kitchen Guide)
2 tablespoons plus 1¾ teaspoons (38 g) still mineral water
¾ cup (150 g) superfine granulated sugar
½ cup plus 1½ tablespoons (50 g) unsweetened cocoa, preferably Valrhona

FOR THE YOGURT GANACHE
14 ounces (400 g) Valrhona Ivoire 35% white chocolate
1½ cups (350 g) plain stirred yogurt
3⅔ ounces (105 g) Sosa powdered Mediterranean acid yogurt
3 tablespoons (25 g) powdered milk

Macaron Velouté Pamplemousse

*I paired this yogurt filling, perfumed
with grapefruit zest, with the subtle
bitterness of grapefruit puree made
with a star anise syrup, vanilla,
and Sarawak black pepper.*

TWO DAYS IN ADVANCE, PREPARE THE CANDIED GRAPEFRUIT PUREE. Wash and dry the grapefruit. Cut off both rounded ends to create a flat top and bottom. Set the grapefruit on a flat end and, using a knife, slice down the grapefruit all the way around from top to bottom to remove the rind in large strips. Leave about ³⁄₈ inch (1 cm) of the pulp attached to each strip.

Place the strips of rind in a saucepan of boiling water. When the water reaches a boil again, boil the strips for 2 minutes then drain. Rinse them under cold water. Repeat these steps twice, boiling and draining the strips, then set the strips aside to dry.

Place the peppercorns in a saucepan along with the mineral water, sugar, lemon juice, and star anise. Scrape the seeds out of the vanilla bean using a knife. Add the seeds and the vanilla bean pod to the pan. Bring to a boil over low heat. Add the strips of grapefruit rind. Cover three-quarters of the top of the saucepan. Simmer very gently for 1 hour 30 minutes.

Transfer to a bowl and let cool. Cover and refrigerate until the next day.

The day before, drain the strips for 1 hour in a sieve set over a bowl. Using an immersion blender, blend them to a fine puree. Refrigerate until needed.

PREPARE THE WHITE MACARON SHELLS. Sift together the confectioners' sugar and almonds.

Dilute the titanium dioxide powder in the warm water then stir it into half of the "liquefied" egg whites. Pour this into the confectioners' sugar–almond mixture without mixing.

Add the remaining "liquefied" egg whites to the bowl of a stand mixer fitted with the wire whisk. In a saucepan, boil the mineral water and granulated sugar to 244°F (118°C). As soon as the syrup reaches 239°F (115°C), begin beating the egg whites on high speed.

When the syrup reaches 244°F (118°C), reduce the mixer speed to medium-high and pour the syrup in a steady stream down the inside edge of the bowl into the beaten egg whites. Beat the meringue until it cools to 122°F (50°C). Fold it with a silicone spatula into the confectioners' sugar–almond mixture until the mixture loses volume. Transfer the batter to a pastry bag fitted with a plain #11, ¹⁄₂-inch (11-mm to 12-mm) pastry tip.

Line baking sheets with parchment paper. Pipe disks about 1¹⁄₂ inches (3.5 cm) in diameter and ³⁄₄ inch (2 cm) apart on the lined baking sheets. Rap the baking sheets on a work surface covered with a clean kitchen towel to gently smooth out the disks. Set aside for at least 30 minutes at room temperature to allow a skin to form.

MAKES ABOUT 72 MACARONS (OR ABOUT 144 SHELLS)

PREPARATION TIME: **5 MINUTES (5 DAYS IN ADVANCE, SEE "MACARON SHELLS STEP-BY-STEP" IN THE KITCHEN GUIDE) + 20 MINUTES (2 DAYS IN ADVANCE) + 1 HOUR 30 MINUTES**

COOKING TIME: **1 HOUR 40 MINUTES (2 DAYS IN ADVANCE) + ABOUT 20 MINUTES**

MACERATION TIME: **24 HOURS**

RESTING TIME: **30 MINUTES (TWICE)**

REFRIGERATION TIME: **4 HOURS + 24 HOURS**

FOR THE CANDIED GRAPEFRUIT PUREE
2 unwaxed grapefruits
10 crushed Sarawak black peppercorns
4¼ cups (1 L) still mineral water
2½ cups (500 g) superfine granulated sugar
¼ cup (62 g) freshly squeezed lemon juice (from 1 lemon)
1 star anise
1 vanilla bean, halved lengthwise

FOR THE WHITE MACARON SHELLS
1½ cups (150 g) confectioners' sugar
1 cup plus 1 tablespoon (150 g) ground almonds
1⅓ teaspoons (8 g) titanium dioxide powder
1 teaspoon (4 g) warm water
3½ large (110 g) "liquefied" egg whites, divided (see "Macaron Shells Step-by-Step" in the Kitchen Guide)
3 tablespoons (43 g) still mineral water
¾ cup (150 g) superfine granulated sugar

FOR THE GRAPEFRUIT MACARON SHELLS
1½ cups (150 g) confectioners' sugar
1 cup plus 1 tablespoon (150 g) ground almonds
Scant ¾ teaspoon (2.5 g) liquid lemon yellow food color
Scant ½ teaspoon (1.5 g) liquid strawberry red food color
Scant ½ teaspoon (1.5 g) liquid carmine red food color
3½ large (110 g) "liquefied" egg whites, divided (see "Macaron Shells Step-by-Step" in the Kitchen Guide)
2 tablespoons plus 1¾ teaspoons (38 g) still mineral water
¾ cup (150 g) superfine granulated sugar

FOR THE YOGURT GANACHE
14 ounces (400 g) Valrhona Ivoire 35% white chocolate
1 tablespoon plus 2 teaspoons (10 g) freshly grated pink grapefruit zest (from 1 grapefruit)
1½ cups (350 g) plain stirred yogurt
3⅔ ounces (105 g) Sosa powdered Mediterranean acid yogurt
3 tablespoons (25 g) powdered milk

PREPARE THE GRAPEFRUIT MACARON SHELLS. Sift together the confectioners' sugar and almonds.

Combine the yellow and both red food colors with half of the "liquefied" egg whites. Pour this into the confectioners' sugar–almond mixture without mixing.

Add the remaining "liquefied" egg whites to the bowl of a stand mixer fitted with the wire whisk. In a saucepan, boil the mineral water and granulated sugar to 244°F (118°C). As soon as the syrup reaches 239°F (115°C), begin beating the egg whites on high speed.

When the syrup reaches 244°F (118°C), reduce the mixer speed to medium-high and pour the syrup in a steady stream down the inside edge of the bowl into the beaten egg whites. Beat the meringue until it cools to 122°F (50°C). Fold it with a silicone spatula into the confectioners' sugar–almond mixture until the mixture loses volume. Transfer the batter to a pastry bag fitted with a plain #11, ½-inch (11-mm to 12-mm) pastry tip.

Line baking sheets with parchment paper. Pipe disks about 1½ inches (3.5 cm) in diameter and ¾ inch (2 cm) apart on the lined baking sheets. Rap the baking sheets on a work surface covered with a clean kitchen towel to gently smooth out the disks. Set aside for at least 30 minutes at room temperature to allow a skin to form.

Preheat a convection oven to 350°F (180°C). Place the baking sheets in the oven. Bake for 12 minutes, quickly opening and closing the oven door twice during baking to release moisture. Remove the shells from the oven and slide them still on the parchment paper onto a work surface.

PREPARE THE YOGURT GANACHE. Chop the white chocolate using a serrated knife then melt it to between 113°F (45°C) and 122°F (50°C) set over a bain-marie or in a microwave.

Wash and dry the grapefruit. Using a microplane grater, zest the grapefruit and measure the quantity of zest needed. In a saucepan, combine it with the yogurt, powdered yogurt, and powdered milk. Heat to 140°F (60°C) while stirring. Pour the hot mixture in thirds into the melted white chocolate, stirring after each addition starting in the center then in increasingly wider concentric circles toward the sides of the bowl. Using an immersion blender, blend the ganache until smooth.

Pour the ganache into a baking dish. Cover it by gently pressing plastic wrap onto its surface. Refrigerate for 4 hours, just until the ganache has developed a creamy consistency.

Transfer the ganache and the grapefruit puree to separate pastry bags fitted with plain #11, ½-inch (11-mm to 12-mm) pastry tips.

Turn the white macaron shells over with the flat sides up onto a new piece of parchment paper. Fill them with the yogurt ganache then pipe a dollop of the grapefruit puree in the center. Pipe a dab of the ganache on top of the puree. Close them with the grapefruit macaron shells, pressing down lightly.

Refrigerate the macarons for 24 hours. Remove them from the refrigerator 2 hours before eating them.

Macaron Velouté Mandarine

The mandarin oranges I prefer come from Sicily. It is in the zest that these oranges best express their powerful, sun-ripened scent of citrus.

MAKES ABOUT 72 MACARONS
(OR ABOUT 144 SHELLS)

PREPARATION TIME: 5 MINUTES (5 DAYS IN ADVANCE, SEE "MACARON SHELLS STEP-BY-STEP" IN THE KITCHEN GUIDE) + 20 MINUTES (2 DAYS IN ADVANCE) + 1 HOUR 30 MINUTES

COOKING TIME: 2 HOURS 15 MINUTES (2 DAYS IN ADVANCE) + ABOUT 20 MINUTES

MACERATION TIME: 24 HOURS

DRAINING TIME: 1 HOUR

RESTING TIME: 30 MINUTES (TWICE)

REFRIGERATION TIME: 4 HOURS + 24 HOURS

FOR THE SEMI-CANDIED MANDARIN ORANGES
10 Sicilian mandarin oranges, preferably from La Tête dans les Olives
4¼ cups (1 L) still mineral water
2½ cups (500 g) superfine granulated sugar

FOR THE WHITE MACARON SHELLS
1½ cups (150 g) confectioners' sugar
1 cup plus 1 tablespoon (150 g) ground almonds
1⅓ teaspoons (8 g) titanium dioxide powder
1 teaspoon (4 g) warm water
3½ large (110 g) "liquefied" egg whites, divided (see "Macaron Shells Step-by-Step" in the Kitchen Guide)
3 tablespoons (43 g) still mineral water
¾ cup (150 g) superfine granulated sugar

PREPARE THE SEMI-CANDIED MANDARIN ORANGES. Two days in advance, wash and dry the oranges. Cut off both rounded ends. Cut the oranges in half from top to bottom. Immerse them three times in boiling water for 20 seconds then leave them to boil for 2 minutes. Rinse them under cold water. Repeat these same steps two times, then drain. In a saucepan, bring the mineral water and sugar to a boil. Place the orange halves in the boiling syrup. Cover and let simmer gently for 2 hours. Set aside to soak until the next day.

The day before, drain the oranges for 1 hour in a sieve set over a bowl then cut them into ¼-inch (5-mm) cubes. Refrigerate until needed.

PREPARE THE WHITE MACARON SHELLS. Sift together the confectioners' sugar and almonds.

Dilute the titanium dioxide powder in the warm water then stir it into half of the "liquefied" egg whites. Pour this into the confectioners' sugar–almond mixture without mixing.

Add the remaining "liquefied" egg whites to the bowl of a stand mixer fitted with the wire whisk. In a saucepan, boil the mineral water and granulated sugar to 244°F (118°C). As soon as the syrup reaches 239°F (115°C), begin beating the egg whites on high speed.

When the syrup reaches 244°F (118°C), reduce the mixer speed to medium-high and pour the syrup in a steady stream down the inside edge of the bowl into the beaten egg whites. Beat the meringue until it cools to 122°F (50°C). Fold it with a silicone spatula into the confectioners' sugar–almond mixture until the mixture loses volume. Transfer the batter to a pastry bag fitted with a plain #11, ½-inch (11-mm to 12-mm) pastry tip.

Line baking sheets with parchment paper. Pipe disks about 1½ inches (3.5 cm) in diameter and ¾ inch (2 cm) apart on the lined baking sheets. Rap the baking sheets on a work surface covered with a clean kitchen towel to gently smooth out the disks. Set aside for at least 30 minutes at room temperature to allow a skin to form.

PREPARE THE MANDARIN MACARON SHELLS. Sift together the confectioners' sugar and almonds.

Combine the yellow and red food colors with half of the "liquefied" egg whites. Pour this into the confectioners' sugar–almond mixture without mixing.

Add the remaining "liquefied" egg whites to the bowl of a stand mixer fitted with the wire whisk. In a saucepan, boil the mineral water and granulated sugar to 244°F (118°C). As soon as the syrup reaches 239°F (115°C), begin beating the egg whites on high speed.

When the syrup reaches 244°F (118°C), reduce the mixer speed to medium–high and pour the syrup in a steady stream down the inside edge of the bowl into the beaten egg whites. Beat the meringue until it cools to 122°F (50°C). Fold it with a silicone spatula into the confectioners' sugar–almond mixture until the mixture loses volume. Transfer the batter to a pastry bag fitted with a plain #11, ¹⁄₂-inch (11-mm to 12-mm) pastry tip.

Line baking sheets with parchment paper. Pipe disks about 1¹⁄₂ inches (3.5 cm) in diameter and ³⁄₄ inch (2 cm) apart on the lined baking sheets. Rap the baking sheets on a work surface covered with a clean kitchen towel to gently smooth out the disks. Set aside for at least 30 minutes at room temperature to allow a skin to form.

Preheat a convection oven to 350°F (180°C). Place the baking sheets in the oven. Bake for 12 minutes, quickly opening and closing the oven door twice during baking to release moisture. Remove the shells from the oven and slide them still on the parchment paper onto a work surface.

PREPARE THE YOGURT GANACHE. Chop the white chocolate using a serrated knife then melt it to between 113°F (45°C) and 122°F (50°C) set over a bain-marie or in a microwave.

Wash and dry the mandarin oranges. Using a microplane grater, zest them and measure the quantity of zest needed. In a saucepan, combine it with the yogurt, yogurt powder, and powdered milk. Heat to 140°F (60°C) while stirring. Pour the hot mixture in thirds into the melted white chocolate, stirring after each addition starting in the center then in increasingly wider concentric circles toward the sides of the bowl. Using an immersion blender, blend the ganache until smooth.

Pour the ganache into a baking dish. Cover it by gently pressing plastic wrap onto its surface. Refrigerate for 4 hours, just until the ganache has developed a creamy consistency. Transfer the ganache to a pastry bag fitted with a plain #11, ¹⁄₂-inch (11-mm to 12-mm) pastry tip.

Turn the white macaron shells over with the flat sides up onto a new piece of parchment paper. Fill them with the yogurt ganache then place three or four pieces of the semi-candied oranges in the center. Pipe a dab of the ganache on top of the orange pieces. Close them with the mandarin macaron shells, pressing down lightly.

Refrigerate the macarons for 24 hours. Remove them from the refrigerator 2 hours before eating them.

FOR THE MANDARIN MACARON SHELLS
1½ cups (150 g) confectioners' sugar
1 cup plus 1 tablespoon (150 g) ground almonds
Scant 1 teaspoon (3.5 g) liquid lemon yellow food color
¼ teaspoon (1 g) liquid strawberry red food color
3½ large (110 g) "liquefied" egg whites, divided (see "Macaron Shells Step-by-Step" in the Kitchen Guide)
2 tablespoons plus 1¾ teaspoons (38 g) still mineral water
¾ cup (150 g) superfine granulated sugar

FOR THE YOGURT GANACHE
14 ounces (400 g) Valrhona Ivoire 35% white chocolate
2 tablespoons (12 g) freshly grated mandarin orange zest (from 2 oranges), preferably from La Tête dans les Olives
1½ cups (350 g) plain stirred yogurt
3⅔ ounces (105 g) Sosa powdered Mediterranean acid yogurt
3 tablespoons (25 g) powdered milk

Macaron Velouté Citron Vert

My favorite limes come from Brazil. I especially like their sharp, almost abrasive, flavor and the different characteristics, the fruity and fragrant notes that are gradually revealed.

PREPARE THE WHITE MACARON SHELLS. The day before, sift together the confectioners' sugar and almonds.

Dilute the titanium dioxide powder in the warm water then stir it into half of the "liquefied" egg whites. Pour this into the confectioners' sugar–almond mixture without mixing.

Add the remaining "liquefied" egg whites to the bowl of a stand mixer fitted with the wire whisk. In a saucepan, boil the mineral water and granulated sugar to 244°F (118°C). As soon as the syrup reaches 239°F (115°C), begin beating the egg whites on high speed.

When the syrup reaches 244°F (118°C), reduce the mixer speed to medium–high and pour the syrup in a steady stream down the inside edge of the bowl into the beaten egg whites. Beat the meringue until it cools to 122°F (50°C). Fold it with a silicone spatula into the confectioners' sugar–almond mixture until the mixture loses volume. Transfer the batter to a pastry bag fitted with a plain #11, ½-inch (11-mm to 12-mm) pastry tip.

Line baking sheets with parchment paper. Pipe disks about 1½ inches (3.5 cm) in diameter and ¾ inch (2 cm) apart on the lined baking sheets. Rap the baking sheets on a work surface covered with a clean kitchen towel to gently smooth out the disks. Set aside for at least 30 minutes at room temperature to allow a skin to form.

PREPARE THE LIME MACARON SHELLS. Sift together the confectioners' sugar and almonds.

Combine the yellow and green food colors with half of the "liquefied" egg whites. Pour this into the confectioners' sugar–almond mixture without mixing.

Add the remaining "liquefied" egg whites to the bowl of a stand mixer fitted with the wire whisk. In a saucepan, boil the mineral water and granulated sugar to 244°F (118°C). As soon as the syrup reaches 239°F (115°C), begin beating the egg whites on high speed.

When the syrup reaches 244°F (118°C), reduce the mixer speed to medium-high and pour the syrup in a steady stream down the inside edge of the bowl into the beaten egg whites. Beat the meringue until it cools to 122°F (50°C). Fold it with a silicone spatula into the confectioners' sugar–almond mixture until the mixture loses volume. Transfer the batter to a pastry bag fitted with a plain #11, ½-inch (11-mm to 12-mm) pastry tip.

Line baking sheets with parchment paper. Pipe disks about 1½ inches (3.5 cm) in diameter and ¾ inch (2 cm) apart on the lined baking sheets. Rap the baking sheets on a work surface covered with a clean kitchen towel to gently smooth out the disks. Set aside for at least 30 minutes at room temperature to allow a skin to form.

Preheat a convection oven to 350°F (180°C). Place the baking sheets in the oven. Bake for 12 minutes, quickly opening and closing the oven door twice during baking to release moisture. Remove the shells from the oven and slide them still on the parchment paper onto a work surface.

PREPARE THE YOGURT GANACHE. Chop the white chocolate using a serrated knife then melt it to between 113°F (45°C) and 122°F (50°C) set over a bain-marie or in a microwave.

Wash and dry the limes. Using a microplane grater, zest them and measure the quantity of zest needed. In a saucepan, combine it with the yogurt, yogurt powder, and powdered milk. Heat to 140°F (60°C) while stirring. Pour the hot mixture in thirds into the melted white chocolate, stirring after each addition starting in the center then in increasingly wider concentric circles toward the sides of the bowl. Using an immersion blender, blend the ganache until smooth.

Pour the ganache into a baking dish. Cover it by gently pressing plastic wrap onto its surface. Refrigerate for 4 hours, just until the ganache has developed a creamy consistency. Transfer the ganache to a pastry bag fitted with a plain #11, ½-inch (11-mm to 12-mm) pastry tip.

Turn the white macaron shells over with the flat sides up onto a new piece of parchment paper. Fill them with the yogurt ganache. Close them with the lime macaron shells, pressing down lightly.

Refrigerate the macarons for 24 hours. Remove them from the refrigerator 2 hours before eating them.

MAKES ABOUT 72 MACARONS (OR ABOUT 144 MACARON SHELLS)
PREPARATION TIME: **5 MINUTES (5 DAYS IN ADVANCE, SEE "MACARON SHELLS STEP-BY-STEP" IN THE KITCHEN GUIDE) + 1 HOUR 30 MINUTES**
COOKING TIME: **ABOUT 20 MINUTES**
RESTING TIME: **30 MINUTES (TWICE)**
REFRIGERATION TIME: **4 HOURS + 24 HOURS**

FOR THE WHITE MACARON SHELLS

1½ cups (150 g) confectioners' sugar
1 cup plus 1 tablespoon (150 g) ground almonds
1⅓ teaspoons (8 g) titanium dioxide powder
1 teaspoon (4 g) warm water
3½ large (110 g) "liquefied" egg whites, divided (see "Macaron Shells Step-by-Step" in the Kitchen Guide)
3 tablespoons (43 g) still mineral water
¾ cup (150 g) superfine granulated sugar

FOR THE LIME MACARON SHELLS

1½ cups (150 g) confectioners' sugar
1 cup plus 1 tablespoon (150 g) ground almonds
¾ teaspoon (3 g) liquid lemon yellow food color
¼ teaspoon (1 g) liquid pistachio green food color
3½ large (110 g) "liquefied" egg whites, divided (see "Macaron Shells Step-by-Step" in the Kitchen Guide)
2 tablespoons plus 1¾ teaspoons (38 g) still mineral water
¾ cup (150 g) superfine granulated sugar

FOR THE YOGURT GANACHE

14 ounces (400 g) Valrhona Ivoire 35% white chocolate
2 tablespoons (12 g) freshly grated lime zest (from 4 limes)
1½ cups (350 g) plain stirred yogurt
3⅔ ounces (105 g) Sosa powdered Mediterranean acid yogurt
3 tablespoons (25 g) powdered milk

THE
"JARDINS"

Macaron Jardin Subtil

This is a subtle and delicate macaron. Mingled with the strong flavor of Espelette pepper, the almost abrasive flavor from the lemon gelée gives this macaron a flavor of both freshness and contrast.

PREPARE THE TINTED SUGAR. The day before, preheat the oven to 140°F (60°C). Put on disposable gloves. Rub the food color into the coarse sugar using your fingertips. Spread the sugar out onto a baking sheet. Place the baking sheet in the oven for 30 minutes to dry the sugar. Set aside to cool to room temperature.

PREPARE THE LEMON *GELÉE*. In a saucepan, combine the sugar with the agar-agar. Add the lemon juice and the lemon zest and bring to a boil while whisking. Let boil for 1 minute. Add the mixture to an airtight container and refrigerate for 12 hours. Just before using, pour the *gelée* into a large bowl and whisk it until smooth. Immediately before using, transfer the *gelée* to a pastry bag fitted with a plain #11, ¹⁄₂-inch (11-mm to 12-mm) pastry tip.

PREPARE THE SUBTLE GARDEN MACARON SHELLS. Sift together the confectioners' sugar and almonds.

Combine the food color with half of the "liquefied" egg whites. Pour this into the confectioners' sugar–almond mixture without mixing.

Add the remaining "liquefied" egg whites to the bowl of a stand mixer fitted with the wire whisk. In a saucepan, boil the mineral water and granulated sugar to 244°F (118°C). As soon as the syrup reaches 239°F (115°C), begin beating the egg whites on high speed.

When the syrup reaches 244°F (118°C), reduce the mixer speed to medium-high and pour the syrup in a steady stream down the inside edge of the bowl into the beaten egg whites. Beat the meringue until it cools to 122°F (50°C). Fold it with a silicone spatula into the confectioners' sugar–almond mixture until the mixture loses volume. Transfer the batter to a pastry bag fitted with a plain #11, ¹⁄₂-inch (11-mm to 12-mm) pastry tip.

MAKES ABOUT 72 MACARONS (OR ABOUT 144 SHELLS)

PREPARATION TIME: **5 MINUTES (5 DAYS IN ADVANCE, SEE "MACARON SHELLS STEP-BY-STEP" IN THE KITCHEN GUIDE) + 1 HOUR 30 MINUTES**

COOKING TIME: **ABOUT 1 HOUR**

INFUSION TIME: **20 MINUTES**

RESTING TIME: **30 MINUTES**

REFRIGERATION TIME: **4 HOURS + 24 HOURS**

FOR THE TINTED SUGAR
Scant ¾ teaspoon **(2.5 g)** liquid glittering (or "pearl") green food color
1¼ cups **(250 g)** coarse sugar
Note: *This will make more tinted sugar than is needed for one batch of macarons.*

FOR THE LEMON *GELÉE*
¾ teaspoon **(10 g)** superfine granulated sugar
2½ teaspoons **(5 g)** agar-agar, preferably PCB Création Texturas or Sosa brand
¾ cup **(200 g)** freshly squeezed lemon juice
½ teaspoon **(1 g)** freshly grated lemon zest

FOR THE SUBTLE GARDEN MACARON SHELLS
3 cups **(300 g)** confectioners' sugar
2 cups plus 2 tablespoons **(300 g)** ground almonds
Scant 1 teaspoon **(3.5 g)** liquid lemon yellow food color
7 large **(220 g)** "liquefied" egg whites, divided (see "Macaron Shells Step-by-Step" in the Kitchen Guide)
¼ cup plus 1 tablespoon **(75 g)** still mineral water
1½ cups **(300 g)** superfine granulated sugar
Tinted Sugar (see above)

Line baking sheets with parchment paper. Pipe disks about 1½ inches (3.5 cm) in diameter and ¾ inch (2 cm) apart on the lined baking sheets. Rap the baking sheets on a work surface covered with a clean kitchen towel to gently smooth out the disks. Sprinkle the disks with the tinted sugar. Set aside for at least 30 minutes at room temperature to allow a skin to form.

Preheat a convection oven to 350°F (180°C). Place the baking sheets in the oven. Bake for 12 minutes, quickly opening and closing the oven door twice during baking to release moisture. Remove the shells from the oven and slide them still on the parchment paper onto a work surface.

PREPARE THE CITRUS CHILE CREAM. Chop the white chocolate using a serrated knife then melt it to between 113°F (45°C) and 122°F (50°C) set over a bain-marie or in a microwave.

In a saucepan, bring the cream to a boil with the lime, orange, and grapefruit zests and the chile. Remove from the heat, then cover and let infuse for 20 minutes.

Pour the hot cream in thirds into the melted white chocolate, stirring after each addition starting in the center then in increasingly wider concentric circles toward the sides of the bowl. Heat the orange juice and hot pepper sauce to about 122°F (50°C) then stir it into the white chocolate. Using an immersion blender, blend the cream until smooth.

Pour the cream into a baking dish. Cover it by gently pressing plastic wrap onto its surface. Refrigerate for 4 hours, just until the cream has developed a creamy consistency. Transfer the cream to a pastry bag fitted with a plain #11, ½-inch (11-mm to 12-mm) pastry tip.

Turn half of the shells over with the flat sides up onto a new piece of parchment paper. Fill them with the chile cream then pipe a dollop of the *gelée* in the center. Pipe a dab of the cream on top of the *gelée*. Close them with the rest of the shells, pressing down lightly.

Refrigerate the macarons for 24 hours. Remove them from the refrigerator 2 hours before eating them.

FOR THE CITRUS CHILE CREAM
10½ ounces (300 g) Valrhona Ivoire 35% white chocolate
¾ cup plus 2 tablespoons (200 g) light whipping cream (32%–35% fat)
1½ teaspoons (3 g) freshly grated lime zest (from 1 lime)
1½ teaspoons (3 g) freshly grated orange zest (from ½ orange)
1½ teaspoons (3 g) freshly grated grapefruit zest (from ¼ grapefruit)
Scant ⅛ ounce (2.5 g) fresh Espelette chile
Scant 2 tablespoons (25 g) freshly squeezed blood orange juice (from ½ orange), or use Tropicana
Several drops hot pepper sauce, preferably Tabasco

Macaron Jardin de Valérie

I created this macaron as homage to the home country of my love, Valérie. The scent of immortelle flowers is, in my opinion, symbolic of Corsica, and powerfully evokes fresh bay and anise. I embedded a few cubes of candied lemon in the center of an immortelle flower cream to create a subtle combination.

PREPARE THE YELLOW MACARON SHELLS. The day before, sift together the confectioners' sugar and almonds.

Combine the food color with half of the "liquefied" egg whites. Pour this into the confectioners' sugar–almond mixture without mixing.

Add the remaining "liquefied" egg whites to the bowl of a stand mixer fitted with the wire whisk. In a saucepan, boil the mineral water and granulated sugar to 244°F (118°C). As soon as the syrup reaches 239°F (115°C), begin beating the egg whites on high speed.

When the syrup reaches 244°F (118°C), reduce the mixer speed to medium-high and pour the syrup in a steady stream down the inside edge of the bowl into the beaten egg whites. Beat the meringue until it cools to 122°F (50°C). Fold it with a silicone spatula into the confectioners' sugar–almond mixture until the mixture loses volume. Transfer the batter to a pastry bag fitted with a plain #11, ½-inch (11-mm to 12-mm) pastry tip.

Line baking sheets with parchment paper. Pipe disks about 1½ inches (3.5 cm) in diameter and ¾ inch (2 cm) apart on the lined baking sheets. Rap the baking sheets on a work surface covered with a clean kitchen towel to gently smooth out the disks. Set aside for at least 30 minutes at room temperature to allow a skin to form.

MAKES ABOUT 72 MACARONS (OR ABOUT 144 SHELLS)
PREPARATION TIME: 5 MINUTES (5 DAYS IN ADVANCE, SEE "MACARON SHELLS STEP-BY-STEP" IN THE KITCHEN GUIDE) + 1 HOUR 50 MINUTES
COOKING TIME: ABOUT 20 MINUTES
RESTING TIME: 30 MINUTES (TWICE)
REFRIGERATION TIME: 4 HOURS + 24 HOURS

○

FOR THE YELLOW MACARON SHELLS
1½ cups (150 g) confectioners' sugar
1 cup plus 1 tablespoon (150 g) ground almonds
½ teaspoon (2 g) liquid lemon yellow food color
3½ large (110 g) "liquefied" egg whites, divided (see "Macaron Shells Step-by-Step" in the Kitchen Guide)
2 tablespoons plus 1¾ teaspoons (38 g) still mineral water
¾ cup (150 g) superfine granulated sugar

FOR THE ORANGE MACARON SHELLS
1½ cups (150 g) confectioners' sugar
1 cup plus 1 tablespoon (150 g) ground almonds
Scant ¾ teaspoon (2.5 g) liquid lemon yellow food color
Scant ½ teaspoon (1.5 g) liquid strawberry red food color
Scant ½ teaspoon (1.5 g) liquid carmine red food color
3½ large (110 g) "liquefied" egg whites, divided (see "Macaron Shells Step-by-Step" in the Kitchen Guide)
2 tablespoons plus 1¾ teaspoons (38 g) still mineral water
¾ cup (150 g) superfine granulated sugar

FOR THE IMMORTELLE FLOWER CREAM
13½ ounces (385 g) Valrhona Ivoire 35% white chocolate
1½ cups (345 g) light whipping cream (32%–35% fat)
2 tablespoons plus 1½ teaspoons (30 g) organic immortelle flower (*Helichrysum italicum*) essential oil, preferably by Stéphane Acquarone, Aléria, Corsica

FOR THE FILLING
7 ounces (200 g) candied citron, preferably from Confiserie Saint-Sylvestre, cut into small cubes

PREPARE THE ORANGE MACARON SHELLS. Sift together the confectioners' sugar and almonds.

Combine the yellow and both red food colors with half of the "liquefied" egg whites. Pour this into the confectioners' sugar–almond mixture without mixing.

Add the remaining "liquefied" egg whites to the bowl of a stand mixer fitted with the wire whisk. In a saucepan, boil the mineral water and granulated sugar to 244°F (118°C). As soon as the syrup reaches 239°F (115°C), begin beating the egg whites on high speed.

When the syrup reaches 244°F (118°C), reduce the mixer speed to medium-high and pour the syrup in a steady stream down the inside edge of the bowl into the beaten egg whites. Beat the meringue until it cools to 122°F (50°C). Fold it with a silicone spatula into the confectioners' sugar–almond mixture until the mixture loses volume. Transfer the batter to a pastry bag fitted with a plain #11, ½-inch (11-mm to 12-mm) pastry tip.

Line baking sheets with parchment paper. Pipe disks about 1½ inches (3.5 cm) in diameter and ¾ inch (2 cm) apart on the lined baking sheets. Rap the baking sheets on a work surface covered with a clean kitchen towel to gently smooth out the disks. Set aside for at least 30 minutes at room temperature to allow a skin to form.

Preheat a convection oven to 350°F (180°C). Place the baking sheets in the oven. Bake for 12 minutes, quickly opening and closing the oven door twice during baking to release moisture. Remove the shells from the oven and slide them still on the parchment paper onto a work surface.

PREPARE THE IMMORTELLE FLOWER CREAM. Chop the white chocolate using a serrated knife then melt it to between 113°F (45°C) and 122°F (50°C) set over a bain-marie or in a microwave.

In a saucepan, bring the cream to a boil. Pour the hot cream in thirds into the melted chocolate, stirring after each addition starting in the center then in increasingly wider concentric circles toward the sides of the bowl. Add the immortelle essential oil. Using an immersion blender, blend the cream until smooth.

Pour the cream into a baking dish. Cover it by gently pressing plastic wrap onto its surface. Refrigerate for 4 hours, just until the cream has developed a creamy consistency. Transfer the immortelle flower cream to a pastry bag fitted with a plain #11, ½-inch (11-mm to 12-mm) pastry tip.

Turn the yellow macaron shells over with the flat sides up onto a new piece of parchment paper. Fill them with the immortelle flower cream then place three cubes of candied citron in the center. Pipe a small dab of the cream on top of the citron. Close them with the orange macaron shells, pressing down lightly.

Refrigerate the macarons for 24 hours. Remove them from the refrigerator 2 hours before eating them.

Macaron Jardin d'Automne

While dining in a French restaurant in Macao, I had the idea for this macaron after tasting a pumpkin and corn velouté whose flavor was very distinct. The two flavors stood out from each other but were also a marvelous blend. I reinterpreted these flavors by seasoning the pumpkin with cinnamon, ginger, and nutmeg.

**MAKES ABOUT 72 MACARONS
(OR ABOUT 144 SHELLS)**

PREPARATION TIME: **5 MINUTES (5 DAYS
IN ADVANCE, SEE "MACARON SHELLS
STEP-BY-STEP" IN THE KITCHEN GUIDE)
+ 2 HOURS**

COOKING TIME: **ABOUT 1 HOUR 10
MINUTES**

RESTING TIME: **30 MINUTES (TWICE)**

REFRIGERATION TIME: **4 HOURS +
24 HOURS**

**FOR THE YELLOW MACARON
SHELLS**
1½ cups (150 g) confectioners'
sugar
1 cup plus 1 tablespoon (150 g)
ground almonds
¾ teaspoon (3 g) liquid lemon
yellow food color
3½ large (110 g) "liquefied" egg
whites, divided (see "Macaron
Shells Step-by-Step" in the Kitchen
Guide)
**2 tablespoons plus 1¾ teaspoons
(38 g)** still mineral water
¾ cup (150 g) superfine granulated
sugar

$\longrightarrow$

PREPARE THE YELLOW MACARON SHELLS. The day before, sift together the confectioners' sugar and almonds.

Combine the food color with half of the "liquefied" egg whites. Pour this into the confectioners' sugar–almond mixture without mixing.

Add the remaining "liquefied" egg whites to the bowl of a stand mixer fitted with the wire whisk. In a saucepan, boil the mineral water and granulated sugar to 244°F (118°C). As soon as the syrup reaches 239°F (115°C), begin beating the egg whites on high speed.

When the syrup reaches 244°F (118°C), reduce the mixer speed to medium-high and pour the syrup in a steady stream down the inside edge of the bowl into the beaten egg whites. Beat the meringue until it cools to 122°F (50°C). Fold it with a silicone spatula into the confectioners' sugar–almond mixture until the mixture loses volume. Transfer the batter to a pastry bag fitted with a plain #11, ½-inch (11-mm to 12-mm) pastry tip.

Line baking sheets with parchment paper. Pipe disks about 1½ inches (3.5 cm) in diameter and ¾ inch (2 cm) apart on the lined baking sheets. Rap the baking sheets on a work surface covered with a clean kitchen towel to gently smooth out the disks. Set aside for at least 30 minutes at room temperature to allow a skin to form.

PREPARE THE ORANGE MACARON SHELLS. Sift together the confectioners' sugar and almonds.

Combine the yellow and red food colors with half of the "liquefied" egg whites. Pour this into the confectioners' sugar–almond mixture without mixing.

Add the remaining "liquefied" egg whites to the bowl of a stand mixer fitted with the wire whisk. In a saucepan, boil the mineral water and granulated sugar to 244°F (118°C). As soon as the syrup reaches 239°F (115°C), begin beating the egg whites on high speed.

When the syrup reaches 244°F (118°C), reduce the mixer speed to medium–high and pour the syrup in a steady stream down the inside edge of the bowl into the beaten egg whites. Beat the meringue until it cools to 122°F (50°C). Fold it with a silicone spatula into the confectioners' sugar–almond mixture until the mixture loses volume. Transfer the batter to a pastry bag fitted with a plain #11, ½-inch (11–mm to 12–mm) pastry tip.

Line baking sheets with parchment paper. Pipe disks about 1½ inches (3.5 cm) in diameter and ¾ inch (2 cm) apart on the lined baking sheets. Rap the baking sheets on a work surface covered with a clean kitchen towel to gently smooth out the disks. Set aside for at least 30 minutes at room temperature to allow a skin to form.

Preheat a convection oven to 350°F (180°C). Place the baking sheets in the oven. Bake for 12 minutes, quickly opening and closing the oven door twice during baking to release moisture. Remove the shells from the oven and slide them still on the parchment paper onto a work surface.

PREPARE THE CORN FILLING. Reduce the temperature of the oven to 175°F (80°C). Cut the corn kernels from the cobs using a knife. Spread the kernels on a baking sheet lined with parchment paper. Place the baking sheet in the oven for 30 minutes to dry the corn.

PREPARE THE PUMPKIN PUREE. Peel the pumpkin and remove the seeds. Cut the flesh into large pieces then place them in a pressure cooker for 20 minutes; remove the pieces to drain. Process the pumpkin to a very fine puree in a blender or food processor, then place the puree in a saucepan with the ginger, cinnamon, and nutmeg.

PREPARE THE PUMPKIN CREAM. Chop the white chocolate and the cocoa butter using a serrated knife then melt them in separate bowls to between 113°F (45°C) and 122°F (50°C) set over a bain–marie or in a microwave then stir them together to combine.

Bring the pumpkin puree to a boil. Pour the hot puree in thirds into the melted chocolate–cocoa butter mixture, stirring after each addition starting in the center then in increasingly wider concentric circles toward the sides of the bowl. Using an immersion blender, blend the cream until smooth.

Pour the cream into a baking dish. Cover it by gently pressing plastic wrap onto its surface. Refrigerate for 4 hours, just until the cream has developed a creamy consistency. Transfer the cream to a pastry bag fitted with a plain #11, ½-inch (11–mm to 12–mm) pastry tip.

Turn the yellow macaron shells over with the flat sides up onto a new piece of parchment paper. Fill them with the pumpkin cream. Gently place four dried corn kernels on top. Pipe a small dab of the cream on top of the corn. Close them with the orange macaron shells, pressing down lightly.

Refrigerate the macarons for 24 hours. Remove them from the refrigerator 2 hours before eating them.

FOR THE ORANGE MACARON SHELLS
1½ cups (150 g) confectioners' sugar
1 cup plus 1 tablespoon (150 g) ground almonds
Scant 1 teaspoon (3.5 g) liquid lemon yellow food color
¼ teaspoon (1 g) liquid strawberry red food color
3½ large (110 g) "liquefied" egg whites, divided (see "Macaron Shells Step-by-Step" in the Kitchen Guide)
2 tablespoons plus 1¾ teaspoons (38 g) still mineral water
¾ cup (150 g) superfine granulated sugar

FOR THE CORN FILLING
2 cobs of corn, cooked sous vide or by steaming or boiling

FOR THE PUMPKIN PUREE
1⅛ pounds (500 g) fresh pumpkin (to make 1½ cups/350 g puree)
1½ teaspoons (8 g) freshly grated ginger
¼ teaspoon (0.5 g) ground Ceylon cinnamon
Pinch freshly grated nutmeg

FOR THE PUMPKIN CREAM
11¾ ounces (335 g) Valrhona Ivoire 35% white chocolate
1¼ ounces (35 g) cocoa butter, preferably Valrhona
12¼ ounces (350 g) Pumpkin Puree (see above)

Macaron Jardin du Sultan

While working on the flavor of coffee with Hippolyte Courty, I wanted to create a flavor combination of coffee and orange blossom. This gave me the idea to incorporate candied orange in the center of the cream. In order to preserve their full flavor, grind the coffee beans just before using them.

MAKES ABOUT 72 MACARONS
(OR ABOUT 144 SHELLS)

PREPARATION TIME: **5 MINUTES (5 DAYS IN ADVANCE, SEE "MACARON SHELLS STEP-BY-STEP" IN THE KITCHEN GUIDE)** + **5 MINUTES (2 DAYS IN ADVANCE)** + **1 HOUR 30 MINUTES**

COOKING TIME: **2 HOURS 10 MINUTES (2 DAYS IN ADVANCE)** + ABOUT **20 MINUTES**

MACERATION TIME: **24 HOURS**

DRAINING TIME: **1 HOUR**

INFUSION TIME: **3 MINUTES**

RESTING TIME: **30 MINUTES (TWICE)**

REFRIGERATION TIME: **6 HOURS +** **24 HOURS**

FOR THE CANDIED ORANGE PUREE

1⅓ pounds (600 g) oranges
2 cups plus 2 tablespoons (500 g) still mineral water
1¼ cups (250 g) superfine granulated sugar

PREPARE THE CANDIED ORANGE PUREE. Two days in advance, wash and dry the oranges. Cut off both rounded ends then quarter the oranges, slicing from top to bottom. Immerse the quarters in a saucepan of boiling water. When the water reaches a boil again, boil the quarters for 2 minutes, then drain. Rinse them under cold water. Repeat these steps twice, boiling and draining the quarters, then set them aside to dry.

In a saucepan, bring the mineral water and the sugar to a boil over low heat. Add the oranges. Cover three-quarters of the top of the saucepan. Simmer very gently for 2 hours.

Transfer to a bowl to cool. Cover and refrigerate until the next day.

The day before, drain the oranges for 1 hour in a sieve set over a bowl then process them in a blender or food processor into a fine puree. Refrigerate until needed.

FOR THE COFFEE MACARON SHELLS

1½ cups (150 g) confectioners' sugar

1 cup plus 1 tablespoon (150 g) ground almonds

¼ teaspoon (1 g) liquid lemon yellow color

1¾ teaspoons (7.5 g) coffee extract, preferably Trablit

3½ large (110 g) "liquefied" egg whites, divided (see "Macaron Shells Step-by-Step" in the Kitchen Guide)

2 tablespoons plus 1¾ teaspoons (38 g) still mineral water

¾ cup (150 g) superfine granulated sugar

FOR THE MANDARIN MACARON SHELLS

1½ cups (150 g) confectioners' sugar

1 cup plus 1 tablespoon (150 g) ground almonds

Scant 1 teaspoon (3.5 g) liquid lemon yellow food color

¼ teaspoon (1 g) liquid strawberry red food color

3½ large (110 g) "liquefied" egg whites, divided (see "Macaron Shells Step-by-Step" in the Kitchen Guide)

2 tablespoons plus 1¾ teaspoons (38 g) still mineral water

¾ cup (150 g) superfine granulated sugar

FOR THE ORANGE FLOWER CREAM

Generous ¼ cup (18 g) lapar rouge du Brésil coffee beans, preferably from l'Arbre à Café

1½ cups plus 1⅔ tablespoons (370 g) light whipping cream (32%–35% fat)

1½ teaspoons (10 g) glucose syrup or corn syrup

11¼ ounces (320 g) Valrhona Ivoire 35% white chocolate

½ teaspoon (2 g) orange flower water

PREPARE THE COFFEE MACARON SHELLS. Sift together the confectioners' sugar and almonds.

Combine the food color and coffee extract with half of the "liquefied" egg whites. Pour this into the confectioners' sugar–almond mixture without mixing.

Add the remaining "liquefied" egg whites to the bowl of a stand mixer fitted with the wire whisk. In a saucepan, boil the mineral water and granulated sugar to 244°F (118°C). As soon as the syrup reaches 239°F (115°C), begin beating the egg whites on high speed.

When the syrup reaches 244°F (118°C), reduce the mixer speed to medium–high and pour the syrup in a steady stream down the inside edge of the bowl into the beaten egg whites. Beat the meringue until it cools to 122°F (50°C). Fold it with a silicone spatula into the confectioners' sugar–almond mixture until the mixture loses volume. Transfer the batter to a pastry bag fitted with a plain #11, ½-inch (11-mm to 12-mm) pastry tip.

Line baking sheets with parchment paper. Pipe disks about 1½ inches (3.5 cm) in diameter and ¾ inch (2 cm) apart on the lined baking sheets. Rap the baking sheets on a work surface covered with a clean kitchen towel to gently smooth out the disks. Set aside for at least 30 minutes at room temperature to allow a skin to form.

PREPARE THE MANDARIN MACARON SHELLS. Sift together the confectioners' sugar and almonds.

Combine the yellow and red food colors with half of the "liquefied" egg whites. Pour this into the confectioners' sugar–almond mixture without mixing.

Add the remaining "liquefied" egg whites to the bowl of a stand mixer fitted with the wire whisk. In a saucepan, boil the mineral water and granulated sugar to 244°F (118°C). As soon as the syrup reaches 239°F (115°C), begin beating the egg whites on high speed.

When the syrup reaches 244°F (118°C), reduce the mixer speed to medium–high and pour the syrup in a steady stream down the inside edge of the bowl into the beaten egg whites. Beat the meringue until it cools to 122°F (50°C). Fold it with a silicone spatula into the confectioners' sugar–almond mixture until the mixture loses volume. Transfer the batter to a pastry bag fitted with a plain #11, 1/2-inch (11-mm to 12-mm) pastry tip.

Line baking sheets with parchment paper. Pipe disks about 1 1/2 inches (3.5 cm) in diameter and 3/4 inch (2 cm) apart on the lined baking sheets. Rap the baking sheets on a work surface covered with a clean kitchen towel to gently smooth out the disks. Set aside for at least 30 minutes at room temperature to allow a skin to form.

Preheat a convection oven to 350°F (180°C). Place the baking sheets in the oven. Bake for 12 minutes, quickly opening and closing the oven door twice during baking to release moisture. Remove the shells from the oven and slide them still on the parchment paper onto a work surface.

PREPARE THE ORANGE FLOWER CREAM. Grind the coffee beans. In a saucepan, bring the cream to a boil then add the ground coffee. Remove from the heat, then cover and let infuse for 3 minutes.

Strain the cream then stir in the syrup. Chop the white chocolate using a serrated knife then melt it to between 113°F (45°C) and 122°F (50°C) set over a bain-marie or in a microwave.

Pour the hot cream in thirds into the melted white chocolate, stirring after each addition starting in the center then in increasingly wider concentric circles toward the sides of the bowl. Stir in the orange flower water. Using an immersion blender, blend the cream until smooth.

Pour the cream into a baking dish. Cover it by gently pressing plastic wrap onto its surface. Refrigerate for 6 hours, just until the cream has developed a creamy consistency.

Transfer the candied orange puree and the orange flower cream to separate pastry bags fitted with plain #11, 1/2-inch (11-mm to 12-mm) pastry tips.

Turn the coffee macaron shells over with the flat sides up onto a new piece of parchment paper. Fill them with the orange flower cream then pipe a dollop of the candied orange puree in the center. Pipe a dab of the cream on top of the puree. Close them with the mandarin macaron shells, pressing down lightly.

Refrigerate the macarons for 24 hours. Remove them from the refrigerator 2 hours before eating them.

Macaron
Jardin Andalou

This is a macaron with an intensely fruity taste—the meeting of a mandarin olive oil–scented cream and a center of red and black fruit compote in which the slightly bitter note of wild strawberries stands out.

PREPARE THE MANDARIN MACARON SHELLS. The day before, sift together the confectioners' sugar and almonds.

Combine the yellow and red food colors with half of the "liquefied" egg whites. Pour this into the confectioners' sugar–almond mixture without mixing.

Add the remaining "liquefied" egg whites to the bowl of a stand mixer fitted with the wire whisk. In a saucepan, boil the mineral water and granulated sugar to 244°F (118°C). As soon as the syrup reaches 239°F (115°C), begin beating the egg whites on high speed.

When the syrup reaches 244°F (118°C), reduce the mixer speed to medium–high and pour the syrup in a steady stream down the inside edge of the bowl into the beaten egg whites. Beat the meringue until it cools to 122°F (50°C). Fold it with a silicone spatula into the confectioners' sugar–almond mixture until the mixture loses volume. Transfer the batter to a pastry bag fitted with a plain #11, ½-inch (11–mm to 12–mm) pastry tip.

Line baking sheets with parchment paper. Pipe disks about 1½ inches (3.5 cm) in diameter and ¾ inch (2 cm) apart on the lined baking sheets. Rap the baking sheets on a work surface covered with a clean kitchen towel to gently smooth out the disks. Set aside for at least 30 minutes at room temperature to allow a skin to form.

MAKES ABOUT 72 MACARONS
(OR ABOUT 144 SHELLS)
PREPARATION TIME: 5 MINUTES (5 DAYS
IN ADVANCE, SEE "MACARON SHELLS
STEP-BY-STEP" IN THE KITCHEN GUIDE)
+ 1 HOUR 50 MINUTES
COOKING TIME: ABOUT 30 MINUTES
RESTING TIME: 30 MINUTES (TWICE)
REFRIGERATION TIME: 4 HOURS +
24 HOURS

**FOR THE MANDARIN
MACARON SHELLS**
1½ cups (150 g) confectioners'
sugar
1 cup plus 1 tablespoon (150 g)
ground almonds
Scant 1 teaspoon (3.5 g) liquid
lemon yellow food color
¼ teaspoon (1 g) liquid strawberry
red food color
3½ large (110 g) "liquefied" egg
whites, divided (see "Macaron
Shells Step-by-Step" in the Kitchen
Guide)
2 tablespoons plus 1¾ teaspoons
(38 g) still mineral water
¾ cup (150 g) superfine granulated
sugar

PREPARE THE RED MACARON SHELLS. Sift together the confectioners' sugar and almonds.

Combine both red food colors with half of the "liquefied" egg whites. Pour this into the confectioners' sugar–almond mixture without mixing.

Add the remaining "liquefied" egg whites to the bowl of a stand mixer fitted with the wire whisk. In a saucepan, boil the mineral water and granulated sugar to 244°F (118°C). As soon as the syrup reaches 239°F (115°C), begin beating the egg whites on high speed.

When the syrup reaches 244°F (118°C), reduce the mixer speed to medium-high and pour the syrup in a steady stream down the inside edge of the bowl into the beaten egg whites. Beat the meringue until it cools to 122°F (50°C). Fold it with a silicone spatula into the confectioners' sugar–almond mixture until the mixture loses volume. Transfer the batter to a pastry bag fitted with a plain #11, ¹/₂-inch (11-mm to 12-mm) pastry tip.

Line baking sheets with parchment paper. Pipe disks about 1¹/₂ inches (3.5 cm) in diameter and ³/₄ inch (2 cm) apart on the lined baking sheets. Rap the baking sheets on a work surface covered with a clean kitchen towel to gently smooth out the disks. Set aside for at least 30 minutes at room temperature to allow a skin to form.

Preheat a convection oven to 350°F (180°C). Place the baking sheets in the oven. Bake for 12 minutes, quickly opening and closing the oven door twice during baking to release moisture. Remove the shells from the oven and slide them still on the parchment paper onto a work surface.

PREPARE THE MANDARIN OLIVE OIL CREAM. Chop the white chocolate using a serrated knife then melt it to between 113°F (45°C) and 122°F (50°C) set over a bain-marie or in a microwave.

In a saucepan, bring the cream to a boil. Pour the hot cream in thirds into the melted white chocolate, stirring after each addition starting in the center then in increasingly wider concentric circles toward the sides of the bowl. Using an immersion blender, blend the cream until smooth.

As soon as the mixture falls below 122°F (50°C), stir in the mandarin olive oil in three parts to combine, then blend again.

Pour the cream into a baking dish. Cover it by gently pressing plastic wrap onto its surface. Refrigerate for 4 hours, just until the cream has developed a creamy consistency.

PREPARE THE FRUIT COMPOTE. Using a food mill, in separate batches, puree the raspberries, strawberries, red currants, black currants, and wild strawberries. In a saucepan, combine the agar-agar with the sugar. Add the fruit purees and lemon juice, then bring to a boil while stirring continuously. Let boil for 1 minute then remove from the heat to cool.

Transfer the mandarin olive oil cream and the compote to separate pastry bags fitted with a plain #11, ¹⁄₂-inch (11-mm to 12-mm) pastry tip.

Turn the mandarin macaron shells over with the flat sides up onto a new piece of parchment paper. Fill them with the mandarin olive oil cream then pipe a dollop of the compote in the center. Pipe a dab of the cream on top of the compote. Close them with the red macaron shells, pressing down lightly.

Refrigerate the macarons for 24 hours. Remove them from the refrigerator 2 hours before eating them.

FOR THE RED MACARON SHELLS
1½ cups (150 g) confectioners' sugar
1 cup plus 1 tablespoon (150 g) ground almonds
Generous 2 teaspoons (10 g) liquid strawberry red food color
¾ teaspoon (3 g) liquid carmine red food color
3½ large (110 g) "liquefied" egg whites, divided (see "Macaron Shells Step-by-Step" in the Kitchen Guide)
2 tablespoons plus 1¾ teaspoons (38 g) still mineral water
¾ cup (150 g) superfine granulated sugar

FOR THE MANDARIN OLIVE OIL CREAM
15¾ ounces (450 g) Valrhona Ivoire 35% white chocolate
¾ cup plus 2 tablespoons (200 g) light whipping cream (32%–35% fat)
1⅓ cups (300 g) mandarin olive oil, preferably from Première Pression Provence

FOR THE FRUIT COMPOTE
Generous ¼ pint (100 g) raspberries
⅔ pint (220 g) strawberries
⅓ cup (50 g) red currants, stems removed
⅓ cup (50 g) black currants, stems removed
⅓ cup (50 g) wild strawberries
1 teaspoon (3 g) agar-agar
¼ cup (50 g) superfine granulated sugar
Generous 1 tablespoon (20 g) freshly squeezed lemon juice (from ½ lemon)

Macaron
Jardin d'Antan

It was when I was working together with Jean-Michel Duriez on Au Coeur du Goût that I combined the old-fashioned flavor of violet with the fresh aroma of anise, creating a macaron with a taste reminiscent of days gone by.

MAKES ABOUT 72 MACARONS
(OR ABOUT 144 SHELLS)

PREPARATION TIME: **5 MINUTES (5 DAYS IN ADVANCE, SEE "MACARON SHELLS STEP-BY-STEP" IN THE KITCHEN GUIDE) + 1 HOUR 50 MINUTES**

COOKING TIME: **ABOUT 30 MINUTES**

RESTING TIME: **30 MINUTES (TWICE)**

REFRIGERATION TIME: **2 HOURS + 24 HOURS**

FOR THE GREEN MACARON SHELLS
1½ cups (150 g) confectioners' sugar
1 cup plus 1 tablespoon (150 g) ground almonds
8 drops / ⅛ teaspoon (0.5 g) liquid chocolate brown food color
8 drops / ⅛ teaspoon (0.5 g) liquid lemon yellow food color
8 drops / ⅛ teaspoon (0.5 g) liquid pistachio green food color
3½ large (110 g) "liquefied" egg whites, divided (see "Macaron Shells Step-by-Step" in the Kitchen Guide)
2 tablespoons plus 1¾ teaspoons (38 g) still mineral water
¾ cup (150 g) superfine granulated sugar

PREPARE THE GREEN MACARON SHELLS. The day before, sift together the confectioners' sugar and almonds.

Combine the brown, yellow, and green food colors with half of the "liquefied" egg whites. Pour this into the confectioners' sugar–almond mixture without mixing.

Add the remaining "liquefied" egg whites to the bowl of a stand mixer fitted with the wire whisk. In a saucepan, boil the mineral water and granulated sugar to 244°F (118°C). As soon as the syrup reaches 239°F (115°C), begin beating the egg whites on high speed.

When the syrup reaches 244°F (118°C), reduce the mixer speed to medium-high and pour the syrup in a steady stream down the inside edge of the bowl into the beaten egg whites. Beat the meringue until it cools to 122°F (50°C). Fold it with a silicone spatula into the confectioners' sugar–almond mixture until the mixture loses volume. Transfer the batter to a pastry bag fitted with a plain #11, ½-inch (11-mm to 12-mm) pastry tip.

Line baking sheets with parchment paper. Pipe disks about 1½ inches (3.5 cm) in diameter and ¾ inch (2 cm) apart on the lined baking sheets. Rap the baking sheets on a work surface covered with a clean kitchen towel to gently smooth out the disks. Set aside for at least 30 minutes at room temperature to allow a skin to form.

PREPARE THE VIOLET MACARON SHELLS. Sift together the confectioners' sugar and almonds.

Combine the food color with half of the "liquefied" egg whites. Pour this into the confectioners' sugar–almond mixture without mixing.

Add the remaining "liquefied" egg whites to the bowl of a stand mixer fitted with the wire whisk. In a saucepan, boil the mineral water and granulated sugar to 244°F (118°C). As soon as the syrup reaches 239°F (115°C), begin beating the egg whites on high speed.

When the syrup reaches 244°F (118°C), reduce the mixer speed to medium–high and pour the syrup in a steady stream down the inside edge of the bowl into the beaten egg whites. Beat the meringue until it cools to 122°F (50°C). Fold it with a silicone spatula into the confectioners' sugar–almond mixture until the mixture loses volume. Transfer the batter to a pastry bag fitted with a plain #11, ¹/₂-inch (11-mm to 12-mm) pastry tip.

Line baking sheets with parchment paper. Pipe disks about 1¹/₂ inches (3.5 cm) in diameter and ³/₄ inch (2 cm) apart on the lined baking sheets. Rap the baking sheets on a work surface covered with a clean kitchen towel to gently smooth out the disks. Set aside for at least 30 minutes at room temperature to allow a skin to form.

Preheat a convection oven to 350°F (180°C). Place the baking sheets in the oven. Bake for 12 minutes, quickly opening and closing the oven door twice during baking to release moisture. Remove the shells from the oven and slide them still on the parchment paper onto a work surface.

PREPARE THE ITALIAN MERINGUE. Add the egg whites to the bowl of a stand mixer fitted with the wire whisk. In a saucepan, boil the mineral water and all but 1¹/₄ teaspoons (5 g) of the granulated sugar. When the syrup starts to boil, wipe down the inside of the saucepan with a dampened pastry brush. As soon as the syrup reaches 239°F (115°C), begin beating the egg whites on high speed with the rest of the granulated sugar until the peaks are almost firm and droop slightly in the shape of a "bird's beak" when the whisk is lifted. When the syrup reaches 250°F (121°C), reduce the mixer speed to medium and slowly pour the syrup in a steady stream into the beaten egg whites, continuing to beat until the meringue has cooled.

PREPARE THE CRÈME ANGLAISE. In a saucepan, bring the milk to a boil. In a separate saucepan, whisk together the egg yolks and granulated sugar until lightened. Slowly add the hot milk to the yolk-sugar mixture while whisking vigorously. Place the saucepan over low heat and cook to 185°F (85°C) while stirring continuously—rich in eggs, this cream has a tendency to stick to the bottom of the saucepan. Strain the cooked cream then transfer it to a stand mixer fitted with the wire whisk. Beat on medium speed until cooled.

PREPARE THE VIOLET AND ANISE BUTTERCREAM. In a stand mixer, beat the butter on high speed for 5 minutes. Add the cooled crème anglaise, the anise, and violet essence. Beat again to combine then transfer this mixture to a bowl.

Using a silicone spatula, fold in the Italian meringue a little at a time.

Pour the buttercream into a baking dish. Cover it by gently pressing plastic wrap onto its surface. Refrigerate for 2 hours, just until the cream has developed a creamy consistency. Transfer the cream to a pastry bag fitted with a plain #11, ¹/₂-inch (11-mm to 12-mm) pastry tip.

Turn the green macaron shells over with the flat sides up onto a new piece of parchment paper. Fill them with the violet and anise buttercream. Close them with the violet macaron shells, pressing down lightly.

Refrigerate the macarons for 24 hours. Remove them from the refrigerator 2 hours before eating them.

FOR THE VIOLET MACARON SHELLS
1½ cups (150 g) confectioners' sugar
1 cup plus 1 tablespoon (150 g) ground almonds
¼ teaspoon (1 g) liquid violet food color
3½ large (110 g) "liquefied" egg whites, divided (see "Macaron Shells Step-by-Step" in the Kitchen Guide)
2 tablespoons plus 1¾ teaspoons (38 g) still mineral water
¾ cup (150 g) superfine granulated sugar

FOR THE ITALIAN MERINGUE
2 large (65 g) egg whites
2 tablespoons plus 1 teaspoon (35 g) still mineral water
⅔ cup (130 g) superfine granulated sugar, divided

FOR THE CRÈME ANGLAISE
⅓ cup plus 2 teaspoons (90 g) fresh whole milk
3½ large (70 g) egg yolks
3 tablespoons plus ½ teaspoon (40 g) superfine granulated sugar

FOR THE VIOLET AND ANISE BUTTERCREAM
2 cups (450 g) fine French unsalted butter, preferably *beurre de la Viette*, room temperature
1 recipe Crème Anglaise (see above)
2 teaspoons (3 g) ground anise seed, preferably from Thiercelin
4 drops / ¹/₁₆ teaspoon (0.25 g) violet essence flavoring, preferably from Sévarôme
1½ cups (175 g) Italian Meringue (see above)

I am inspired by the things I desire.

Macaron Jardin d'Été

This macaron evokes the feelings of summer, with the lively freshness of lemon zest and lemon juice and subtle anise notes from the fennel that I caramelize with butter and Muscovado sugar then season with Sarawak black pepper.

PREPARE THE LEMON CREAM. Two days in advance, wash and dry the lemons. Using a microplane grater, zest the lemons over a bowl and measure the quantity needed. Add the sugar and rub it into the zest by pinching it with your fingers. Whisk in the eggs and lemon juice then cook to between 181°F (83°C) and 183°F (84°C) over a bain-marie, whisking the mixture from time to time.

Place the bowl inside a larger bowl containing ice water and stir until the cream cools to 140°F (60°C). Whisk in the butter in small pieces until incorporated, then blend the cream for 10 minutes until smooth using an immersion blender.

Pour the cream into a baking dish. Cover it by gently pressing plastic wrap onto its surface. Refrigerate until the next day.

The day before, finish the lemon cream. Chop the cocoa butter using a serrated knife then melt it to between 113°F (45°C) and 122°F (50°C) set over a bain-marie or in a microwave.

Stir the lemon cream prepared the day before to smooth it out. Stir the melted cocoa butter into the lemon cream then stir in the almonds. Cover and refrigerate until needed.

MAKES ABOUT 72 MACARONS
(OR ABOUT 144 SHELLS)
PREPARATION TIME: 5 MINUTES (5 DAYS
IN ADVANCE, SEE "MACARON SHELLS
STEP-BY-STEP" IN THE KITCHEN GUIDE)
+ 30 MINUTES (2 DAYS IN ADVANCE) +
1 HOUR 30 MINUTES
COOKING TIME: 20 MINUTES (2 DAYS
IN ADVANCE) + ABOUT 1 HOUR
30 MINUTES
RESTING TIME: 30 MINUTES (TWICE)
REFRIGERATION TIME: 4 HOURS +
24 HOURS (TWICE)

○

FOR THE LEMON CREAM
1 tablespoon plus 1 teaspoon
(8 g) freshly grated lemon zest
(from 2 lemons)
1¼ cups minus 2 teaspoons
(240 g) superfine granulated sugar
4½ large (225 g) eggs
½ cup plus 2 tablespoons (160 g)
freshly squeezed lemon juice (from
2 lemons)
1½ cups plus 2 teaspoons
(350 g) fine French unsalted butter,
preferably *beurre de la Viette*,
room temperature
6⅛ ounces (175 g) cocoa butter,
preferably Valrhona
⅔ cup (95 g) ground blanched
almonds

→ PREPARE THE FENNEL PUREE. Preheat the oven to 212°F (100°C). Rinse and dry the fennel then dice it into ³⁄₈-inch (1-cm) cubes. In a sauté pan, cook the butter and sugar until it caramelizes, about 1 minute. Add the fennel, lemon juice, and the pepper (about one turn of the peppermill). Stir to combine then spread this mixture, including the juices, out onto a baking sheet lined with parchment paper. Place the baking sheet in the oven for 30 minutes. Remove from the oven and let cool. Transfer the roasted fennel, with juice, to a small bowl and blend to a fine puree using an immersion blender.

PREPARE THE YELLOW MACARON SHELLS. Sift the confectioners' sugar and almonds together in a bowl.

Combine the food color with half of the "liquefied" egg whites. Pour this into the confectioners' sugar–almond mixture without mixing.

Add the remaining "liquefied" egg whites to the bowl of a stand mixer fitted with the wire whisk. In a saucepan, boil the mineral water and granulated sugar to 244°F (118°C). As soon as the syrup reaches 239°F (115°C), begin beating the egg whites on high speed.

When the syrup reaches 244°F (118°C), reduce the mixer speed to medium-high and pour the syrup in a steady stream down the inside edge of the bowl into the beaten egg whites. Beat the meringue until it cools to 122°F (50°C). Fold it with a silicone spatula into the confectioners' sugar–almond mixture until the mixture loses volume. Transfer the batter to a pastry bag fitted with a plain #11, ¹⁄₂-inch (11-mm to 12-mm) pastry tip.

Line baking sheets with parchment paper. Pipe disks about 1¹⁄₂ inches (3.5 cm) in diameter and ³⁄₄ inch (2 cm) apart on the lined baking sheets. Rap the baking sheets on a work surface covered with a clean kitchen towel to gently smooth out the disks. Set aside for at least 30 minutes at room temperature to allow a skin to form.

PREPARE THE GREEN ANISE MACARON SHELLS. Sift the confectioners' sugar and almonds together in a bowl.

Combine the brown, yellow, and green food colors with half of the "liquefied" egg whites. Pour this into the confectioners' sugar–almond mixture without mixing.

Add the remaining "liquefied" egg whites to the bowl of a stand mixer fitted with the wire whisk. In a saucepan, boil the mineral water and granulated sugar to 244°F (118°C). As soon as the syrup reaches 239°F (115°C), begin beating the egg whites on high speed.

When the syrup reaches 244°F (118°C), reduce the mixer speed to medium-high and pour the syrup in a steady stream down the inside edge of the bowl into the beaten egg whites. Beat the meringue until it cools to 122°F (50°C). Fold it with a silicone spatula into the confectioners' sugar–almond mixture until the mixture loses volume. Transfer the batter to a pastry bag fitted with a plain #11, ¹⁄₂-inch (11-mm to 12-mm) pastry tip.

Line baking sheets with parchment paper. Pipe disks about 1¹⁄₂ inches (3.5 cm) in diameter and ³⁄₄ inch (2 cm) apart on the lined baking sheets. Rap the baking sheets on a work surface covered with a clean kitchen towel to gently smooth out the disks. Set aside for at least 30 minutes at room temperature to allow a skin to form.

Preheat a convection oven to 350°F (180°C). Place the baking sheets in the oven. Bake for 12 minutes, quickly opening and closing the oven door twice during baking to release moisture. Remove the shells from the oven and slide them still on the parchment paper onto a work surface.

Transfer the lemon cream and the fennel puree to separate pastry bags fitted with plain #11, ¹/₂-inch (11-mm to 12-mm) pastry tips.

Turn the yellow macaron shells over with the flat sides up onto a new piece of parchment paper. Fill them with the lemon cream then pipe a dollop of fennel puree in the center. Pipe a dab of the cream on top of the puree. Close them with the green macaron shells, pressing down lightly.

Refrigerate the macarons for 24 hours. Remove them from the refrigerator 2 hours before eating them.

FOR THE FENNEL PUREE
8¾ ounces (250 g) fresh fennel
3 tablespoons plus 1 teaspoon (50 g) fine French unsalted butter, preferably *beurre de la Viette*
¼ cup (40 g) Muscovado sugar
Scant 2 tablespoons (25 g) freshly squeezed lemon juice (from ½ lemon)
Freshly ground Sarawak black pepper

FOR THE YELLOW MACARON SHELLS
1½ cups (150 g) confectioners' sugar
1 cup plus 1 tablespoon (150 g) ground almonds
Scant 1 teaspoon (3.5 g) liquid lemon yellow food color
3½ large (110 g) "liquefied" egg whites, divided (see "Macaron Shells Step-by-Step" in the Kitchen Guide)
2 tablespoons plus 1¾ teaspoons (38 g) still mineral water
¾ cup (150 g) superfine granulated sugar

FOR THE GREEN ANISE MACARON SHELLS
1½ cups (150 g) confectioners' sugar
1 cup plus 1 tablespoon (150 g) ground almonds
8 drops / ⅛ teaspoon (0.5 g) liquid chocolate brown food color
8 drops / ⅛ teaspoon (0.5 g) liquid lemon yellow food color
8 drops / ⅛ teaspoon (0.5 g) liquid pistachio green food color
3½ large (110 g) "liquefied" egg whites, divided (see "Macaron Shells Step-by-Step" in the Kitchen Guide)
2 tablespoons plus 1¾ teaspoons (38 g) still mineral water
¾ cup (150 g) superfine granulated sugar

Macaron Jardin dans les Nuages

Smoked-salt butter, which lends the distinctive flavor of this macaron, was conceived by Jean-Yves Bordier, master butter maker from Saint-Malo, France, who inspired me to create a chocolate bonbon that I named Nuage. This butter releases hints of smoke, pepper, and curry, which brings it an incredible aroma suggestive of the smoking process, and a beautifully aromatic and delicate touch.

MAKES ABOUT 72 MACARONS
(OR ABOUT 144 SHELLS)

PREPARATION TIME: 5 MINUTES (5 DAYS
IN ADVANCE, SEE "MACARON SHELLS
STEP-BY-STEP" IN THE KITCHEN GUIDE)
+ 1 HOUR 30 MINUTES

COOKING TIME: ABOUT 20 MINUTES

RESTING TIME: 30 MINUTES (TWICE)

REFRIGERATION TIME: 2 HOURS +
24 HOURS

**FOR THE CHOCOLATE
MACARON SHELLS**
2⅛ ounces (60 g) Valrhona 100%
cocoa paste
1½ cups (150 g) confectioners'
sugar
1 cup plus 1 tablespoon (150 g)
ground almonds
4 drops / ¹/₁₆ teaspoon (0.25 g)
liquid carmine red food color
3½ large (110 g) "liquefied" egg
whites, divided (see "Macaron
Shells Step-by-Step" in the Kitchen
Guide)
3 tablespoons (43 g) still mineral
water
¾ cup (150 g) superfine granulated
sugar
½ cup plus 1½ tablespoons
(50 g) unsweetened cocoa,
preferably Valrhona

PREPARE THE CHOCOLATE MACARON SHELLS. The day before, chop the cocoa paste using a serrated knife then melt it to between 113°F (45°C) and 122°F (50°C) set over a bain-marie or in a microwave.

Sift together the confectioners' sugar and almonds.

Combine the food color with half of the "liquefied" egg whites. Pour this into the confectioners' sugar–almond mixture without mixing.

Add the remaining "liquefied" egg whites to the bowl of a stand mixer fitted with the wire whisk. In a saucepan, boil the mineral water and granulated sugar to 244°F (118°C). As soon as the syrup reaches 239°F (115°C), begin beating the egg whites on high speed.

When the syrup reaches 244°F (118°C), reduce the mixer speed to medium-high and pour the syrup in a steady stream down the inside edge of the bowl into the beaten egg whites. Beat the meringue until it cools to 122°F (50°C). Fold about one-third of the meringue into the melted cocoa paste then add this mixture to the confections' sugar–almond mixture along with the rest of the meringue. Fold it with a silicone spatula until the mixture loses volume. Transfer the batter to a pastry bag fitted with a plain #11, ¹/₂-inch (11-mm to 12-mm) pastry tip.

Line baking sheets with parchment paper. Pipe disks about 1½ inches (3.5 cm) in diameter and ¾ inch (2 cm) apart on the lined baking sheets. Rap the baking sheets on a work surface covered with a clean kitchen towel to gently smooth out the disks. Dust the disks with cocoa. Set aside for at least 30 minutes at room temperature to allow a skin to form.

In the end, my work is about the architecture of tastes and sensations, with the single goal of providing pleasure to those who taste it.

PREPARE THE PLAIN MACARON SHELLS. Sift together the confectioners' sugar and almonds.

Pour half of the "liquefied" egg whites into the confectioners' sugar–almond mixture without mixing.

Add the remaining "liquefied" egg whites to the bowl of a stand mixer fitted with the wire whisk. In a saucepan, boil the mineral water and granulated sugar to 244°F (118°C). As soon as the syrup reaches 239°F (115°C), begin beating the egg whites on high speed.

When the syrup reaches 244°F (118°C), reduce the mixer speed to medium–high and pour the syrup in a steady stream down the inside edge of the bowl into the beaten egg whites. Beat the meringue until it cools to 122°F (50°C). Fold it with a silicone spatula into the confectioners' sugar–almond mixture until the mixture loses volume. Transfer the batter to a pastry bag fitted with a plain #11, ¹⁄₂-inch (11-mm to 12-mm) pastry tip.

Line baking sheets with parchment paper. Pipe disks about 1¹⁄₂ inches (3.5 cm) in diameter and ³⁄₄ inch (2 cm) apart on the lined baking sheets. Rap the baking sheets on a work surface covered with a clean kitchen towel to gently smooth out the disks. Set aside for at least 30 minutes at room temperature to allow a skin to form.

Preheat a convection oven to 350°F (180°C). Place the baking sheets in the oven. Bake for 12 minutes, quickly opening and closing the oven door twice during baking to release moisture. Remove the shells from the oven and slide them still on the parchment paper onto a work surface.

PREPARE THE SMOKED-SALT BUTTER GANACHE. Chop the chocolate using a serrated knife then place it in a bowl.

In a saucepan, bring the cream to a boil. Pour the hot cream in thirds into the chocolate, stirring after each addition starting in the center then in increasingly wider concentric circles toward the sides of the bowl. Stir in the smoked sea salt, if using. When the ganache cools to 122°F (50°C), stir in the butter a little at a time. Using an immersion blender, blend the ganache until smooth.

Pour the ganache into a baking dish. Cover it by gently pressing plastic wrap onto its surface. Refrigerate for 2 hours, just until the ganache has developed a creamy consistency. Transfer the ganache to a pastry bag fitted with a plain #11, ¹⁄₂-inch (11-mm to 12-mm) pastry tip.

Turn the chocolate macaron shells over with the flat sides up onto a new piece of parchment paper. Fill them with the ganache. Close them with the plain macaron shells, pressing down lightly.

Refrigerate the macarons for 24 hours. Remove them from the refrigerator 2 hours before eating them.

FOR THE PLAIN MACARON SHELLS
1½ cups (150 g) confectioners' sugar
1 cup plus 1 tablespoon (150 g) ground almonds
3½ large (110 g) "liquefied" egg whites, divided (see "Macaron Shells Step-by-Step" in the Kitchen Guide)
2 tablespoons plus 1¾ teaspoons (38 g) still mineral water
¾ cup (150 g) superfine granulated sugar

FOR THE SMOKED-SALT BUTTER GANACHE
12 ounces (340 g) Valrhona Manjari 64% cacao dark chocolate
1⅓ cups (300 g) light whipping cream (32%–35% fat)
¼ cup plus 1½ tablespoons (75 g) smoked-salt butter, preferably Bordier, or fine French unsalted butter plus 1 teaspoon fine smoked sea salt, room temperature, cut into small pieces

Macaron Jardin du Maquis

After tasting honey produced by Alain Valentini in Corsica, I wanted to make a chocolate bonbon and a macaron using this particular honey. To highlight its unique and complex flavor derived from the Corsican maquis, I combined it with two chocolates that have little bitterness: Valrhona Jivara milk chocolate and Valrhona Caraïbe dark chocolate.

PREPARE THE TINTED SUGAR. The day before, preheat the oven to 140°F (60°C). Put on disposable gloves. Rub the gold dust into the coarse sugar using your fingertips. Spread the sugar out on a baking sheet and place the baking sheet in the oven for 30 minutes to dry the sugar. Set aside to cool to room temperature.

MAKES ABOUT 72 MACARONS
(OR ABOUT 144 SHELLS)
PREPARATION TIME: **5 MINUTES (5 DAYS IN ADVANCE, SEE "MACARON SHELLS STEP-BY-STEP" IN THE KITCHEN GUIDE) + 1 HOUR 30 MINUTES**
COOKING TIME: **ABOUT 50 MINUTES**
RESTING TIME: **30 MINUTES (TWICE)**
REFRIGERATION TIME: **2 HOURS + 24 HOURS**

○

FOR THE TINTED SUGAR
2½ teaspoons (2.5 g) edible gold dust
1¼ cups (250 g) coarse sugar
Note: *This will make more tinted sugar than is needed for one batch of macarons.*

PREPARE THE CHOCOLATE MACARON SHELLS. Chop the cocoa paste using a serrated knife then melt it to between 113°F (45°C) and 122°F (50°C) set over a bain-marie or in a microwave.

Sift together the confectioners' sugar and almonds.

Combine the food color with half of the "liquefied" egg whites. Pour this into the confectioners' sugar–almond mixture without mixing.

Add the remaining "liquefied" egg whites to the bowl of a stand mixer fitted with the wire whisk. In a saucepan, boil the mineral water and granulated sugar to 244°F (118°C). As soon as the syrup reaches 239°F (115°C), begin beating the egg whites on high speed.

When the syrup reaches 244°F (118°C), reduce the mixer speed to medium-high and pour the syrup in a steady stream down the inside edge of the bowl into the beaten egg whites. Beat the meringue until it cools to 122°F (50°C). Fold about one-third of the meringue into the melted cocoa paste then add this mixture to the confections' sugar–almond mixture along with the rest of the meringue. Fold it with a silicone spatula until the mixture loses volume. Transfer the batter to a pastry bag fitted with a plain #11, ¹/₂-inch (11-mm to 12-mm) pastry tip.

Line baking sheets with parchment paper. Pipe disks about 1¹/₂ inches (3.5 cm) in diameter and ³/₄ inch (2 cm) apart on the lined baking sheets. Rap the baking sheets on a work surface covered with a clean kitchen towel to gently smooth out the disks. Set aside for at least 30 minutes at room temperature to allow a skin to form.

PREPARE THE HONEY MACARON SHELLS. Sift together the confectioners' sugar and almonds.

Combine the food color with half of the "liquefied" egg whites. Pour this into the confectioners' sugar–almond mixture without mixing.

Add the remaining "liquefied" egg whites to the bowl of a stand mixer fitted with the wire whisk. In a saucepan, boil the mineral water and granulated sugar to 244°F (118°C). As soon as the syrup reaches 239°F (115°C), begin beating the egg whites on high speed.

When the syrup reaches 244°F (118°C), reduce the mixer speed to medium-high and pour the syrup in a steady stream down the inside edge of the bowl into the beaten egg whites. Beat the meringue until it cools to 122°F (50°C). Fold it into the confectioners' sugar–almond mixture until the mixture loses volume. Transfer the batter to a pastry bag fitted with a plain #11, ¹/₂-inch (11-mm to 12-mm) pastry tip.

Line baking sheets with parchment paper. Pipe disks about 1¹/₂ inches (3.5 cm) in diameter and ³/₄ inch (2 cm) apart on the lined baking sheets. Rap the baking sheets on a work surface covered with a clean kitchen towel to gently smooth out the disks. Sprinkle the disks with tinted sugar. Set aside for at least 30 minutes at room temperature to allow a skin to form.

Preheat a convection oven to 350°F (180°C). Place the baking sheets in the oven. Bake for 12 minutes, quickly opening and closing the oven door twice during baking to release moisture. Remove the shells from the oven and slide them still on the parchment paper onto a work surface.

PREPARE THE MAQUIS HONEY GANACHE. Chop the dark and milk chocolates using a serrated knife then melt them together to between 113°F (45°C) and 122°F (50°C) set over a bain-marie or in a microwave.

In a saucepan, bring the cream to a boil. In a separate saucepan, heat the honey to between 113°F (45°C) and 122°F (50°C). Pour the hot cream in thirds into the melted chocolate, stirring after each addition starting in the center then in increasingly wider concentric circles toward the sides of the bowl. Stir in the honey. Using an immersion blender, blend the ganache until smooth.

Pour the ganache into a baking dish. Cover it by gently pressing plastic wrap onto its surface. Refrigerate for 2 hours, just until the ganache has developed a creamy consistency. Transfer the ganache to a pastry bag fitted with a plain #11, ¹/₂-inch (11-mm to 12-mm) pastry tip.

Turn the chocolate macaron shells over with the flat sides up onto a new piece of parchment paper. Fill them with the ganache. Close them with the honey macaron shells, pressing down lightly.

Refrigerate the macarons for 24 hours. Remove them from the refrigerator 2 hours before eating them.

FOR THE CHOCOLATE MACARON SHELLS
2⅛ ounces (60 g) Valrhona 100% cocoa paste
1½ cups (150 g) confectioners' sugar
1 cup plus 1 tablespoon (150 g) ground almonds
4 drops / ¹/₁₆ teaspoon (0.25 g) liquid carmine red food color
3½ large (110 g) "liquefied" egg whites, divided (see "Macaron Shells Step-by-Step" in the Kitchen Guide)
3 tablespoons (43 g) still mineral water
¾ cup (150 g) superfine granulated sugar

FOR THE HONEY MACARON SHELLS
1½ cups (150 g) confectioners' sugar
1 cup plus 1 tablespoon (150 g) ground almonds
Scant ½ teaspoon (1.5 g) liquid lemon yellow food color
3½ large (110 g) "liquefied" egg whites, divided (see "Macaron Shells Step-by-Step" in the Kitchen Guide)
2 tablespoons plus 1¾ teaspoons (38 g) still mineral water
¾ cup (150 g) superfine granulated sugar
Tinted Sugar (see above)

FOR THE MAQUIS HONEY GANACHE
11¾ ounces (330 g) Valrhona Caraibe 66% cacao dark chocolate
8¾ ounces (250 g) Valrhona Jivara 40% cacao milk chocolate
1 cup plus 2 teaspoons (240 g) light whipping cream (32%–35% fat)
¼ cup plus 2 tablespoons (120 g) Corsican maquis spring honey, preferably from Alain Valentini, Corsica

Macaron Jardin de Lou

This is a macaron with well-rounded and smooth flavors, filled with the delicious caramelized notes of milk chocolate ganache highlighted by the heat of the candied ginger.

MAKES ABOUT 72 MACARONS
(OR ABOUT 144 SHELLS)
PREPARATION TIME: **5 MINUTES (5 DAYS IN ADVANCE, SEE "MACARON SHELLS STEP-BY-STEP" IN THE KITCHEN GUIDE)** + **10 MINUTES (2 DAYS IN ADVANCE)** + **1 HOUR 30 MINUTES**
COOKING TIME: **ABOUT 50 MINUTES**
RESTING TIME: **30 MINUTES (TWICE)**
REFRIGERATION TIME: **2 HOURS** + **24 HOURS**

FOR THE CANDIED GINGER
1 generous cup (180 g) crystallized ginger pieces

FOR THE GINGER SUGAR
3 tablespoons (20 g) ground ginger, preferably from Thiercelin
1¼ cups (250 g) coarse sugar, preferably Biffar brand

PREPARE THE CANDIED GINGER. Two days in advance, rinse the crystallized ginger pieces for 3 minutes under warm water. Place them on a rack to drain until the next day.

THE DAY BEFORE, PREPARE THE GINGER SUGAR. Preheat the oven to 140°F (60°C). Put on disposable gloves. Rub the ginger into the coarse sugar using your fingertips. Spread the sugar out on a baking sheet. Place the baking sheet in the oven for 30 minutes to dry the sugar. Set aside to cool to room temperature.

PREPARE THE CHOCOLATE MACARON SHELLS. Chop the cocoa paste using a serrated knife then melt it to between 113°F (45°C) and 122°F (50°C) set over a bain-marie or in a microwave.

Sift together the confectioners' sugar and almonds.

Combine the food color with half of the "liquefied" egg whites. Pour this into the confectioners' sugar–almond mixture without mixing.

Add the remaining "liquefied" egg whites to the bowl of a stand mixer fitted with the wire whisk. In a saucepan, boil the mineral water and granulated sugar to 244°F (118°C). As soon as the syrup reaches 239°F (115°C), begin beating the egg whites on high speed.

When the syrup reaches 244°F (118°C), reduce the mixer speed to medium-high and pour the syrup in a steady stream down the inside edge of the bowl into the beaten egg whites. Beat the meringue until it cools to 122°F (50°C). Fold about one-third of the meringue into the melted cocoa paste then add this mixture to the confections' sugar–almond mixture along with the rest of the meringue. Fold it with a silicone spatula until the mixture loses volume. Transfer the batter to a pastry bag fitted with a plain #11, ¹/₂-inch (11-mm to 12-mm) pastry tip.

Line baking sheets with parchment paper. Pipe disks about 1¹/₂ inches (3.5 cm) in diameter and ³/₄ inch (2 cm) apart on the lined baking sheets. Rap the baking sheets on a work surface covered with a clean kitchen towel to gently smooth out the disks. Set aside for at least 30 minutes at room temperature to allow a skin to form.

PREPARE THE PLAIN MACARON SHELLS. Sift together the confectioners' sugar and almonds.

Pour half of the "liquefied" egg whites into the confectioners' sugar–almond mixture without mixing.

Add the remaining "liquefied" egg whites to the bowl of a stand mixer fitted with the wire whisk. In a saucepan, boil the mineral water and granulated sugar to 244°F (118°C). As soon as the syrup reaches 239°F (115°C), begin beating the egg whites on high speed.

When the syrup reaches 244°F (118°C), reduce the mixer speed to medium-high and pour the syrup in a steady stream down the inside edge of the bowl into the beaten egg whites. Beat the meringue until it cools to 122°F (50°C). Fold it with a silicone spatula into the confectioners' sugar–almond mixture until the mixture loses volume. Transfer the batter to a pastry bag fitted with a plain #11, ¹/₂-inch (11-mm to 12-mm) pastry tip.

Line baking sheets with parchment paper. Pipe disks about 1¹/₂ inches (3.5 cm) in diameter and ³/₄ inch (2 cm) apart on the lined baking sheets. Rap the baking sheets on a work surface covered with a clean kitchen towel to gently smooth out the tops of the disks. Sprinkle the disks with the ginger sugar. Set aside for at least 30 minutes at room temperature to allow a skin to form.

Preheat a convection oven to 350°F (180°C). Place the baking sheets in the oven. Bake for 12 minutes, quickly opening and closing the oven door twice during baking to release moisture. Remove the shells from the oven and slide them still on the parchment paper onto a work surface.

PREPARE THE CHOCOLATE GINGER GANACHE. Chop the chocolate using a serrated knife then melt it to between 113°F (45°C) and 122°F (50°C) set over a bain-marie or in a microwave.

Peel the ginger and grate it into the cream. Bring the cream to a boil then pour it in thirds into the melted chocolate, stirring after each addition starting in the center then in increasingly wider concentric circles toward the sides of the bowl. When the ganache cools to 122°F (50°C), stir in the butter. Using an immersion blender, blend the ganache until smooth.

Pour the ganache into a baking dish. Cover it by gently pressing plastic wrap onto its surface. Refrigerate for 2 hours, just until the ganache has developed a creamy consistency. Transfer the ganache to a pastry bag fitted with a plain #11, ½-inch (11-mm to 12-mm) pastry tip.

Turn the chocolate macaron shells over with the flat sides up onto a new piece of parchment paper. Fill them with the ganache. Gently place four or five pieces of the candied ginger in the center. Pipe a dab of the ganache on top of the ginger pieces. Close them with the plain macaron shells, pressing down lightly.

Refrigerate the macarons for 24 hours. Remove them from the refrigerator 2 hours before eating them.

FOR THE CHOCOLATE MACARON SHELLS
2⅛ ounces (60 g) Valrhona 100% cocoa paste
1½ cups (150 g) confectioners' sugar
1 cup plus 1 tablespoon (150 g) ground almonds
4 drops / ¹⁄₁₆ teaspoon (0.25 g) liquid carmine red food color
3½ large (110 g) "liquefied" egg whites, divided (see "Macaron Shells Step-by-Step" in the Kitchen Guide)
3 tablespoons (43 g) still mineral water
¾ cup (150 g) superfine granulated sugar

FOR THE PLAIN MACARON SHELLS
1½ cups (150 g) confectioners' sugar
1 cup plus 1 tablespoon (150 g) ground almonds
3½ large (110 g) "liquefied" egg whites, divided (see "Macaron Shells Step-by-Step" in the Kitchen Guide)
2 tablespoons plus 1¾ teaspoons (38 g) still mineral water
¾ cup (150 g) superfine granulated sugar
Ginger Sugar (see page 223)

FOR THE CHOCOLATE GINGER GANACHE
1 pound (475 g) Valrhona Jivara 40% cacao milk chocolate
1 ounce (30 g) fresh ginger
1 cup minus 1½ teaspoons (225 g) light whipping cream (32%–35% fat)
1 tablespoon (15 g) fine French butter, lightly salted, preferably *beurre de la Viette demi-sel*, room temperature

Macaron Jardin Enchanté

MAKES ABOUT 72 MACARONS
(OR ABOUT 144 SHELLS)

PREPARATION TIME: **5 MINUTES (5 DAYS
IN ADVANCE, SEE "MACARON SHELLS
STEP-BY-STEP" IN THE KITCHEN GUIDE)
+ 2 HOURS**

COOKING TIME: **ABOUT 2 HOURS +
30 MINUTES + 20 MINUTES**

INFUSION TIME: **30 MINUTES**

RESTING TIME: **30 MINUTES (TWICE)**

REFRIGERATION TIME: **12 HOURS +
24 HOURS**

◯

**FOR THE DRIED
RASPBERRIES**
Generous ½ pint (200 g) fresh
raspberries, or ¼ cup plus
1 tablespoon **(40 g)** dried

◖◗

FOR THE TINTED SUGAR
Scant ¾ teaspoon (2.5 g) liquid
strawberry red food color
1¼ cups (250 g) coarse sugar
Note: *This will make more tinted
sugar than is needed for one
batch of macarons.*

*This macaron is the
first in the "Jardins"
macaron collection that
I envisioned in 2011.
I incorporated the
smooth acidity of the
zest and juice from
limes with the spicy
hint of Espelette
pepper. I surrounded
the spiciness of this
cream, whose taste is
warm but not burning,
with a fruity and acidic
raspberry center.*

PREPARE THE DRIED RASPBERRIES. The day before, if using fresh raspberries, preheat the oven to 195°F (90°C). Spread the berries out on a baking sheet and place them in the oven. Let dry for 2 hours, stirring every 30 minutes. Set aside to cool then place them in an airtight container until needed.

PREPARE THE TINTED SUGAR. Preheat the oven to 140°F (60°C). Put on disposable gloves. Rub the food color into the coarse sugar using your finger-tips. Spread the sugar out on a baking sheet. Place the baking sheet in the oven for 30 minutes to dry the sugar. Set aside to cool to room temperature.

FOR THE GREEN MACARON SHELLS
1½ cups (150 g) confectioners' sugar
1 cup plus 1 tablespoon (150 g) ground almonds
¾ teaspoon (3 g) liquid lemon yellow food color
¼ teaspoon (1 g) liquid pistachio green food color
3½ large (110 g) "liquefied" egg whites, divided (see "Macaron Shells Step-by-Step" in the Kitchen Guide)
2 tablespoons plus 1¾ teaspoons (38 g) still mineral water
¾ cup (150 g) superfine granulated sugar

FOR THE PLAIN MACARON SHELLS
1½ cups (150 g) confectioners' sugar
1 cup plus 1 tablespoon (150 g) ground almonds
3½ large (110 g) "liquefied" egg whites, divided (see "Macaron Shells Step-by-Step" in the Kitchen Guide)
2 tablespoons plus 1¾ teaspoons (38 g) still mineral water
¾ cup (150 g) superfine granulated sugar
Tinted Sugar (see page 227)

FOR THE LIME CHILE CREAM
14 ounces (400 g) Valrhona Ivoire 35% white chocolate
1⅓ cups plus 1⅓ tablespoons (320 g) light whipping cream (32%–35% fat)
1 tablespoon plus 1 teaspoon (8 g) freshly grated lime zest (from 2 limes)
⅛ ounce (4 g) fresh Espelette chile
2 tablespoons plus 1½ teaspoons (40 g) freshly squeezed lime juice (from 1 lime)

PREPARE THE GREEN MACARON SHELLS. Sift together the confectioners' sugar and almonds.

Combine the yellow and green food colors with half of the "liquefied" egg whites. Pour this into the confectioners' sugar–almond mixture without mixing.

Add the remaining "liquefied" egg whites to the bowl of a stand mixer fitted with the wire whisk. In a saucepan, boil the mineral water and granulated sugar to 244°F (118°C). As soon as the syrup reaches 239°F (115°C), begin beating the egg whites on high speed.

When the syrup reaches 244°F (118°C), reduce the mixer speed to medium–high and pour the syrup in a steady stream down the inside edge of the bowl into the beaten egg whites. Beat the meringue until it cools to 122°F (50°C). Fold it with a silicone spatula into the confectioners' sugar–almond mixture until the mixture loses volume. Transfer the batter to a pastry bag fitted with a plain #11, ½-inch (11-mm to 12-mm) pastry tip.

Line baking sheets with parchment paper. Pipe disks about 1½ inches (3.5 cm) in diameter and ¾ inch (2 cm) apart on the lined baking sheets. Rap the baking sheets on a work surface covered with a clean kitchen towel to gently smooth out the disks. Set aside for at least 30 minutes at room temperature to allow a skin to form.

PREPARE THE PLAIN MACARON SHELLS. Sift together the confectioners' sugar and almonds.

Pour half of the "liquefied" egg whites into the confectioners' sugar–almond mixture without mixing.

Add the remaining "liquefied" egg whites to the bowl of a stand mixer fitted with the wire whisk. In a saucepan, boil the mineral water and granulated sugar to 244°F (118°C). As soon as the syrup reaches 239°F (115°C), begin beating the egg whites on high speed.

When the syrup reaches 244°F (118°C), reduce the mixer speed to medium–high and pour the syrup in a steady stream down the inside edge of the bowl into the beaten egg whites. Beat the meringue until it cools to 122°F (50°C). Fold it with a silicone spatula into the confectioners' sugar–almond mixture until the mixture loses volume. Transfer the batter to a pastry bag fitted with a plain #11, ½-inch (11-mm to 12-mm) pastry tip.

Line baking sheets with parchment paper. Pipe disks about 1½ inches (3.5 cm) in diameter and ¾ inch (2 cm) apart on the lined baking sheets. Rap the baking sheets on a work surface covered with a clean kitchen towel to gently smooth out the disks. Sprinkle the disks with tinted sugar. Set aside for at least 30 minutes at room temperature to allow a skin to form.

Preheat a convection oven to 350°F (180°C). Place the baking sheets in the oven. Bake for 12 minutes, quickly opening and closing the oven door twice during baking to release moisture. Remove the shells from the oven and slide them still on the parchment paper onto a work surface.

PREPARE THE LIME CHILE CREAM. Chop the white chocolate using a serrated knife then melt it to between 113°F (45°C) and 122°F (50°C) set over a bain-marie or in a microwave.

In a saucepan, bring the cream to a boil. Remove from the heat and add the lime zest and chile. Cover the saucepan and let infuse for 30 minutes.

Heat the cream through again then pour it in thirds into the melted white chocolate, stirring after each addition starting in the center then in increasingly wider concentric circles toward the sides of the bowl. Bring the lime juice to a boil and stir it into the cream. Using an immersion blender, blend the cream until smooth.

Pour the cream into a baking dish. Cover it by gently pressing plastic wrap onto its surface. Refrigerate for 12 hours, just until the cream has developed a creamy consistency. Transfer the cream to a pastry bag fitted with a plain #11, ½-inch (11-mm to 12-mm) pastry tip.

Turn the green macaron shells over with the flat sides up onto a new piece of parchment paper. Fill them with the lime chile cream then gently place a dried raspberry in the center. Pipe a dab of the cream on top of the raspberry. Close them with the plain macaron shells, pressing down lightly.

Refrigerate the macarons for 24 hours. Remove them from the refrigerator 2 hours before eating them.

Macaron Jardin Japonais

My idea with this macaron was to re-create the flavor of the Japanese cherry blossoms that are used in Japan in savory dishes. I made a cream by combining the sour notes of morello cherries with a hint of tonka bean, which has a strong flavor of almond and freshly cut bay. The cream's flavor is awakened with the slight acidity of lemon.

PREPARE THE CHERRY MACARON SHELLS. The day before, sift together the confectioners' sugar and almonds.

Combine the red and black food colors with half of the "liquefied" egg whites. Pour this into the confectioners' sugar–almond mixture without mixing.

Add the remaining "liquefied" egg whites to the bowl of a stand mixer fitted with the wire whisk. In a saucepan, boil the mineral water and granulated sugar to 244°F (118°C). As soon as the syrup reaches 239°F (115°C), begin beating the egg whites on high speed.

When the syrup reaches 244°F (118°C), reduce the mixer speed to medium–high and pour the syrup in a steady stream down the inside edge of the bowl into the beaten egg whites. Beat the meringue until it cools to 122°F (50°C). Fold it with a silicone spatula into the confectioners' sugar–almond mixture until the mixture loses volume. Transfer the batter to a pastry bag fitted with a plain #11, ½-inch (11-mm to 12-mm) pastry tip.

Line baking sheets with parchment paper. Pipe disks about 1½ inches (3.5 cm) in diameter and ¾ inch (2 cm) apart on the lined baking sheets. Rap the baking sheets on a work surface covered with a clean kitchen towel to gently smooth out the disks. Lightly dust the disks with red dust. Set aside for at least 30 minutes at room temperature to allow a skin to form.

MAKES ABOUT 72 MACARONS
(OR ABOUT 144 SHELLS)
PREPARATION TIME: **5 MINUTES (5 DAYS IN ADVANCE, SEE "MACARON SHELLS STEP-BY-STEP" IN THE KITCHEN GUIDE)** + 1 HOUR 30 MINUTES
COOKING TIME: **ABOUT 20 MINUTES**
INFUSION TIME: **20 MINUTES**
RESTING TIME: **30 MINUTES (TWICE)**
REFRIGERATION TIME: **4 HOURS + 24 HOURS**

FOR THE CHERRY MACARON SHELLS
1½ cups (150 g) confectioners' sugar
1 cup plus 1 tablespoon (150 g) ground almonds
½ teaspoon (2 g) liquid carmine red food color
1 drop liquid charcoal black food color
3½ large (110 g) "liquefied" egg whites, divided (see "Macaron Shells Step-by-Step" in the Kitchen Guide)
2 tablespoons plus 1¾ teaspoons (38 g) still mineral water
¾ cup (150 g) superfine granulated sugar
Edible glittering (or "pearl") red dust, for sprinkling

PREPARE THE PLAIN MACARON SHELLS. Sift together the confectioners' sugar and almonds.

Pour half of the "liquefied" egg whites into the confectioners' sugar–almond mixture without mixing.

Add the remaining "liquefied" egg whites to the bowl of a stand mixer fitted with the wire whisk. In a saucepan, boil the mineral water and granulated sugar to 244°F (118°C). As soon as the syrup reaches 239°F (115°C), begin beating the egg whites on high speed.

When the syrup reaches 244°F (118°C), reduce the mixer speed to medium–high and pour the syrup in a steady stream down the inside edge of the bowl into the beaten egg whites. Beat the meringue until it cools to 122°F (50°C). Fold it with a silicone spatula into the confectioners' sugar–almond mixture until the mixture loses volume. Transfer the batter to a pastry bag fitted with a plain #11, ½-inch (11-mm to 12-mm) pastry tip.

Line baking sheets with parchment paper. Pipe disks about 1½ inches (3.5 cm) in diameter and ¾ inch (2 cm) apart on the lined baking sheets. Rap the baking sheets on a work surface covered with a clean kitchen towel to gently smooth out the disks. Lightly dust the disks with the red dust. Set aside for at least 30 minutes at room temperature to allow a skin to form.

Preheat a convection oven to 350°F (180°C). Place the baking sheets in the oven. Bake for 12 minutes, quickly opening and closing the oven door twice during baking to release moisture. Remove the shells from the oven and slide them still on the parchment paper onto a work surface.

PREPARE THE MORELLO CHERRY CREAM. Chop the white chocolate and the cocoa butter using a serrated knife then melt them in separate bowls to between 113°F (45°C) and 122°F (50°C) set over a bain–marie or in a microwave then stir them together to combine.

In a saucepan, bring the cream, lemon zest, and tonka bean to a boil. Remove from the heat then cover the saucepan and let infuse for 20 minutes.

Strain the cream then heat it through again. Pour it in thirds into the melted white chocolate–cocoa butter mixture, stirring after each addition starting in the center then in increasingly wider concentric circles toward the sides of the bowl. Heat the cherry puree and lemon juice to about 140°F (60°C). Stir this mixture into the chocolate. Using an immersion blender, blend until smooth.

Pour the cream into a baking dish. Cover it by gently pressing plastic wrap onto its surface. Refrigerate for 4 hours, just until the cream has developed a creamy consistency. Transfer the cream to a pastry bag fitted with a plain #11, ½-inch (11-mm to 12-mm) pastry tip.

Turn the cherry macaron shells over with the flat sides up onto a new piece of parchment paper. Fill them with the morello cherry cream. Close them with the plain macaron shells, pressing down lightly.

Refrigerate the macarons for 24 hours. Remove them from the refrigerator 2 hours before eating them.

FOR THE PLAIN MACARON SHELLS
1½ cups (150 g) confectioners' sugar
1 cup plus 1 tablespoon (150 g) ground almonds
3½ large (110 g) "liquefied" egg whites, divided (see "Macaron Shells Step-by-Step" in the Kitchen Guide)
2 tablespoons plus 1¾ teaspoons (38 g) still mineral water
¾ cup (150 g) superfine granulated sugar
Edible glittering (or "pearl") red dust, for sprinkling

FOR THE MORELLO CHERRY CREAM
14½ ounces (415 g) Valrhona Ivoire 35% white chocolate
1¼ ounces (35 g) cocoa butter, preferably Valrhona
½ cup plus 1 tablespoon (135 g) light whipping cream (32%–35% fat)
¾ teaspoon (1.5 g) freshly grated lemon zest (from ½ lemon)
2 teaspoons (1 g) grated tonka bean, preferably from Thiercelin
2½ cups (400 g) fresh morello cherries (to make 1 cup plus 2 tablespoons/250 g puree), or use Boiron brand frozen morello cherry puree
3 tablespoons plus 1 teaspoon (50 g) freshly squeezed lemon juice (from 1 lemon)

Macaron Jardin Merveilleux

After my discussions with Jean-Michel Duriez, the perfumer of Rochas, I combined cucumber water with a delicate mandarin olive oil. The taste of this macaron is a reinterpretation of the seascape aromas that come from the collection of the Rochas perfumery.

MAKES ABOUT 72 MACARONS
(OR ABOUT 144 SHELLS)

PREPARATION TIME: **5 MINUTES (5 DAYS IN ADVANCE, SEE "MACARON SHELLS STEP-BY-STEP" IN THE KITCHEN GUIDE) + 1 HOUR 30 MINUTES**

COOKING TIME: **ABOUT 45 MINUTES**

RESTING TIME: **30 MINUTES (TWICE)**

REFRIGERATION TIME: **4 HOURS + 24 HOURS**

FOR THE GREEN MACARON SHELLS

1½ cups (150 g) confectioners' sugar
1 cup plus 1 tablespoon (150 g) ground almonds
8 drops / ⅛ teaspoon (0.5 g) liquid lemon yellow food color
6 drops / scant ⅛ teaspoon (0.35 g) liquid pistachio green food color
3½ large (110 g) "liquefied" egg whites, divided (see "Macaron Shells Step-by-Step" in the Kitchen Guide)
3 tablespoons (43 g) still mineral water
¾ cup (150 g) superfine granulated sugar

PREPARE THE GREEN MACARON SHELLS. The day before, sift together the confectioners' sugar and almonds.

Combine the yellow and green food colors with half of the "liquefied" egg whites. Pour this into the confectioners' sugar–almond mixture without mixing.

Add the remaining "liquefied" egg whites to the bowl of a stand mixer fitted with the wire whisk. In a saucepan, boil the mineral water and granulated sugar to 244°F (118°C). As soon as the syrup reaches 239°F (115°C), begin beating the egg whites on high speed.

When the syrup reaches 244°F (118°C), reduce the mixer speed to medium–high and pour the syrup in a steady stream down the inside edge of the bowl into the beaten egg whites. Beat the meringue until it cools to 122°F (50°C). Fold it with a silicone spatula into the confectioners' sugar–almond mixture until the mixture loses volume. Transfer the batter to a pastry bag fitted with a plain #11, ½-inch (11-mm to 12-mm) pastry tip.

Line baking sheets with parchment paper. Pipe disks about 1½ inches (3.5 cm) in diameter and ¾ inch (2 cm) apart on the lined baking sheets. Rap the baking sheets on a work surface covered with a clean kitchen towel to gently smooth out the disks. Set aside for at least 30 minutes at room temperature to allow a skin to form.

I practice my craft by being a gourmand.

FOR THE MANDARIN MACARON SHELLS

1½ cups (150 g) confectioners' sugar

1 cup plus 1 tablespoon (150 g) ground almonds

Scant 1 teaspoon (3.5 g) liquid lemon yellow food color

¼ teaspoon (1 g) liquid strawberry red food color

3½ large (110 g) "liquefied" egg whites, divided (see "Macaron Shells Step-by-Step" in the Kitchen Guide)

2 tablespoons plus 1¾ teaspoons (38 g) still mineral water

¾ cup (150 g) superfine granulated sugar

FOR THE CUCUMBER WATER CREAM

10½ ounces (300 g) cucumbers (to make ⅓ cup plus 1¾ teaspoons/ 85 g cucumber water), peeled and seeded

14 ounces (400 g) Valrhona Ivoire 35% white chocolate

⅓ cup plus 1¾ teaspoons (85 g) light whipping cream (32%–35% fat)

1¼ cups (250 g) mandarin olive oil, preferably from Première Pression Provence

PREPARE THE MANDARIN MACARON SHELLS. Sift together the confectioners' sugar and almonds.

Combine the yellow and red food colors with half of the "liquefied" egg whites. Pour this into the confectioners' sugar–almond mixture without mixing.

Add the remaining "liquefied" egg whites to the bowl of a stand mixer fitted with the wire whisk. In a saucepan, boil the mineral water and granulated sugar to 244°F (118°C). As soon as the syrup reaches 239°F (115°C), begin beating the egg whites on high speed.

When the syrup reaches 244°F (118°C), reduce the mixer speed to medium-high and pour the syrup in a steady stream down the inside edge of the bowl into the beaten egg whites. Beat the meringue until it cools to 122°F (50°C). Fold it with a silicone spatula into the confectioners' sugar–almond mixture until the mixture loses volume. Transfer the batter to a pastry bag fitted with a plain #11, ½-inch (11-mm to 12-mm) pastry tip.

Line baking sheets with parchment paper. Pipe disks about 1½ inches (3.5 cm) in diameter and ¾ inch (2 cm) apart on the lined baking sheets. Rap the baking sheets on a work surface covered with a clean kitchen towel to gently smooth out the disks. Set aside for at least 30 minutes at room temperature to allow a skin to form.

Preheat a convection oven to 350°F (180°C). Place the baking sheets in the oven. Bake for 12 minutes, quickly opening and closing the oven door twice during baking to release moisture. Remove the shells from the oven and slide them still on the parchment paper onto a work surface.

PREPARE THE CUCUMBER WATER CREAM. Process the cucumber flesh through a juicer to extract about ⅓ cup (85 g) of liquid.

Chop the white chocolate using a serrated knife then melt it to between 113°F (45°C) and 122°F (50°C) set over a bain-marie or in a microwave.

In a saucepan, bring the cream and cucumber water to a boil. Pour the hot mixture in thirds into the melted chocolate, stirring after each addition starting in the center then in increasingly wider concentric circles toward the sides of the bowl. As soon as the cream falls below 122°F (50°C), stir in the mandarin olive oil in thirds. Using an immersion blender, blend the cream until smooth.

Pour the cream into a baking dish. Cover it by gently pressing plastic wrap onto its surface. Refrigerate for 4 hours, just until the cream has developed a creamy consistency. Transfer the cream to a pastry bag fitted with a plain #11, ½-inch (11-mm to 12-mm) pastry tip.

Turn the cucumber macaron shells over with the flat sides up onto a new piece of parchment paper. Fill them with the cucumber water cream. Close them with the mandarin macaron shells, pressing down lightly.

Refrigerate the macarons for 24 hours. Remove them from the refrigerator 2 hours before eating them.

Macaron Jardin Pamplemousse

This is the second macaron I created in the "Jardins" collection. I wanted to create a subtle grapefruit flavor seasoned with clove and nutmeg. I was inspired by a familiar and favorite perfume by Hermès that is made from concentrated grapefruit.

PREPARE THE CANDIED GRAPEFRUIT. Two days in advance, wash and dry the grapefruit. Cut off both rounded ends to create a flat top and bottom. Set the grapefruit on a flat end and, using a knife, slice down the grapefruit all the way around from top to bottom to remove the rind in large strips. Leave about ³/₈ inch (1 cm) of the pulp attached to each strip.

Place the strips of rind in a saucepan of boiling water. When the water reaches a boil again, cook the strips for 2 minutes then drain. Rinse them under cold water. Repeat these steps twice, boiling and draining the strips, then set the strips aside to dry.

Place the peppercorns in a saucepan along with the mineral water, sugar, lemon juice, and star anise. Scrape the seeds out of the vanilla bean using a knife. Add the seeds and the vanilla bean pod to the pan. Bring to a boil over low heat. Add the strips of grapefruit rind. Cover three-quarters of the top of the saucepan. Simmer very gently for 1 hour 30 minutes.

Transfer to a bowl and let cool. Cover and refrigerate until the next day.

The day before, drain the strips for 1 hour in a sieve set over a bowl. Cut the strips into ¹/₈-inch (3-mm) cubes.

MAKES ABOUT 72 MACARONS (OR ABOUT 144 SHELLS)

PREPARATION TIME: 5 MINUTES (5 DAYS IN ADVANCE, SEE "MACARON SHELLS STEP-BY-STEP" IN THE KITCHEN GUIDE) + 40 MINUTES (2 DAYS IN ADVANCE) + 1 HOUR 30 MINUTES

COOKING TIME: 1 HOUR 35 MINUTES (2 DAYS IN ADVANCE) + ABOUT 30 MINUTES

MACERATION TIME: 24 HOURS (2 DAYS IN ADVANCE)

DRAINING TIME: 1 HOUR

INFUSION TIME: 15 MINUTES

RESTING TIME: 30 MINUTES (TWICE)

REFRIGERATION TIME: 6 HOURS + 24 HOURS (TWICE)

FOR THE CANDIED GRAPEFRUIT
2 unwaxed grapefruits
10 crushed Sarawak black peppercorns
4¼ cups (1 L) still mineral water
2½ cups (500 g) superfine granulated sugar
¼ cup (62 g) freshly squeezed lemon juice (from 1 lemon)
1 star anise
1 vanilla bean, halved lengthwise

FOR THE ORANGE MACARON SHELLS

1½ cups (150 g) confectioners' sugar

1 cup plus 1 tablespoon (150 g) ground almonds

Scant 1 teaspoon (3.5 g) liquid lemon yellow food color

¼ teaspoon (1 g) liquid strawberry red food color

3½ large (110 g) "liquefied" egg whites, divided (see "Macaron Shells Step-by-Step" in the Kitchen Guide)

2 tablespoons plus 1¾ teaspoons (38 g) still mineral water

¾ cup (150 g) superfine granulated sugar

FOR THE GRAPEFRUIT MACARON SHELLS

1½ cups (150 g) confectioners' sugar

1 cup plus 1 tablespoon (150 g) ground almonds

Scant ¾ teaspoon (2.5 g) liquid lemon yellow food color

Scant ½ teaspoon (1.5 g) liquid strawberry red food color

Scant ½ teaspoon (1.5 g) liquid carmine red food color

3½ large (110 g) "liquefied" egg whites, divided (see "Macaron Shells Step-by-Step" in the Kitchen Guide)

2 tablespoons plus 1¾ teaspoons (38 g) still mineral water

¾ cup (150 g) superfine granulated sugar

FOR THE GRAPEFRUIT CREAM

1 pound plus 1 ounce (480 g) Valrhona Ivoire 35% white chocolate

2½ teaspoons (5 g) freshly grated grapefruit zest (from ½ grapefruit)

Scant 1 cup (235 g) freshly squeezed grapefruit juice

2 tablespoons (35 g) freshly squeezed lemon juice (from 1 lemon)

½ teaspoon (1.2 g) ground cloves, preferably from Thiercelin

⅛ teaspoon (0.3 g) freshly grated nutmeg, preferably from Thiercelin

 PREPARE THE ORANGE MACARON SHELLS. Sift together the confectioners' sugar and almonds.

Combine the yellow and red food colors with half of the "liquefied" egg whites. Pour this into the confectioners' sugar–almond mixture without mixing.

Add the remaining "liquefied" egg whites to the bowl of a stand mixer fitted with the wire whisk. In a saucepan, boil the mineral water and granulated sugar to 244°F (118°C). As soon as the syrup reaches 239°F (115°C), begin beating the egg whites on high speed.

When the syrup reaches 244°F (118°C), reduce the mixer speed to medium–high and pour the syrup in a steady stream down the inside edge of the bowl into the beaten egg whites. Beat the meringue until it cools to 122°F (50°C). Fold it with a silicone spatula into the confectioners' sugar–almond mixture until the mixture loses volume. Transfer the batter to a pastry bag fitted with a plain #11, ½-inch (11-mm to 12-mm) pastry tip.

Line baking sheets with parchment paper. Pipe disks about 1½ inches (3.5 cm) in diameter and ¾ inch (2 cm) apart on the lined baking sheets. Rap the baking sheets on a work surface covered with a clean kitchen towel to gently smooth out the disks. Set aside for at least 30 minutes at room temperature to allow a skin to form.

PREPARE THE GRAPEFRUIT MACARON SHELLS.
Sift together the confectioners' sugar and almonds.

Combine the yellow and both red food colors with half of the "liquefied" egg whites. Pour this into the confectioners' sugar–almond mixture without mixing.

Add the remaining "liquefied" egg whites to the bowl of a stand mixer fitted with the wire whisk. In a saucepan, boil the mineral water and granulated sugar to 244°F (118°C). As soon as the syrup reaches 239°F (115°C), begin beating the egg whites on high speed.

When the syrup reaches 244°F (118°C), reduce the mixer speed to medium-high and pour the syrup in a steady stream down the inside edge of the bowl into the beaten egg whites. Beat the meringue until it cools to 122°F (50°C). Fold it with a silicone spatula into the confectioners' sugar–almond mixture until the mixture loses volume. Transfer the batter to a pastry bag fitted with a plain #11, ½-inch (11-mm to 12-mm) pastry tip.

Line baking sheets with parchment paper. Pipe disks about 1½ inches (3.5 cm) in diameter and ¾ inch (2 cm) apart on the lined baking sheets. Rap the baking sheets on a work surface covered with a clean kitchen towel to gently smooth out the disks. Set aside for at least 30 minutes at room temperature to allow a skin to form.

Preheat a convection oven to 350°F (180°C). Place the baking sheets in the oven. Bake for 12 minutes, quickly opening and closing the oven door twice during baking to release moisture. Remove the shells from the oven and slide them still on the parchment paper onto a work surface.

PREPARE THE GRAPEFRUIT CREAM. Chop the white chocolate using a serrated knife then melt it to between 113°F (45°C) and 122°F (50°C) set over a bain-marie or in a microwave.

Wash and dry the grapefruit then zest it using a microplane grater and measure the quantity of zest needed. Heat the grapefruit juice, lemon juice, grapefruit zest, cloves, and nutmeg to 140°F (60°C). Remove from the heat then cover and let infuse for 15 minutes.

Pour the hot mixture in thirds into the melted white chocolate, stirring after each addition starting in the center then in increasingly wider concentric circles toward the sides of the bowl. Using an immersion blender, blend the cream until smooth.

Pour the cream into a baking dish. Cover it by gently pressing plastic wrap onto its surface. Refrigerate for 6 hours, just until the cream has developed a creamy consistency. Transfer the cream to a pastry bag fitted with a plain #11, ½-inch (11-mm to 12-mm) pastry tip.

Turn the orange macaron shells over with the flat sides up onto a new piece of parchment paper. Fill them with the grapefruit cream. Gently place three candied grapefruit cubes in the center. Pipe a dab of the cream on top of the cubes. Close them with the grapefruit macaron shells, pressing down lightly.

Refrigerate the macarons for 24 hours. Remove them from the refrigerator 2 hours before eating them.

Macaron Jardin Potager

This macaron is composed in the way that a bartender creates a cocktail. A fragrant mixture of flavors from the garden—arugula, mint, green apple, and cucumber that I season with clear rum, tequila, and lime.

PREPARE THE TINTED COOKIE CRUMBLE. Two days in advance, place the cookie crumbs in a bowl. Sprinkle with the green dust then delicately mix them together. Spread the crumbs out onto a baking sheet to dry at room temperature until the next day.

PREPARE THE VEGETABLE GARDEN JUICE. Remove any hard membrane from the apple cores. Process the apples and cucumbers separately through a juicer and measure the quantity of juice needed from each. Immediately in a blender or food processor, process the apple juice with the lime zest, mint, and arugula. Add the cucumber juice, lime juice, rum, and tequila then process again. Add the mixture to a saucepan and bring to a boil.

PREPARE THE VEGETABLE GARDEN CREAM. Chop the cocoa butter using a serrated knife then melt it set over a bain-marie or in a microwave. Add the white chocolate. Pour the hot vegetable juice in thirds into the cocoa butter–white chocolate mixture, stirring after each addition starting in the center then in increasingly wider concentric circles toward the sides of the bowl. Add the yogurt powder then blend with an immersion blender until smooth.

Pour the cream into a baking dish. Cover it by gently pressing plastic wrap onto its surface. Refrigerate until the next day, then transfer the cream to a pastry bag fitted with a plain #11, ½-inch (11-mm to 12-mm) pastry tip.

MAKES ABOUT 72 MACARONS (OR ABOUT 144 SHELLS)
PREPARATION TIME: 5 MINUTES (5 DAYS IN ADVANCE, SEE "MACARON SHELLS STEP-BY-STEP" IN THE KITCHEN GUIDE) + 40 MINUTES (2 DAYS IN ADVANCE) + 1 HOUR 30 MINUTES
COOKING TIME: 18 TO 20 MINUTES
RESTING TIME: 30 MINUTES (TWICE)
REFRIGERATION TIME: 24 HOURS (TWICE)

FOR THE TINTED COOKIE CRUMBLE
3½ ounces (100 g) plain Gavottes crêpe cookies, crumbled
1 tablespoon plus 2 teaspoons (5 g) edible glittering (or "pearl") green dust

FOR THE VEGETABLE GARDEN JUICE
15¾ ounces (450 g) Granny Smith apples (to make 1¼ cups/300 g juice), peeled, seeded, and halved
10½ ounces (300 g) cucumbers (to make ¾ cup/200 g juice), peeled, seeded, and halved
½ teaspoon (1 g) freshly grated lime zest (from ½ lime)
2½ tablespoons (6 g) mint leaves
1½ tablespoons (4 g) arugula leaves
¼ cup plus 1 tablespoon (80 g) freshly squeezed lime juice (from 2 limes)
Scant 1 tablespoon (10 g) clear rum, preferably Clément
2 tablespoons (30 g) tequila

FOR THE VEGETABLE GARDEN CREAM
1 ounce (25 g) cocoa butter, preferably Valrhona
15¾ ounces (450 g) Valrhona Ivoire 35% white chocolate, chopped
Scant 2 cups (430 g) Vegetable Garden Juice (see above)
1 ounce (25 g) Sosa powdered Mediterranean acid yogurt

PREPARE THE WHITE MACARON SHELLS. The day before, sift together the confectioners' sugar and almonds.

Dilute the titanium dioxide powder in the warm water then stir it into half of the "liquefied" egg whites. Pour this into the confectioners' sugar–almond mixture without mixing.

Add the remaining "liquefied" egg whites to the bowl of a stand mixer fitted with the wire whisk. In a saucepan, boil the mineral water and granulated sugar to 244°F (118°C). As soon as the syrup reaches 239°F (115°C), begin beating the egg whites on high speed.

When the syrup reaches 244°F (118°C), reduce the mixer speed to medium–high and pour the syrup in a steady stream down the inside edge of the bowl into the beaten egg whites. Beat the meringue until it cools to 122°F (50°C). Fold it with a silicone spatula into the confectioners' sugar–almond mixture until the mixture loses volume. Transfer the batter to a pastry bag fitted with a plain #11, ¹/₂-inch (11-mm to 12-mm) pastry tip.

Line baking sheets with parchment paper. Pipe disks about 1¹/₂ inches (3.5 cm) in diameter and ³/₄ inch (2 cm) apart on the lined baking sheets. Rap the baking sheets on a work surface covered with a clean kitchen towel to gently smooth out the tops of the disks. Sprinkle the disks with the tinted cookie crumbs. Set aside for at least 30 minutes at room temperature to allow a skin to form.

PREPARE THE GREEN MACARON SHELLS. Sift together the confectioners' sugar and almonds.

Combine the food color with half of the "liquefied" egg whites. Pour this into the confectioners' sugar–almond mixture without mixing.

Add the remaining "liquefied" egg whites to the bowl of a stand mixer fitted with the wire whisk. In a saucepan, boil the mineral water and granulated sugar to 244°F (118°C). As soon as the syrup reaches 239°F (115°C), begin beating the egg whites on high speed.

When the syrup reaches 244°F (118°C), reduce the mixer speed to medium–high and pour the syrup in a steady stream down the inside edge of the bowl into the beaten egg whites. Beat the meringue until it cools to 122°F (50°C). Fold it with a silicone spatula into the confectioners' sugar–almond mixture until the mixture loses volume. Transfer the batter to a pastry bag fitted with a plain #11, ¹/₂-inch (11-mm to 12-mm) pastry tip.

Line baking sheets with parchment paper. Pipe disks about 1¹/₂ inches (3.5 cm) in diameter and ³/₄ inch (2 cm) apart on the lined baking sheets. Rap the baking sheets on a work surface covered with a clean kitchen towel to gently smooth out the tops of the disks. Set aside for at least 30 minutes at room temperature to allow a skin to form.

Preheat a convection oven to 350°F (180°C). Place the baking sheets in the oven. Bake for 12 minutes, quickly opening and closing the oven door twice during baking to release moisture. Remove the shells from the oven and slide them still on the parchment paper onto a work surface.

Turn the green macaron shells over with the flat sides up onto a new piece of parchment paper. Fill them with the vegetable garden cream. Close them with the white macaron shells, pressing down lightly.

Refrigerate the macarons for 24 hours. Remove them from the refrigerator 2 hours before eating them.

FOR THE WHITE MACARON SHELLS
1½ cups (150 g) confectioners' sugar
1 cup plus 1 tablespoon (150 g) ground almonds
1⅓ teaspoons (8 g) titanium dioxide powder
1 teaspoon (4 g) warm water
3½ large (110 g) "liquefied" egg whites, divided (see "Macaron Shells Step-by-Step" in the Kitchen Guide)
2 tablespoons plus 1¾ teaspoons (38 g) still mineral water
¾ cup (150 g) superfine granulated sugar
Tinted Cookie Crumble (see page 242)

FOR THE GREEN MACARON SHELLS
1½ cups (150 g) confectioners' sugar
1 cup plus 1 tablespoon (150 g) ground almonds
½ teaspoon (2 g) liquid pistachio green food color
3½ large (110 g) "liquefied" egg whites, divided (see "Macaron Shells Step-by-Step" in the Kitchen Guide)
2 tablespoons plus 1¾ teaspoons (38 g) still mineral water
¾ cup (150 g) superfine granulated sugar

Learn, understand, compare. I always felt a constant need to sharpen my knowledge through unique sensory experiences. You must master the subtleties of all of the fundamentals of your education to be able to one day, hopefully, break free of them.

Macaron
Jardin Secret

The perfumer Jean-Michel Duriez introduced me to the aroma of carnations, with notes of rose and spices. For this macaron, I combined rose and vanilla with clove to create a single and harmonious flavor.

MAKES ABOUT 72 MACARONS
(OR ABOUT 144 SHELLS)

PREPARATION TIME: **5 MINUTES (5 DAYS IN ADVANCE, SEE "MACARON SHELLS STEP-BY-STEP" IN THE KITCHEN GUIDE)** + **1 HOUR 50 MINUTES**

COOKING TIME: **ABOUT 20 MINUTES**

INFUSION TIME: **30 MINUTES**

RESTING TIME: **30 MINUTES (TWICE)**

REFRIGERATION TIME: **24 HOURS**

FOR THE ROSE MACARON SHELLS
1½ cups (150 g) confectioners' sugar
1 cup plus 1 tablespoon (150 g) ground almonds
Scant ½ teaspoon (1.5 g) liquid carmine red food color
3½ large (110 g) "liquefied" egg whites, divided (see "Macaron Shells Step-by-Step" in the Kitchen Guide)
2 tablespoons plus 1¾ teaspoons (38 g) still mineral water
¾ cup (150 g) superfine granulated sugar

PREPARE THE ROSE MACARON SHELLS. The day before, sift together the confectioners' sugar and almonds.

Combine the food color with half of the "liquefied" egg whites. Pour this into the confectioners' sugar–almond mixture without mixing.

Add the remaining "liquefied" egg whites to the bowl of a stand mixer fitted with the wire whisk. In a saucepan, boil the mineral water and granulated sugar to 244°F (118°C). As soon as the syrup reaches 239°F (115°C), begin beating the egg whites on high speed.

When the syrup reaches 244°F (118°C), reduce the mixer speed to medium–high and pour the syrup in a steady stream down the inside edge of the bowl into the beaten egg whites. Beat the meringue until it cools to 122°F (50°C). Fold it with a silicone spatula into the confectioners' sugar–almond mixture until the mixture loses volume. Transfer the batter to a pastry bag fitted with a plain #11, ½-inch (11-mm to 12-mm) pastry tip.

Line baking sheets with parchment paper. Pipe disks about 1½ inches (3.5 cm) in diameter and ¾ inch (2 cm) apart on the lined baking sheets. Rap the baking sheets on a work surface covered with a clean kitchen towel to gently smooth out the disks. Set aside for at least 30 minutes at room temperature to allow a skin to form.

PREPARE THE VANILLA MACARON SHELLS. Sift together the confectioners' sugar, almonds, and vanilla powder.

Pour half of the "liquefied" egg whites into the confectioners' sugar–almond–vanilla mixture without mixing.

Add the remaining "liquefied" egg whites to the bowl of a stand mixer fitted with the wire whisk. In a saucepan, boil the mineral water and granulated sugar to 244°F (118°C). As soon as the syrup reaches 239°F (115°C), begin beating the egg whites on high speed.

When the syrup reaches 244°F (118°C), reduce the mixer speed to medium-high and pour the syrup in a steady stream down the inside edge of the bowl into the beaten egg whites. Beat the meringue until it cools to 122°F (50°C). Fold it with a silicone spatula into the confectioners' sugar–almond mixture until the mixture loses volume. Transfer the batter to a pastry bag fitted with a plain #11, ½-inch (11-mm to 12-mm) pastry tip.

Line baking sheets with parchment paper. Pipe disks about 1½ inches (3.5 cm) in diameter and ¾ inch (2 cm) apart on the lined baking sheets. Rap the baking sheets on a work surface covered with a clean kitchen towel to gently smooth out the disks. Set aside for at least 30 minutes at room temperature to allow a skin to form.

Preheat a convection oven to 350°F (180°C). Place the baking sheets in the oven. Bake for 12 minutes, quickly opening and closing the oven door twice during baking to release moisture. Remove the shells from the oven and slide them still on the parchment paper onto a work surface.

PREPARE THE ITALIAN MERINGUE. Add the egg whites to the bowl of a stand mixer fitted with the wire whisk. In a saucepan, boil the mineral water and all but 1¼ teaspoons (5 g) of the granulated sugar. When the syrup starts to boil, wipe down the inside of the saucepan with a dampened pastry brush. As soon as the syrup reaches 239°F (115°C), begin beating the egg whites on high speed with the rest of the granulated sugar until the peaks are almost firm and droop slightly in the shape of a "bird's beak" when the whisk is lifted. When the syrup reaches 250°F (121°C), reduce the mixer speed to medium and slowly pour the syrup in a steady stream into the beaten egg whites continuing to beat until the meringue has cooled.

PREPARE THE CRÈME ANGLAISE. Add the milk and cloves to a saucepan. Scrape the seeds out of the vanilla bean using a knife. Add the seeds and the vanilla bean pod to the pan. Bring to a boil. Remove from the heat then cover the saucepan and let infuse for 30 minutes.

Strain the infused milk. In a separate saucepan, whisk together the egg yolks and granulated sugar until lightened. Slowly add the hot milk to the yolk-sugar mixture while whisking vigorously. Place the saucepan over low heat and cook to 185°F (85°C) while stirring continuously—rich in eggs, this cream has a tendency to stick to the bottom of the saucepan. Strain the cooked cream then transfer it to a stand mixer fitted with the wire whisk. Beat on medium speed until cooled.

PREPARE THE ROSE BUTTERCREAM. In a stand mixer, beat the butter on high speed for 5 minutes. Add the cooled crème anglaise, rose extract, and rose syrup. Beat again to combine, then transfer to a bowl. Using a silicone spatula, fold in the Italian meringue a little at a time. Transfer the mixture to a pastry bag fitted with a plain #11, ½-inch (11-mm to 12-mm) pastry tip.

Turn the rose macaron shells over with the flat sides up onto a new piece of parchment paper. Fill them with the rose buttercream. Close them with the vanilla macaron shells, pressing down lightly.

Refrigerate the macarons for 24 hours. Remove them from the refrigerator 2 hours before eating them.

FOR THE VANILLA MACARON SHELLS
1½ cups (150 g) confectioners' sugar
1 cup plus 1 tablespoon (150 g) ground almonds
Scant 1 teaspoon (1.5 g) vanilla powder
3½ large (110 g) "liquefied" egg whites, divided (see "Macaron Shells Step-by-Step" in the Kitchen Guide)
2 tablespoons plus 1¾ teaspoons (38 g) still mineral water
¾ cup (150 g) superfine granulated sugar

FOR THE ITALIAN MERINGUE
2 large (65 g) egg whites
2 tablespoons plus 1 teaspoon (35 g) still mineral water
⅔ cup (130 g) superfine granulated sugar, divided

FOR THE CRÈME ANGLAISE
⅓ cup plus 2 teaspoons (90 g) fresh whole milk
1 teaspoon (2 g) ground cloves
4 Mexican vanilla beans, halved lengthwise
3½ large (70 g) egg yolks
3 tablespoons plus ½ teaspoon (40 g) superfine granulated sugar

FOR THE ROSE BUTTERCREAM
2 cups (450 g) fine French unsalted butter, preferably *beurre de la Viette*, room temperature
1 recipe Crème Anglaise (see above)
1 teaspoon (4.4 g) rose extract
1 tablespoon plus 2 teaspoons (30 g) rose syrup
1½ cups (175 g) Italian Meringue (see above)

Macaron Jardin sur la Baie d'Along

It was by request of Hélène Darroze and Caroline Rostang that I created this macaron to raise money for their Les Enfants du Vietnam foundation. This is a macaron with exotic flavors, consisting of a coconut and lime cream seasoned with ginger, and a center of fresh cilantro compote.

MAKES ABOUT 72 MACARONS
(OR ABOUT 144 SHELLS)

PREPARATION TIME: 5 MINUTES (5 DAYS IN ADVANCE, SEE "MACARON SHELLS STEP-BY-STEP" IN THE KITCHEN GUIDE)
+ 1 HOUR 50 MINUTES

COOKING TIME: ABOUT 30 MINUTES

RESTING TIME: 30 MINUTES

REFRIGERATION TIME: 6 HOURS + 24 HOURS

FOR THE COCONUT MACARON SHELLS

2¼ cups plus 2 tablespoons (240 g) confectioners' sugar
1¾ cups (240 g) ground almonds
1½ cups (120 g) freshly grated coconut, plus more for sprinkling
7 large (220 g) "liquefied" egg whites, divided (see "Macaron Shells Step-by-Step" in the Kitchen Guide)
¼ cup plus 1 tablespoon (75 g) still mineral water
1½ cups (300 g) superfine granulated sugar

MAKE THE COCONUT MACARON SHELLS. The day before, sift together the confectioners' sugar and almonds.

Stir the coconut into half of the "liquefied" egg whites. Pour this into the confectioners' sugar–almond mixture without mixing.

Add the remaining "liquefied" egg whites to the bowl of a stand mixer fitted with the wire whisk. In a saucepan, boil the mineral water and granulated sugar to 244°F (118°C). As soon as the syrup reaches 239°F (115°C), begin beating the egg whites on high speed.

When the syrup reaches 244°F (118°C), reduce the mixer speed to medium–high and pour the syrup in a steady stream down the inside edge of the bowl into the beaten egg whites. Beat the meringue until it cools to 122°F (50°C). Fold it into the confectioners' sugar–almond mixture until the mixture loses volume. Transfer the batter to a pastry bag fitted with a plain #11, ½-inch (11-mm to 12-mm) pastry tip.

Line baking sheets with parchment paper. Pipe disks about 1½ inches (3.5 cm) in diameter and ¾ inch (2 cm) apart on the lined baking sheets. Rap the baking sheets on a work surface covered with a clean kitchen towel to gently smooth out the disks. Lightly sprinkle the disks with grated coconut. Set aside for at least 30 minutes at room temperature to allow a skin to form.

Preheat a convection oven to 350°F (180°C). Place the baking sheets in the oven. Bake for 12 minutes, quickly opening and closing the oven door twice during baking to release moisture. Remove the shells from the oven and slide them still on the parchment paper onto a work surface.

PREPARE THE COCONUT AND LIME CREAM. Chop the white chocolate using a serrated knife then melt it to between 113°F (45°C) and 122°F (50°C) set over a bain-marie or in a microwave.

Heat the coconut puree, lime zest, and lime juice to about 140°F (60°C). Pour the hot mixture in thirds into the melted white chocolate, stirring after each addition starting in the center then in increasingly wider concentric circles toward the sides of the bowl. Using an immersion blender, blend the cream until smooth.

Pour the cream into a baking dish. Cover it by gently pressing plastic wrap onto its surface. Refrigerate for 6 hours, just until the cream has developed a creamy consistency. Transfer the cream to a pastry bag fitted with a plain #11, ¹/₂-inch (11-mm to 12-mm) pastry tip.

PREPARE THE CILANTRO JUICE. Rinse the cilantro leaves three times. Place them on paper towels to dry. In a saucepan, bring the mineral water, sugar, lime zest, ginger, and pepper to a boil. Add the cilantro leaves. Using an immersion blender, puree thoroughly.

PREPARE THE CILANTRO COMPOTE. Mix together the agar-agar and the sugar. Stir in the cilantro juice. Bring the mixture to a boil while whisking continuously; let boil for 1 minute. Let cool then transfer the mixture to a pastry bag fitted with a plain #11, ¹/₂-inch (11-mm to 12-mm) pastry tip.

Turn half of the shells over with the flat sides up onto a new piece of parchment paper. Fill them with the coconut and lime cream then pipe a dollop of cilantro compote in the center. Pipe a dab of the cream on top. Close them with the rest of the shells, pressing down lightly.

Refrigerate the macarons for 24 hours. Remove them from the refrigerator 2 hours before eating them.

FOR THE COCONUT AND LIME CREAM
1¹/₈ **pounds (500 g)** Valrhona Ivoire 35% white chocolate
10½ **ounces (300 g)** coconut puree, preferably Boiron brand
1 **tablespoon plus 1 teaspoon (8 g)** freshly grated lime zest (from 2 limes)
3 **tablespoons plus 1 teaspoon (50 g)** freshly squeezed lime juice (from 1 lime)

FOR THE CILANTRO JUICE
¾ **cup (30 g)** fresh cilantro leaves
¾ **cup plus 2½ tablespoons (215 g)** still mineral water
2 **teaspoons (8 g)** superfine granulated sugar
½ **teaspoon (1 g)** freshly grated lime zest (from ½ lime)
4 **thin strips** fresh ginger
Scant ¼ teaspoon (0.5 g) ground Sarawak black pepper, preferably from Thiercelin

FOR THE CILANTRO COMPOTE
1 **teaspoon (2.5 g)** agar-agar
2½ **teaspoons (10 g)** superfine granulated sugar
1 **cup plus 1 tablespoon (250 g)** Cilantro Juice (see above)

Macaron Jardin d'Éden

Vanilla and basil form a perfect marriage. Large green basil leaves have a prominent flavor, but by combining vanilla from Madagascar, Tahiti, and Mexico, the flavors are softened and the finish enhanced.

PREPARE THE BASIL SUGAR. Two days in advance, preheat the oven to 120°F (50°C). Wash and dry the basil leaves then tear them into large pieces. Using your hands, combine the coarse sugar with the basil leaves. Spread them on a baking sheet lined with parchment paper. Place the baking sheet in the oven until the next day.

PREPARE THE VANILLA MACARON SHELLS. The day before, sift together the confectioners' sugar, almonds, and vanilla powder.

Pour half of the "liquefied" egg whites into the confectioners' sugar–almond-vanilla mixture without mixing.

Add the remaining "liquefied" egg whites to the bowl of a stand mixer fitted with the wire whisk. In a saucepan, boil the mineral water and granulated sugar to 244°F (118°C). As soon as the syrup reaches 239°F (115°C), begin beating the egg whites on high speed.

When the syrup reaches 244°F (118°C), reduce the mixer speed to medium-high and pour the syrup in a steady stream down the inside edge of the bowl into the beaten egg whites. Beat the meringue until it cools to 122°F (50°C). Fold it with a silicone spatula into the confectioners' sugar–almond mixture until the mixture loses volume. Transfer the batter to a pastry bag fitted with a plain #11, ¹/₂-inch (11-mm to 12-mm) pastry tip.

Line baking sheets with parchment paper. Pipe disks about 1¹/₂ inches (3.5 cm) in diameter and ³/₄ inch (2 cm) apart on the lined baking sheets. Rap the baking sheets on a work surface covered with a clean kitchen towel to gently smooth out the disks. Lightly sprinkle them with basil sugar. Set aside for at least 30 minutes at room temperature to allow a skin to form.

MAKES ABOUT 72 MACARONS
(OR ABOUT 144 SHELLS)
PREPARATION TIME: 5 MINUTES (5 DAYS
IN ADVANCE, SEE "MACARON SHELLS
STEP-BY-STEP" IN THE KITCHEN GUIDE)
+ 1 HOUR 40 MINUTES
COOKING TIME: 12 HOURS (2 DAYS IN
ADVANCE) + ABOUT 30 MINUTES
INFUSION TIME: 30 MINUTES
RESTING TIME: 30 MINUTES (TWICE)
REFRIGERATION TIME: 6 HOURS +
24 HOURS

FOR THE BASIL SUGAR
²/₃ cup (25 g) fresh basil leaves
1¼ cups (250 g) coarse sugar

FOR THE VANILLA MACARON SHELLS
1½ cups (150 g) confectioners' sugar
1 cup plus 1 tablespoon (150 g) ground almonds
Scant 1 teaspoon (1.5 g) vanilla powder
3½ large (110 g) "liquefied" egg whites, divided (see "Macaron Shells Step-by-Step" in the Kitchen Guide)
2 tablespoons plus 1¾ teaspoons (38 g) still mineral water
¾ cup (150 g) superfine granulated sugar
Basil Sugar (see above)

→ PREPARE THE PLAIN MACARON SHELLS. Sift together the confectioners' sugar and almonds.

Pour half of the "liquefied" egg whites into the confectioners' sugar–almond mixture without mixing.

Add the remaining "liquefied" egg whites to the bowl of a stand mixer fitted with the wire whisk. In a saucepan, boil the mineral water and granulated sugar to 244°F (118°C). As soon as the syrup reaches 239°F (115°C), begin beating the egg whites on high speed.

When the syrup reaches 244°F (118°C), reduce the mixer speed to medium–high and pour the syrup in a steady stream down the inside edge of the bowl into the beaten egg whites. Beat the meringue until it cools to 122°F (50°C). Fold it with a silicone spatula into the confectioners' sugar–almond mixture until the mixture loses volume. Transfer the batter to a pastry bag fitted with a plain #11, ½-inch (11-mm to 12-mm) pastry tip.

Line baking sheets with parchment paper. Pipe disks about 1½ inches (3.5 cm) in diameter and ¾ inch (2 cm) apart on the lined baking sheets. Rap the baking sheets on a work surface covered with a clean kitchen towel to gently smooth out the disks. Lightly sprinkle them with basil sugar. Set aside for at least 30 minutes at room temperature to allow a skin to form.

Preheat a convection oven to 350°F (180°C). Place the baking sheets in the oven. Bake for 12 minutes, quickly opening and closing the oven door twice during baking to release moisture. Remove the shells from the oven and slide them still on the parchment paper onto a work surface.

MAKE THE VANILLA BASIL CREAM. Wash and dry the basil leaves then tear them into large pieces. Using the blade of a knife, scrape out the seeds from the vanilla beans. Add the seeds to the cream with the empty vanilla pods and the basil.

Bring the cream to a boil. Remove from the heat then cover and let infuse for 30 minutes.

Chop the white chocolate using a serrated knife then melt it to between 113°F (45°C) and 122°F (50°C) set over a bain-marie or in a microwave.

Remove the empty vanilla pods from the cream then bring the cream back to a boil. Using an immersion blender, blend the cream until smooth. Heat the cream to between 131°F (55°C) and 140°F (60°C) and pour it in thirds into the melted white chocolate stirring after each addition starting in the center then in increasingly wider concentric circles toward the sides of the bowl. Using an immersion blender, blend the cream until smooth.

Pour the cream into a baking dish. Cover it by gently pressing plastic wrap onto its surface. Refrigerate for 6 hours, just until the cream has developed a creamy consistency. Transfer the vanilla basil cream to a pastry bag fitted with a plain #11, ½-inch (11-mm to 12-mm) pastry tip.

Turn the vanilla macaron shells over with the flat sides up onto a new piece of parchment paper. Fill them with the vanilla basil cream. Close them with the plain shells, pressing down lightly.

Refrigerate the macarons for 24 hours. Remove them from the refrigerator 2 hours before eating them.

FOR THE PLAIN MACARON SHELLS
1½ cups (150 g) confectioners' sugar
1 cup plus 1 tablespoon (150 g) ground almonds
3½ large (110 g) "liquefied" egg whites, divided (see "Macaron Shells Step-by-Step" in the Kitchen Guide)
2 tablespoons plus 1¾ teaspoons (38 g) still mineral water
¾ cup (150 g) superfine granulated sugar

FOR THE VANILLA BASIL CREAM
Scant ½ cup (16 g) large basil leaves
1½ Tahitian vanilla beans, halved lengthwise
1½ Madagascar vanilla beans, halved lengthwise
1½ Mexican vanilla beans, halved lengthwise
1½ cups (345 g) light whipping cream (32%–35% fat)
13½ ounces (385 g) Valrhona Ivoire 35% white chocolate

Macaron Jardin Épicé

The warm flavors of this macaron are reminiscent of Alsace. I filled the chocolate ganache with an almost-oozing, salted-butter caramel center flavored with gingerbread spice.

MAKES ABOUT 72 MACARONS
(OR ABOUT 144 SHELLS)

PREPARATION TIME: **5 MINUTES (5 DAYS IN ADVANCE, SEE "MACARON SHELLS STEP-BY-STEP" IN THE KITCHEN GUIDE) + 1 HOUR 50 MINUTES**

COOKING TIME: **ABOUT 25 MINUTES**

RESTING TIME: **30 MINUTES (TWICE)**

REFRIGERATION TIME: **4 HOURS + 24 HOURS**

◯

FOR THE CHOCOLATE MACARON SHELLS

2⅛ ounces (60 g) Valrhona 100% cocoa paste
1½ cups (150 g) confectioners' sugar
1 cup plus 1 tablespoon (150 g) ground almonds
4 drops / ¹⁄₁₆ teaspoon (0.25 g) liquid carmine red food color
3½ large (110 g) "liquefied" egg whites, divided (see "Macaron Shells Step-by-Step" in the Kitchen Guide)
2 tablespoons plus 1¾ teaspoons (38 g) still mineral water
¾ cup (150 g) superfine granulated sugar

PREPARE THE CHOCOLATE MACARON SHELLS. The day before, chop the cocoa paste using a serrated knife then melt it to between 113°F (45°C) and 122°F (50°C) set over a bain-marie or in a microwave.

Sift together the confectioners' sugar and almonds.

Combine the food color with half of the "liquefied" egg whites. Pour this into the confectioners' sugar–almond mixture without mixing.

Add the remaining "liquefied" egg whites to the bowl of a stand mixer fitted with the wire whisk. In a saucepan, boil the mineral water and granulated sugar to 244°F (118°C). As soon as the syrup reaches 239°F (115°C), begin beating the egg whites on high speed.

When the syrup reaches 244°F (118°C), reduce the mixer speed to medium-high and pour the syrup in a steady stream down the inside edge of the bowl into the beaten egg whites. Beat the meringue until it cools to 122°F (50°C). Fold about one-third of the meringue into the melted cocoa paste then add this mixture to the confections' sugar–almond mixture along with the rest of the meringue. Fold it with a silicone spatula until the mixture loses volume. Transfer the batter to a pastry bag fitted with a plain #11, ½-inch (11-mm to 12-mm) pastry tip.

Line baking sheets with parchment paper. Pipe disks about 1½ inches (3.5 cm) in diameter and ¾ inch (2 cm) apart on the lined baking sheets. Rap the baking sheets on a work surface covered with a clean kitchen towel to gently smooth out the disks. Set aside for at least 30 minutes at room temperature to allow a skin to form.

PREPARE THE GINGERBREAD SUGAR. Combine the sugar with the gingerbread spice and set aside.

PREPARE THE GINGERBREAD MACARON SHELLS. Sift together the confectioners' sugar and almonds.

Combine the food color and coffee extract with half of the "liquefied" egg whites. Pour this into the confectioners' sugar–almond mixture without mixing.

Add the remaining "liquefied" egg whites to the bowl of a stand mixer fitted with the wire whisk. In a saucepan, boil the mineral water and granulated sugar to 244°F (118°C). As soon as the syrup reaches 239°F (115°C), begin beating the egg whites on high speed.

When the syrup reaches 244°F (118°C), reduce the mixer speed to medium–high and pour the syrup in a steady stream down the inside edge of the bowl into the beaten egg whites. Beat the meringue until it cools to 122°F (50°C). Fold it with a silicone spatula into the confectioners' sugar–almond mixture until the mixture loses volume. Transfer the batter to a pastry bag fitted with a plain #11, ¹/₂-inch (11-mm to 12-mm) pastry tip.

Line baking sheets with parchment paper. Pipe disks about 1¹/₂ inches (3.5 cm) in diameter and ³/₄ inch (2 cm) apart on the lined baking sheets. Rap the baking sheets on a work surface covered with a clean kitchen towel to gently smooth out the disks. Lightly sprinkle the disks with the gingerbread sugar. Set aside for at least 30 minutes at room temperature to allow a skin to form.

Preheat a convection oven to 350°F (180°C). Place the baking sheets in the oven. Bake for 12 minutes, quickly opening and closing the oven door twice during baking to release moisture. Remove the shells from the oven and slide them still on the parchment paper onto a work surface.

PREPARE THE CHOCOLATE GANACHE. Chop the chocolate using a serrated knife then melt it to between 113°F (45°C) and 122°F (50°C) set over a bain-marie or in a microwave.

In a saucepan, bring the cream to a boil. Pour the hot cream in thirds into the melted chocolate, stirring after each addition starting in the center then in increasingly wider concentric circles toward the sides of the bowl. Stir in the butter in small pieces. Using an immersion blender, blend the ganache until smooth.

Pour the ganache into a baking dish. Cover it by gently pressing plastic wrap onto its surface. Refrigerate for 4 hours, just until the ganache has developed a creamy consistency.

PREPARE THE GINGERBREAD SALTED-BUTTER CARAMEL. In a saucepan, bring the cream and gingerbread spice to a boil. In a separate heavy-bottomed saucepan over medium heat, melt ¹/₄ cup (50 g) of the sugar. Add another ¹/₄ cup (50 g) of the sugar then continue in the same way with the rest of the sugar. Cook just until the caramel develops a deep amber color. Off the heat, add the butter in small pieces and stir to combine using a silicone spatula.

Stir in the hot cream in two parts. Place the saucepan back over the heat and cook the caramel to 226°F (108°C). Blend the caramel with an immersion blender, then pour it into a heat-resistant baking dish. Cover and refrigerate to cool. Transfer the ganache and the gingerbread salted-butter caramel into separate pastry bags fitted with plain #11, ¹/₂-inch (11-mm to 12-mm) pastry tips.

Turn the chocolate macaron shells over with the flat sides up onto a new piece of parchment paper. Fill them with the ganache then pipe a dollop of the caramel in the center. Close them with the gingerbread shells, pressing down lightly.

Refrigerate the macarons for 24 hours. Remove them from the refrigerator 2 hours before eating them.

FOR THE GINGERBREAD SUGAR
1¼ cups (250 g) coarse sugar
¼ cup (25 g) ground gingerbread spice, preferably from Thiercelin

FOR THE GINGERBREAD MACARON SHELLS
1½ cups (150 g) confectioners' sugar
1 cup plus 1 tablespoon (150 g) ground almonds
¼ teaspoon (1 g) liquid lemon yellow food color
1¾ teaspoons (7.5 g) coffee extract, preferably Trablit
3½ large (110 g) "liquefied" egg whites, divided (see "Macaron Shells Step-by-Step" in the Kitchen Guide)
2 tablespoons plus 1¾ teaspoons (38 g) still mineral water
¾ cup (150 g) superfine granulated sugar
Gingerbread Sugar (see above)

FOR THE CHOCOLATE GANACHE
14 ounces (400g) Valrhona Extra-bitter 61% cacao dark chocolate
1 cup plus 1 tablespoon (250 g) light whipping cream (32%–35% fat)
¼ cup plus 1 tablespoon (75 g) fine French unsalted butter, preferably *beurre de la Viette*, room temperature

FOR THE GINGERBREAD SALTED-BUTTER CARAMEL
1½ cups minus 1 tablespoon (335 g) light whipping cream (32%–35% fat)
1 teaspoon (2.5 g) ground gingerbread spice, preferably from Thiercelin
1¼ cups (250 g) superfine granulated sugar
2 tablespoons plus 2 teaspoons (40 g) fine French butter, lightly salted, preferably *beurre de la Viette demi-sel*

Recipe
Name
Index

Acknowledgments

I would like to sincerely thank my friend and associate Charles Znaty as well as Coco Jobard and Laurent Fau.

Thanks also to Mickaël Marsollier, Camille Moënne-Loccoz, Charlotte Bruneau, and Delphine Baussan.

Pierre Hermé

Warm thanks to photographers Laurent Fau and Bernhard Winkelmann as well as my dear collaborator Sarah Vasseghi, all of the pastry chef teams of Pierre Hermé, Camille Moënne-Loccoz, Mickaël Marsollier, and Charlotte Bruneau.

Coco Jobard

Photo Credits

All of the photographs in this book are by Laurent Fau, with the exception of the following:

© Bernhard Winkelmann: pages 14, 42, 90, 98, 118, 135, 143, 154, 203, 206, 211, 214, 219, 226, 231, 234, 239, 243, 246, 255.

FRENCH EDITION
Design: Grégory Bricout
Proofreading: Colette Malandain
Editorial team: Art de vie

ENGLISH EDITION
Editor: Laura Dozier
Designer: Shawn Dahl, dahlimama inc
Production Manager: Denise LaCongo

Published in 2015 by Abrams

Originally published in French under the title *Pierre Hermé Macaron* by Éditions de la Martinière

Copyright © 2014 Éditions de la Martinière, an imprint of La Martinière Groupe, Paris

English translation copyright © 2015 Abrams, New York

Library of Congress Control Number: 2014959143
ISBN: 978-1-61769-171-3

Printed and bound in China
10 9 8 7 6 5 4 3

Abrams books are available at special discounts when purchased in quantity for premiums and promotions as well as fundraising or educational use. Special editions can also be created to specification. For details, contact specialsales@abramsbooks.com or the address below.

ABRAMS The Art of Books
195 Broadway, New York, NY 10007
abramsbooks.com